Time Out for God

A Bible-Based Daily Devotional and Personal Story
Showing God's Life-Changing Transformations.

Amos Martin

Copyright(C) 2019 By Amos Martin Ministries

Published by Amos Martin Ministries

All rights reserved.

ISBN: 9781728694702

i

Amos Martin

Amos played pro football for six years, participating in 3 Super Bowls, and he founded a construction company that has been successful for over 30 years. With all that, nothing, according to Amos, compares to what happened to him in Oakland, California in 1974 – the day Amos asked Jesus Christ into his life.

Amos was born in Indianapolis but lived most of his life in Kentucky where he attended Bardstown High School. He later earned a football scholarship to the University of Louisville. At U of L, Amos played for current ESPN College Gameday Analyst Lee Corso. Amos was drafted in the sixth round of the 1972 NFL draft by the Minnesota Vikings. Amos, a linebacker, played six seasons from 1972-1977. His career year came in 1974 when he recorded three interceptions and scored one touchdown on a fumble recovery. While with the Vikings, Amos played in three Super Bowls; in 1973, '74 and '76. He was traded to the Seattle Seahawks the next year and was forced into retirement after suffering a severe knee injury.

He is a Board Member of the Fellowship of Christian Athletes, past chairman of the FCA Golf Tournament and served as Chairperson for the Youth for Christ Golf Tournament for 20 years. Additionally, he has spent over two decades coaching youth football. He and his wife are active members of Southeast Christian Church. Amos has three children, Rick, Amy and Krissy, and four grandchildren.

Amos wrote this book because he believes that spiritual exercise is non-negotiable. He hopes to inspire people to spend more time with God through his life story, short devotionals, and opportunities for reflection.

FOREWORD

"Let us draw near to God with a sincere heart in full assurance of faith, having our hearts sprinkled to cleanse us from a guilty conscience and having our bodies washed with pure water." (Hebrews 10:22)

A grasp of the fundamentals is essential to success in nearly every endeavor. That's true whether you're building a house, coaching football, or flying a plane. You have to know and apply the basics to be effective.

Dr. Matthew Sleeth, an emergency room doctor, pointed out that this is especially true in medicine. He says in the trauma center when the pressure is on and a life hangs in the balance, there is a formula to remind everyone of the most important priorities. He identified them as the "ABCs of trauma: **A**irway, **B**reathing, **C**irculation, **D**isability, and **E**xposure."

To illustrate, he recalled an incident in which a seriously injured patient was rushed into the ER after an accident. Her leg was jutting out at a 90° angle below the knee. This was an incredibly bad injury, and everyone in the ER was paying close attention to the obvious fracture, which, using the ABCs of trauma paradigm, would be referred to as a "D" (disability). While focusing on the obvious injury, the ER staff had forgotten a more important medical priority, "A" (airway) which, in this case, was blocked. Obviously, the lack of oxygen will kill you before the more noticeable wounded leg.

"As the one running the trauma center," Dr. Sleeth explained, "it's my job not to get preoccupied with what looks terrible and neglect the more serious, eminent threat. The patient couldn't breathe. So we secured her airway, assisted her breathing, and got IVs in to support the circulation. Then, we eventually gave attention to "D" (disability), her fractured leg."

In many respects, Christians in America are facing a similar dilemma. We are rightfully concerned about the obviously increasing immorality in our culture, decreased church attendance, and the disintegration of the family. But while these issues are important, there is an even more basic "A" priority we are missing, which has to do with cementing our personal relationship with God through daily devotions, Bible study, and prayer.

Jesus taught us to pray, "Give me today my daily bread." Clearly, the Lord intended prayer to be a daily exercise. If we are going to grow as believers, it is imperative that we "meditate on God's word day and night" (Joshua 1:8). Or, as the Apostle John pleaded with his readers, "See that what you heard from the beginning remains in you" (1 John 2:24).

I think Christians in America desperately need to reinvigorate our commitment to daily devotions and to Bible study. If we're going to survive spiritually, it's vital that believers have a solid grasp of the Biblical fundamentals.

Amos Martin knows about the importance of fundamentals on the football field. He is a former college football star and an ex-NFL standout, having played as a linebacker for the Minnesota Vikings. After his NFL career was over, Amos became a respected homebuilder, Godly husband and father, church member, and community leader in Louisville, Kentucky. He knows from his broad experience on and off the field that enduring faith has to be more than an inspirational moment; it must be based on solid convictions that we hold at the core of our being, and it has to be exercised regularly.

It's not surprising that Amos' book is about returning to the fundamentals of spending daily time alone with the Lord. That's the best way I know to get your day started off right. And that's the primary reason I am happy to endorse this book and recommend that you read it daily, as Amos shares a practical guide for men to get involved in spending time alone with God every day.

I don't care if you are a morning person, an evening person, or you're at your best somewhere in between. Time alone with God is essential, and Amos has provided you an inspirational, helpful tool to meet with God each day and strengthen your faith.

This book provides a practical, daily devotional guide that will restore you to the basic principles of meeting God every day in your devotional life. Amos' devotions are personal, readable, and insightful. They provide a practical step-by-step blueprint for you to begin a daily quiet time and draw near to the Lord with a glad and sincere heart.

Bob Russell – Retired Minister, Southeast Christian Church, Louisville, Kentucky

OPENING REMARKS

I had been a Christian for few years, but I was struggling with expanding my faith. I had been reading a Living Bible and mostly the New Testament. At that time, I still hadn't figured out why God had written the Old Testament, but I was searching for answers. My reading plan was erratic, and my time in the Word was random. Basically, if I had some dead time and nothing was on television and other activities weren't taking place, I would have time for God.

I'll never forget the seminar I went to in Minneapolis in 1975. I heard some great Bible teaching about the Holy Spirit, and on that day, He would touch my soul. As the lesson ended, the speaker asked several questions: How much time do you spend watching TV? How much time you spend reading newspapers and magazines? Then, he asked one of the most important questions I would ever hear: How much time do you spend with God? This question absolutely stopped me in my tracks, and after I had paused to contemplate, I felt ashamed of my neglect of my God. I was too occupied with the world to take time for the Lord.

So, the speaker continued after I caught my breath, and he asked us to make a promise to the Lord to spend five minutes a day with the God of the universe for a year. This was not only a promise but a covenant, a blood covenant, with the Lord to commit five minutes a day to Him.

The speaker then asked us to raise our hands if we were ready to make that promise. There were 5,000 people in the stands, and many arms went up. So did mine. I left that stadium with a new motivation and was so excited with my new covenant. I knew I had to have a daily plan for my reading, so I went to the bookstore looking for answers. I was looking for something that was short and sweet, and I found it in the devotional section with a book by Max Lucado. The book had a reading for every day, and none of them seemed very long. This gave me the direction I needed. Some days, I would be busy and forget my promise, but just before I went to bed, the Holy Spirit would prompt me to get up and abide by my covenant.

This promise has followed me since that day, and those five minutes have expanded over the years. If I am too busy for God, then I am just too busy! If I do not start my day with the Lord, then I am basically saying, "Lord I got this today, and I can handle it without you!" I know I am not capable of being the man God wants me to be if I am not in His word every day. Romans 12 tells us to be "transformed by the renewing of the mind," and I need that each and every day. I cannot begin to count how many times the Lord has answered my prayers through the devotional I read every day. God will speak to us if we only give Him a little time.

My goal in writing this book was to inspire readers to commit a few minutes each day to the Lord our God. Once you spend some consistent time with God, you will realize that He speaks to us through His word. Each of my devotionals are connected to scripture, and according to Hebrews 4:12, His word is living and active, and it penetrates and judges. I present my personal story to reveal the transformation God has made in my life. I have not led a perfect life, and I've made many mistakes along my journey. There will be more in the future. However, only through my daily time in God's word have I found my strength. His Holy Word has prevented many of my blunders from becoming disastrous. During these trials, I questioned God's involvement, but as I look back, I would not change anything. I needed those experiences to grow my faith and really trust His omnipresence. This is one of my favorite scriptures:

Proverbs 3:5–6

Trust in the Lord with all your heart, and lean not unto your own understanding; in all your ways acknowledge Him, and He will direct your paths.

Trust.

Don't try to understand.

Acknowledge Him.

He will direct you.

If you have read this far and want to continue, here is my suggestion on how to proceed.

Priority #1: Commit, promise, or, ideally, make a covenant with the Lord to read one of the devotionals five days a week, i.e., Monday through Friday, for a month. Wednesday will be a two-minute drill of scripture and will present thought-provoking ideas or questions. Allow God's word to saturate your mind.

If you won't commit five minutes to God, why should He take time out of His schedule to speak to you?

Priority #2: On Saturday, there is a designated page with a scripture to review the previous week. Take a few minutes to journal and reflect on the past several days. When you write your thoughts down, if your pen is moving, you are focused on the task at hand. Don't worry about being neat and legible.

Just write and share with God the happenings of the week, and keep the pen moving.

Priority #3: On Sunday, there is another individual page with scripture to prepare for worship. After all, we only have one day a week to assemble in His house. Hopefully, you have filled yourself with God's word for the previous six days because Sunday should be the day we worship the living God. In the morning, get up a little early and write down all the things you are thankful for. Maybe it has been tough week, so concentrate on all your blessings. As the kids get up and are truly awake, maybe you pause and pray as a family. You want to be ready to honor our God and Savior Jesus Christ on this holy day.

On Monday, back to take five. See you then!

One last thing... Since you can start this book any time of the year and there are no specific dates on the devotionals, I have designated week #48 through week #52 for significant holidays:

Weeks #48 and #49: Easter

Weeks #50 and #51: Christmas

Week #52: New Year

Introduction

Growing up in the small town of Bardstown, Kentucky, was a unique experience that very few kids today have the opportunity to enjoy. All the major attractions were within walking or biking distance, so there was always something to do. There were no video games or fantastic television shows, so the most desirable place to be was something unheard of in todays' culture... the outdoors. This remarkable little community had everything. Baseball fields, gymnasiums, basketball goals, sandlot football, a swimming pool, an ice cream shop, pinball machines, a movie theatre, and the pool hall were all available, so what else could you possibly need?

Since I do not remember anything before age five, here are a few interesting events that happened during my childhood.

Week #1
Monday
TGIM: Thank God It's Monday
Psalm 119:176
I have strayed like a lost sheep.
5 years old

My mom, sister, and I used to go into Louisville to shop and go to the Blue Boar cafeteria. I loved that place, but I would soon have a distaste for downtown Louisville. When I was younger, my mom made me wear one of those chest harness contraptions and a leash so I wouldn't run off. (Just think if a parent put their child in one of those things today. They would be in jail before they left the house.)

We were shopping in the lower level of Woolworths or some other dime store. I guess I had proved myself worthy of harness release by this time, and as we shopped, I was infatuated by some trinket. When I looked up, my mom and sister were gone. I looked around and searched the aisle, and they were not to be found. I wandered for a little while and nobody showed up, so I decided to go back to the car at the Starks parking garage. I remembered the route as I walked the busy sidewalks and eventually took the stairs up to the level our car was on. I thought I might be able to get inside the car, but I was mistaken. I wasn't leaving, and my mom's old 1956 Plymouth and I would become inseparable. I took a nap on the trunk of the car, and after a couple of hours, my mom and sister finally showed up. Needless to say, they were happy to see me and ran to welcome me back from captivity. After hugs and kisses, I immediately asked my mom, "Do I have to wear the harness again?"

Fortunately not.

Free at last!

MONDAY

"The Challenge"

Psalm 105:4

Look to the Lord and His strength; seek his face always.

I went to a seminar years ago, and the speaker asked the question, "How much time do you spend with God?" My first reaction to the question was surprise and shock. Then the speaker asked, "What are you going to do about it?" He then issued a challenge to commit to five minutes with God every day for a month. **Five minutes!** He asked us to make not only a promise, but a covenant, with God that we would honor our decision. He then asked us to raise our hands to acknowledge that all-binding agreement with our God. I slowly lifted my hand that day, and that has to be one of the greatest moments of my life. That promise has extended to this very day. The time has increased, and the rewards have been absolutely unbelievable. God will speak if only we listen.

Jesus endured the rejection of his followers, the antagonistic words of the religious leaders, and, eventually, an agonizing death on the cross so that we might live. The easiest and simplest gift we have to give back is time. I want to challenge you to sacrifice one of your most precious commodities every day: time. Here are some suggestions:

- Five minutes in his word
- Five minutes in prayer
- Five minutes meditating
- Five minutes looking at a sunrise or sunset
- Five minutes listening to praise music
- Five minutes on your knees
- Five dedicated minutes to the living God

Will you promise?

Hosea 10:12

For it is time to seek the Lord...

TUESDAY
"Commitment"

2 Timothy 1:7
For the spirit God gave us does not make us timid, but gives us power, love and self-discipline.

The seminar I mentioned yesterday challenged me to make a commitment to spend five minutes a day with God. I made a covenant with God that I would abide by that special promise. I quickly realized in order to keep my binding arrangement, I would need several items.

Item #1: I needed a quiet place where I would not be disturbed. This required getting up earlier and a focusing my mind on God's word and not business.

Item #2: It was absolutely critical to find a version of the Bible that I could understand and enjoy. There are several places to sample Bible translations, including a local Christian book store or Bible apps on your smartphone, computer, iPad, or Kindle.

Item #3: I needed a systematic way to approach my Bible study. Max Lucado's devotionals open with scripture and then follow with the writer's inspirational thoughts. There are many more writers like this, and you can sample them or get on a daily program by using a Bible app. One of my Facebook friends put me on Rick Warren's daily devotional list, and he has an outstanding message every day.

Item #4: Somedays, you are going to oversleep and be in a rush. A variety of Bible tapes are available, and some Bible apps have audio versions. There are many Christian radio stations. For outstanding speakers, go to 94.7. For Christian music, you have 105.4 and Sirius channel 63, called The Message.

Item #5: This really should be at the top of the list. You need an overwhelming desire to honor God. We are so very blessed, so your time with God must become a non-negotiable priority. Your time with the Lord will reap countless blessings. After all, God promised, that he would reward those who seek him *(Hebrews 11:6).*

Proverbs 16:3
Commit to the Lord whatever you do, and he will establish your plans.

WEDNESDAY
Two-Minute Drill

KNOWLEDGE
Proverbs 1:7
The fear of the Lord is the beginning of <u>knowledge</u>,
But fools despise wisdom and instruction.

Psalms 2:6
For the Lord gives wisdom,
And from His mouth come <u>knowledge</u> and understanding.

Colossians 1:10
So that you may live a life worthy of the Lord and may please him in every way: bearing fruit in every good work, growing in the <u>knowledge</u> of God.

2 Peter 1:2
Grace and peace be yours in abundance through the <u>knowledge</u> of God and of Jesus our Lord.

2 Peter 3:18
But grow in grace and <u>knowledge</u> of our Lord and Savior Jesus Christ. To Him be the glory both now and forever! Amen.

ARE YOU GROWING IN GRACE AND KNOWLEDGE?

THURSDAY
"Visualization"

John 20:16

Again Jesus said, "Simon son of John, do you truly love me?"

Many athletes practice a technique called visualization. This requires focusing your mind on a specific phase of the athletic event, such as making a game-winning interception, catching a touchdown pass with no time on the clock, or blocking a jump shot as time expired, prior to game time.

After making a game-winning free throw, Larry Bird said that he made that shot a hundred times in his mind. after holing out an impossible chip shot that helped him win the US Open Tom Watson also said he envisioned that same shot many times.

I read a few questions recently that stopped me in my tracks and made me pause and reflect. I really had to slow my mind and focus.

Relax and take time to visualize the question. Take a deep breath. Here goes...

Create a mental picture of Jesus.

Now, imagine Jesus walking toward you. He wants to ask you a question.

He speaks very softly and asks, "Do you love me?"

Then, as His eyes gaze into your very soul, He asks, "Why do you love me?"

What would you say?

Matthew 22:37

Love the Lord your God with all your heart and with all your soul and with all your mind.

FRIDAY
"Physical and Mental Preparation"

1 Peter 5:8
Your enemy the devil prowls around like a roaring lion looking for someone to devour.

Most sports require tremendous amounts of physical and mental preparation. How does our spiritual life compare to the physical aspects of football? This sport requires extensive conditioning and training. Exercises consist of warmups, stretching, strength drills, planks, up/downs, sprinting, and endurance and stamina training. Players go through countless hours of practice in order to defeat their opponents. We have a very capable opponent too. His name is Satan, and he has plenty of demon assistants.

Ephesians 6:17
Take the helmet of salvation and the sword of the Spirit, which is the Word of God.

The Spirit within us and football both require substantial training. Repetitious drills are essential for both endeavors. You cannot play football if your body is not prepared properly. So, why do people think our battle against Satan is any different? In fact, Satan wants you to think you are competent without adequate conditioning. Isn't enough that I go to church? Does a football team practice once a week? We all need a daily connection with the source of our power, God's word.

Ephesians 6:13
Therefore put on the full armor of God, so that when the day of evil comes, you may be able to stand your ground...

As a coach, my responsibility is to train my football players to maximize their abilities. As Christians, it is our responsibility to "transform" ourselves every day to anticipate the devious schemes of the devil.

SATURDAY REFLECTIONS
Philippians 4:12–13

I know what it is to be in need,

And I know what it is to have plenty.

I have learned the secret of being content in any and every situation,

Whether well fed or hungry,

Whether living in plenty or in want.

I can do all things through Christ who strengthens me.

Lord, as I review the past week, I remember:

....

....

....

....

....

....

....

....

....

....

....

....

....

....

....

....

SUNDAY
Psalm 103:1

Praise the Lord, my soul;
All my inmost being,
Praise His holy name.

I WILL PRAISE HIS NAME FOREVER.

Prepare to worship and count your blessings.

....

....

....

....

....

....

....

....

....

....

....

....

....

....

....

....

Isaiah 35:5

Then will the eyes of the blind be opened and the ears of the deaf unstopped.

5 and a half years old

We were playing by a tree next to the parking lot. I decided to stand on the bumper of the truck and jump, catch a branch, and swing from limb to limb. I caught the first limb, missed the second, and fell backward, landing on a large iron pipe and fracturing my skull. My mom's brothers owned a funeral home in Taylorsville and rushed to my rescue. They drove the hearse to the hospital in Louisville. On the way, I went in and out of consciousness and opened my eyes one time and asked my mom if I was going to die. I survived but suffered nerve damage and lost the hearing in my left ear. I love it when my grandkids whisper something into my deaf ear. I then whisper back that I cannot hear in that ear.

When I became eligible for Medicare in addition to my great NFL supplement insurance plan, I decided to get an updated hearing test.

The doctor tested me, and yes, there was absolutely nothing in my left ear. The doctor came in and informed me that they have a small hearing aid they could put in the bad ear that would transfer sound to the good ear. Hallelujah! I would be able to hear again. Not so fast... It cost $3,500. I have been deaf in that ear a long time, and I would rather have a new set of golf clubs.

The Doctor continued and informed me that there was another option. There was a type of new technology in which a doctor can drill a small hole into your skull just behind the ear and install a post that attaches to a small box that transfers sound to a hearing aid in the good ear. I could let my hair grow to cover the box.

"Okay, doc," I asked. "How much for the drilling?" His answer floored me. ZERO, absolutely nothing because it is classified as cosmetic surgery. So, I want to thank all you taxpayers for giving me this opportunity to hear again.

Frankenstein post here I come... (Just kidding).

Today, I am still deaf in my left ear, and I have the same old golf clubs.

MONDAY

"Hard Heart?"

Exodus 9:35

So Pharaoh's heart was hard and he would not let the Israelites go...

Throughout my first 25 years of life, I had experienced many miracles. But just like Pharaoh, my heart was hardened. I had recovered from several major injuries and was still drafted to play for the Minnesota Vikings. What a remarkable blessing! But I still ignored God's calling. I was intrigued by some of my Christian teammates, but I thought I was too bad of a person to ask Jesus to be my Lord and Savior. I cussed a lot, drank too much, went to dishonorable places, and treated others with disrespect, including my family. I decided I should clean up my act so Jesus would consider taking me into His kingdom. I struggled to eliminate my un-Christ-like actions. The harder I tried, the more I failed. I was on the verge of giving up, but fortunately, I kept attending chapel service.

One Sunday morning, the speaker began to explain what I needed to do to ask Jesus to come into my life. As I anticipated his strict requirements, he totally surprised me and said, "Jesus wants you just the way you are!" He continued, "He doesn't care what you have done, where you have been, or where you are going. All He wants is your heart!"

All this time, I thought I had to be a better person, and this speaker said Jesus loves me just like I am. What a shocker! How could He love me that much?

That day, despite all my imperfections, I asked Jesus Christ to be my Lord and Savior. I left that conference room and wasn't sure what I had done. But I know that day, the Holy Spirit took control of my life.

Ephesians 1:13

When you believed, you were marked in Him with a seal, the promised Holy Spirit.

Prayer: Lord, I know there are people reading this who believe they are unworthy of your amazing grace. Please make them aware of your all-consuming love, and accept them just like they are. All you want is for them to trust you and ask you to take control of their lives.

Romans 10:13

Everyone who calls on the name of the Lord will be saved.

TUESDAY
"The Choice"

Romans 12:2

Do not conform to the pattern of this world, but be transformed by the renewing of your mind.

The devil's goal is to distract us with the things of this world: television, music, pornography, alcohol, drugs, sex, anger, bitterness, etc. We must realize that Satan has supernatural powers.

Ephesians 6:12

We wrestle not against flesh and blood, but against the rulers, against the authorities, against the powers of this dark world and against the spiritual forces of evil in the heavenly realms.

I struggled for years with various sins and kept telling myself I could eliminate my flaws with my own power. I thought I was strong and disciplined enough to avoid the temptations that confronted me. I finally realized that I was not capable of fighting the forces of evil without spiritual assistance. My only hope was to put on the full armor of God and the sword of the spirit, which is the word of God (Ephesians 6:13–18).

The holy spirit within us (Ephesians 1:13) must be fed in order to grow and mature. We go to church, sing praise music, worship the living God, and fill ourselves with his miraculous strength and power. During the week, we are enticed with worldly allurements, so we *must* continually fortify our defense system by filling our minds with God's almighty word.

Ephesians 6:16

Take up the shield of faith, with which you can extinguish all the flaming arrows of the evil one.

The choice is ours: conform... or be transformed.

Psalm 119:11

I have hidden your word in my heart that I might not sin against you.

WEDNESDAY
Two-Minute Drill

Philippians 4:6–7

Do not be anxious about anything, but in every situation, by prayer and petition, with thanksgiving, present your requests to God. And the peace of God, which transcends all understanding, will guard your hearts and your minds in Christ Jesus.

Now take a moment and absorb a few of the words of this dynamic scripture.

Do not be anxious about *anything*,

But in *everything*,

With *thanksgiving*,

***Present* your requests to God.**

And the *peace* of God, which transcends all understanding,

WILL GUARD YOUR HEARTS AND MINDS

IN CHRIST JESUS.

THURSDAY
"Let It Go!"

Luke 6:37

Do not condemn, and you will not be condemned. Forgive, and you will be forgiven.

I've been helping an older gentleman who is 78 years old and has a slight case of dementia. Occasionally, he gets obnoxious and snaps at me, but I know that inside, he has a good heart. He once sent me a derogatory text message, and I was going to rip him. I read the response I was planning to send him to my wife, and she said," Now Amos!" After a lengthy discussion, I modified the message to say, "I am sorry you are upset." What a reversal of my original reaction! Later that day, he apologized for his previous comments.

Colossians 3:13

Bear with each other and forgive one another if any of you has a grievance against someone. Forgive as the Lord forgave you.

I have a friend who created some personal financial hardships for my family. I was bitter and sent him a somewhat negative letter. After several weeks and no response, my resentment had continually expanded. I didn't like those vindictive thoughts going through my mind every day, so there was only one thing to do... go kick his butt (just kidding). The only option was forgiveness! Without forgiveness, this cancer within my soul would destroy my peace and joy and restrict my relationship with the living God. My anger and bitterness damages me more than the other person.

I went through some tough teenage years with my alcoholic father. Many of you reading this have various family issues. For years, I thought restricting my communication and avoiding my dad was the answer... wrong. *Forgiveness* is the only answer. Release your anger and let it go. It only harms you!

Ephesians 4:31

Get rid of all bitterness, rage and anger... forgiving each other, just as in Christ God forgave you.

"Enoch"

Genesis 5:24

Enoch walked faithfully with God.

When we wake up in the morning, we have a choice: walk with God or not. We can immediately start preparing ourselves for our daily responsibilities and ignore God's presence in our lives, or we can allow some time for God to speak and provide his power and his revelation for the day's activities.

Our choices are stated in Romans 12:2:

1. Conform to the pattern of the world, or
2. Be transformed by the renewing of your mind.

Genesis 6:9

Noah was a righteous man, blameless among the people of his time, and he walked faithfully with God.

I picture Noah walking hand in hand with the creator of the universe every day. God was not necessarily in bodily form, but Noah felt his presence. It was like walking in a celestial park with your best friend. Just listen to Noah's conversation: "Lord, your power and majesty are beyond compare, and your creation is absolutely magnificent. Forgive my sinful thoughts and actions, for I want nothing to affect our walk together. I am so very thankful for you being in my life, and I will worship you every day. Lord, I am anxious to listen to your sovereign whisper and what you have planned for me today and for the rest of my life."

Why was Noah a "righteous man?" Because every day, he walked with God and listened to his voice.

Joni Eareckson Tada, who became a quadriplegic from a diving accident has said that "The longer the tea bag sits in the cup, the stronger the tea. The more God's word saturates our minds, the clearer our grasp on what's important to Him and the stronger our prayers."

SATURDAY REFLECTIONS
Philippians 4:12–13

I know what it is to be in need,

And I know what it is to have plenty.

I have learned the secret of being content in any and every situation,

Whether well fed or hungry,

Whether living in plenty or in want.

I can do all things through Christ who strengthens me.

Lord, as I review the past week, I remember:

....

....

....

....

....

....

....

....

....

....

....

....

....

....

....

....

....

....

SUNDAY
Psalm 145:1–2

I will exalt you, my God the King;
I will praise your name for ever and ever.
Every day I will praise you
And extol your name for ever and ever.

EVER AND EVER

Prepare to worship and count your blessings.

....
....
....
....
....
....
....
....
....
....
....
....
....
....
....
....
....

Week #3

Monday: TGIM

Ecclesiastes 8:11

When the sentence for a crime is not quickly carried out, people's hearts are filled with schemes to do wrong.

10 years old

We were riding bikes one day, and there were some younger girls riding theirs too. We harassed and chased them, and as I was passing one girl, I knocked her off her bike. She fell and screamed bloody murder. What was I going to do? You guessed it... make a run for it! This was my first and last hit and run, and as soon as I got home, my Dad wanted to see me. How could he know already? He asked me about the details, and I wasn't going to compound my mistakes by lying, even though it did cross my mind. Next thing I knew, we are in the car headed for the hospital (just kidding) her house.

The moment of truth had arrived, and I assumed the girl's dad was going to kick my butt and then my dad was going to finish me off. We got out of the car and walked to the door. I didn't think we were ever going to get there, and it was only 50 feet. My dad knocked on the door, and a relatively small man (thank you, Jesus) came forward. He opened the door. As we walked in, I saw the girl I had sideswiped. There were no crutches or bandages anywhere, and I thanked God again. My dad signaled me, and I stepped forward and apologized to her and her dad for being so inconsiderate. Of course, I was crying as I told her it was an accident and that I did not mean to hurt her. Everyone accepted my apology, and we left.

The ride home was quiet at first. Then, my dad very lovingly explained the error of my ways. This was a monumental experience in my life as a kid and as a parent. When you mess up, there needs to be a consequence. Had my Dad not taken me back to apologize, who knows what direction my life would have taken?

MONDAY

"Fighting Impulses"

1 Corinthians 2:16
But we have the mind of Christ.

Sin is constantly at our doorstep. Satan's objective is to separate us from our Lord. Our thoughts are constantly bombarded by the desires of the world. More money, work, worries, lust, anger, bitterness, envy, and the list goes on. How do we fight? Yes, I know what Jesus would do, but many times, I ignore His request. I thought I would try something else. The moment the sinful thought or action enters my brain and I am pondering the ultimate decision, I respond internally by saying, "I love Jesus more!"

When my kids are out of control and I_____? _____I love Jesus more.

When nobody is watching and I_____? _____I love Jesus more.

When I glance at a sexually explicit picture ....I love Jesus more.

When I know I should stop or leave...........................I love Jesus more.

When my boss or client misleads me.........................I love Jesus more.

When I am tired on Sunday morning and it's time for church..............

I love Jesus more!

Galatians 2:20
Christ lives in me.

TUESDAY
"Lies"

Psalm 32:3

When I refused to confess my sin, my body wasted away, and I groaned all day long.

I remember lying to my dad. I was doomed because I knew eventually Judgement Day was coming and that there would be no place to hide. My dad told me to go to my room and that he would be in shortly. I waited and waited and waited. It must have been at least five minutes before he came in. We sat down and discussed my behavior. He was not angry, but I could see his hurt, and I felt his disappointment.

I know I have hurt God too. I couldn't see His hurt, but in my soul, I could feel His disappointment. I have done bad things, and I didn't care about the consequences. I have lied to my God too. For years, I ignored His calling and told myself I could handle things on my own. I finally came to the understanding that without Jesus in my life, there was no hope. I humbly came before Him and asked him to forgive me and my many lies. Amazingly enough, my God didn't even review all my blunders and previous sins. He accepted me just like I was, welcomed me into His kingdom, and gave me eternal life.

Psalm 32:5

Finally, I confessed all my sins to you…. And you forgave me! All my guilt is gone.

I told so many lies, and He gave me love and redemption.

Romans 5:8

But God demonstrates his own love for us in this: while we were still sinners, Christ died for us.

WEDNESDAY
Two-Minute Drill

Isaiah 40:28–31

The Lord is the everlasting God, the Creator of the ends of the earth.

He will not grow tired or weary, and His understanding no one can fathom.

He gives strength to the weary and increases the power of the weak.

Even youths grow tired and weary, and young men stumble and fall;

But those who HOPE in the Lord will renew their strength.

They will SOAR on wings like eagles;

They will RUN and not grow weary,

They will WALK and not be faint.

BUT THOSE WHO HOPE IN THE LORD WILL RENEW THEIR STRENGTH

THURSDAY
"Denial"

Matthew 26:34

Before the rooster crows today, you will disown me three times.

We have all done despicable things in our lives. We all have hurt people we love. At the time, we thought we were doing the right thing, but after days, months, and sometimes years, we doubt our decisions. Sometimes, we can't change the deep wounds and scars left behind by our sinful actions or words.

Mark 14:71

[Peter] began to call down curses, and he swore to them, "I don't know this man you're talking about."

We have all betrayed our Lord at some time in our lives. We didn't stand up for him or we didn't consult him for Godly wisdom. Sometimes, we feel like we heard his voice, but in reality, our desires outweighed his. Hopefully, the awareness of our mistakes creates a similar action to Peter's after denying the Lord three times.

Luke 22:62

He went outside and wept bitterly.

The damage has been done, so where do we go from here? Our Lord comes to us just like he did to Peter, and all he asks is this:

John 21:17

Do you love me?

Our answer should be just like Peter's: "Lord, you know that I love you."

If our hearts are just like Peter's and we have wept for forgiveness, Jesus purifies us from our sins (1 John 1:7). Our challenge is to accept the fact that the Lord of the universe has cleansed us from all unrighteousness. We cannot let the past control our future and prevent God from using us.

Did Peter look back at his denial? Did he let it stop him from being the man of God he was destined to be? No, he did exactly what Jesus asked him to do...

Feed my sheep.

FRIDAY
"What Is Repentance?"

Football coaches give constructive criticism so players maximize their abilities. Some athletes listen and excel, and others never reach their potential because they did it their way. God wants the absolute best for us, but our Heavenly Father (coach) has a different system. It's called a conscience. God has installed an active internal alarm clock that goes off every time we are violating his laws. He is trying to get our attention, and our job is to see why the alarm clock went off. Once we have recognized our sin, we must confess and ask God for forgiveness.

Proverbs 28:13
He who conceals his sins doesn't prosper, but whoever confesses and renounces them finds mercy.

Many times, I have asked God for forgiveness, but I was not truly committed to preventing the sin again. My mind was confessing, but not my heart. The sincerer confessions took place when I realized that if I repeated the offense in question, I was truly hurting my Lord and my God. Potiphar's wife told Joseph, "Come to bed with me," and he responded, "How then could I do such a wicked thing and sin against God?" (Genesis 39:9)

Acts 3:19
Repent, then, and turn to God, so that your sins may be wiped out...

The footnote in my Bible states. "Repentance is a change of mind and will arising from sorrow for sin and leading to transformation of life." We have all sinned (Romans 3:23), and we will continue to sin, but we need to continually commune with God to make ourselves aware of our transgressions so we may confess and truly repent.

Jeremiah 15:19
This is what the Lord says: "If you repent, I will restore you..."

SATURDAY REFLECTIONS
Philippians 4:12–13

I know what it is to be in need,

And I know what it is to have plenty.

I have learned the secret of being content in any and every situation,

Whether well fed or hungry,

Whether living in plenty or in want.

I can do all things through Christ who strengthens me.

Lord, as I review the past week, I remember:

....

....

....

....

....

....

....

....

....

....

....

....

....

....

....

....

SUNDAY
Psalm 138:2

I will bow down toward your holy temple
And will praise your name for your love and your faithfulness,
For you have exalted above all things your name and your word.

EXALTED ABOVE ALL THINGS

Prepare to worship and count your blessings.

....

....

....

....

....

....

....

....

....

....

....

....

....

....

....

....

Monday: TGIM

2 Timothy 3:2

People will be lovers of themselves, lovers of money, boastful, proud, abusive, disobedient to their parents...

11 years old

My buddy and I were riding our bikes (my vehicles always caused trouble), and I completely forgot about the time and was late for supper. I knew I was in trouble, but I was going to pretend I wasn't aware of the time. As I walked in the door, my mom was waiting for me, and she had her hand behind her back. She held out one arm and said, "Give me your hand." Hesitantly, I slowly reached out my arm, and she clamped on my wrist like she was possessed.

Then, I saw it. She pulled her arm around, and she had whittled the limbs off a small flexible branch so it had become a whipping machine. I couldn't get away because of the vise grip on my arm, so all I could do was spin around and dodge as many blows as possible. Praise the Lord I finally escaped the death grip and, fortunately, the upstairs door was open. I bolted, and she came after me, wailing away. There was a bedroom upstairs with one window and two beds. Decision time. Should I bust through the window and sustain certain injury if not death or crawl under the bed and see if she would come after me? She didn't scramble under the bed, but she did everything in her power to bend down and nail me with that demonic switch. She would go to one side of the bed and reach over and wail, and I would slide to the other side as I heard the whoosh of that branch just miss my flesh. Eventually, she got tired and stormed down the stairs. I came out from under the bed a week later (just kidding). Needless to say, I was never late again.

I know my mom is laughing in heaven as I tell this story. She was just a little woman, and praise God I kept growing so she couldn't put the death grip on me again. I did pay her back in my later high school years as my size and strength increased. As she was cooking dinner, I would go over and give her a hug and tell her how much I appreciated her. Then, I would lift her up and sit her down on top of the refrigerator. Paybacks were great. She couldn't get down without breaking an ankle, so eventually, I would let her down a few days later (just kidding). The only reason I let her down was because it was supper time.

MONDAY

"How Much Do You Love Your Children?"

Proverbs 13:24

Those who love their children care enough to discipline them.

Policemen, counselors, and administrators all agree our youth problem today is due to lack of discipline. I spoke with a policeman regarding this issue, and he said he has a terrible time with middle school kids. He apprehends this age group and calls their parents or guardians, and nothing happens. He commented, "There are no consequences for misbehavior!"

Proverbs 29:17

Discipline your children, and they will give you peace of mind and will make your heart glad.

Incarceration is a penalty, but our prisons are overflowing because inside the penitentiary walls, there are few requirements. Three square meals, gymnasiums, exercise equipment, libraries, computers, and no job responsibilities. Why do you think there are so many repeat offenders?

Proverbs 19:18

Discipline your children while there is hope. Otherwise you will ruin their lives.

My parents made the rules, and if I disobeyed them, there would be a consequence. Many times, I disagreed or had an excuse for my behavior, but the punishment was enforced. Without a mandatory requirement for obedience, why should anyone respect society's rules and regulations?

Proverbs 22:6

Direct your children on the right path, and when they are older, they will not leave it.

TUESDAY

"Letter to Our Children"

Exodus 20:12

Honor your father and mother.

Yesterday's devotional reviewed several scriptures emphasizing the importance of parental discipline. Moms and dads have a divine responsibility to enforce the rules and control their child's behavior. Parents must also inform their children that they are accountable too.

Colossians 3:20

Children, obey your parents in everything, for this pleases the Lord.

Here is an easy project. Reproduce the following letter and mail it to your individual children (kids, teenagers, and adults). Grandparents, send to your children and grandchildren (if their parents don't). On the return address, write:

God

Heaven

Dear _____

Proverbs 6:20–23

My son, obey your father's commands, and don't neglect your mother's instruction.

Keep their words always in your heart. Tie them around your neck.

When you walk, their counsel will lead you. When you sleep, they will protect you. When you wake up, they will advise you.

For their command is a lamp and their instruction a light; their corrective discipline is the way to life.

Signed,

Your Heavenly Father

P.S. Children, obey your parents (Ephesians 6:1).

WEDNESDAY
Two-Minute Drill

Today's scripture is for all you moms, dads, grandparents, guardians, babysitters, and all others in our society.

Ecclesiastes 8:11
When the sentence for a crime is not quickly carried out,
The hearts of the people are filled with schemes to do wrong.

Just think about when you were a kid.
If you got away with something, didn't you usually try to do it again?

Think about our justice system today.
Is prison really a punishment?
Why are there so many repeat offenders?
Should there always be a consequence?

Proverbs 13:24
The one who loves their children is careful to discipline them.

THURSDAY
"What's Important"

Proverbs 22:6

Train up a child in the way he should go, and when he is old he will not depart from it.

Every parent is concerned about their child's future. I just spoke with a friend of mine whose son is struggling with selecting a high school. So many decisions... academics, athletics, friends, administration, and many times, finances. We all want our kids to have everything better than what we had. I went to public schools, and my kids all had private education. I had $10 Chucks, and kids today have $125 Kevin Durant tennis shoes. Society wants us to believe that if we make more money, we can buy more happiness. But scripture tells us to be content with what we have... not what we want.

Hebrews 13:5

Don't love money; be satisfied with what you have.

Our children's futures are also dependent on how we apply biblical principles to their everyday living. We must share the benefits of following God's word and provide a loving discipline and awareness of the consequences of disobedience.

2 John 1:6

And this is love: that we walk in obedience to His commands.

We can shower our kids with gifts, provide fantastic schools, and make sure they eat the right foods and wear fashionable clothes, but in the end, there is only one thing that is important: Jesus.

We must not only spread the gospel, but we must _be_ the gospel.

3 John 1:4

I have no greater joy than to hear that my children are walking in the truth.

FRIDAY
"Do You Remember?"

Judges 2:10

After that generation died, another generation grew up who did not acknowledge the Lord or remember the mighty things he had done...

As I review the history of the Israelites, I find some interesting comparisons between their lives and our current society. God had led them from captivity and blessed them with some unbelievable resources. They were entrusted with the land of milk and honey with fertile land and magnificent beauty. After living there one generation (approximately 40 years), they did not remember the mighty things God had done.

Why didn't the older generation tell their children the great events that took place previously? The parting of the Red Sea, the plagues, the manna and quail, water from the rock, the walls of Jericho, and fighting the giants.

Is our society any different? Have we told our children and our grandchildren about God's magnificence and how our nation has been so tremendously blessed? The Old Testament miracles must also be explained, taught, and reviewed so they can understand the unlimited power of our great God. It is our responsibility to present the past in order to protect the future.

I am picking up my grandson tomorrow to take him to a football camp. I look forward to spending time with him and sharing football stories as well as other life experiences. Most importantly, I am excited to share God's story from Genesis to Revelation.

If we don't "remember the mighty things He has done," then our destiny will be the same as the Israelites.

Judges 2:11

The Israelites did evil in the Lord's sight and served the images of Baal. They abandoned the Lord, the God of their ancestors.

SATURDAY REFLECTIONS
Philippians 4:12–13

I know what it is to be in need,

And I know what it is to have plenty.

I have learned the secret of being content in any and every situation,

Whether well fed or hungry,

Whether living in plenty or in want.

I can do all things through Christ who strengthens me.

Lord, as I review the past week, I remember:

....

....

....

....

....

....

....

....

....

....

....

....

....

....

....

SUNDAY
Psalm 145:3

Great is the Lord and most worthy of praise;
His greatness no one can fathom.
One generation commends your works to another;
They tell of your mighty acts.
They speak of the glorious splendor of your majesty—
And I will mediate on your wonderful works.

I WILL MEDITATE ON YOUR WONDERFUL WORKS.

Prepare to worship and count your blessings.

....
....
....
....
....
....
....
....
....
....
....
....
....
....

Acts 2:41

Those who accepted his message were baptized...

12 years old

We went to the Christian church, sometimes called the B&B church because we were next to the local B&B ice cream shop. On Easter morning, we went to sunrise service and came back to church for breakfast and Sunday school. After that, I was to be baptized. I had been up since 5 a.m., so I was extremely tired, and I fell asleep prior to the ceremony. Fortunately, one of my buddies awakened me so I could follow the group behind the baptistery to get ready.

I do not remember too much about that day. I had been through the religion classes, absorbed the information, and mentally confirmed my belief in Jesus. I said the words, "I accept Jesus as my Lord and Savior," but nothing really happened that day. Where this fits into my salvation experience, I am not exactly sure. Did this event have a bearing on my future acceptance? Not sure... I guess I will have to wait and ask Jesus.

Where you baptized as a child?

Do you remember the details?

Did you just accept the facts?

Have you accepted Him into your heart?

Romans 10:9

If you confess with your mouth that Jesus is Lord and believe in your heart that God raised Him from the dead, you will be saved.

MONDAY
"Blondin"

John 14:6

I am the way and the truth and the life. No one comes to the Father except through me.

I remember the story of Charles Blondin, the famous tightrope walker. After many daring events, he decided to stretch his tightrope across Niagara Falls. Many people gathered to watch the event as Blondin made his first attempt to cross the mighty falls. As he arrived at the finish, he exclaimed, "Do you believe in me?" The crowd roared and exclaimed, "We believe!" Blondin now asked the crowd if they thought he could push a wheelbarrow across. They again applauded and said, "We believe." Blondin made the trip once again, and upon completion, he again asked the crowd, "Do you believe in me?" And again, the crowd shouted, "We believe!"

He then asked, "Who wants to get in the wheelbarrow?"

We must realize that we are sinners and the only way to God is through his Son, Jesus Christ.

Romans 3:23

All have sinned and fall short of the glory of God.

Romans 5:8

But God demonstrates His own love for us in this: While we were still sinners, Christ died for us.

Romans 6:23

For the wages of sin is death, but the gift of God is eternal life in Christ Jesus our Lord.

The belief that Jesus Christ is your Lord cannot be a mental acceptance of fact. It must be decision of the heart.

Romans 10:9–10

If you confess with your mouth that Jesus is Lord and believe in your heart that God raised Him from the dead, you will be saved. For with the heart one believes and is justified, and with the mouth one confesses and is saved.

Are you in the wheelbarrow?

TUESDAY

"What Is God's Plan For You?"

Proverbs 16:3

Commit to the Lord whatever you do, and He will establish your plans.

God's plan, not mine, will provide the maximum joy in my life.

Jeremiah 29:11

For I know the plans I have for you... Plans to prosper you and not to harm you, plans to give you hope and a future.

How do I determine God's plan for my life?

Every close relationship you have is dictated by the quality time you spend with someone. If they live in a distant city, you must communicate by phone, email, letter, Facebook, etc. Haven't you heard someone say, "We used to be close, but we lost track of each other, and we just grew apart"? You cannot maintain that closeness without some form of fellowship.

God is no different.

He wants to be my closest friend and help me plan my daily activities as well as my entire future. The only way for me to advance my relationship with the God of all creation is by spending more time with him. Not just Sundays, but every day.

1 Corinthians 2:9

However, as it is written: "What no eye has seen, what no ear has heard, and what no human mind has conceived"—the things God has prepared for those who love him...

Hebrews 11:6

He rewards those who earnestly seek him.

WEDNESDAY
Two-Minute Drill

NO GOD
NO PEACE
KNOW GOD
KNOW PEACE

It's so simple, and yet, we continually try to do things without him.
Think about your activities this past week.
How many times were there

NO GOD
NO PEACE?

Did you consult God?
You went to church, but what about the rest of the week?
We have the answer, but every day, we have to make the choice.

KNOW GOD
KNOW PEACE

THURSDAY
"The Vine"

John 15:5

I am the vine; you are the branches. If you remain in me and I in you, you will bear much fruit; apart from me you can do nothing.

Every day when we wake up, we have a choice to make. Are we going to be a functioning part of the vine or not? If we are too busy preparing for the world and don't pause to spend time with the Lord, then we have decided we can handle our daily responsibilities on our own. We have declared our independence from the power of the vine. We are telling our God, "I don't need you today. I can handle this."

The following verse reminds me about my priorities each day:

Joshua 24:15

Then choose for yourselves this day whom you will serve...

Hopefully, my answer is the same as Joshua's:

Joshua 24:15

But as for me and my household, we will serve the Lord.

Prayer: Lord, I need you. Forgive my neglect because I know you want to speak to me every day. I can't be the man you want me to be if I ignore your word and your voice. Help me start my day by reading your word, a short devotional, praying, or just listening. I need to focus on you and not the distractions of the world.

1 Chronicles 28:9

If you seek Him, He will be found by you...

Hebrews 11:6

He rewards those who earnestly seek Him.

FRIDAY

"I Love You"

Psalm 36:7

How priceless is your unfailing love...

One morning this week as I was driving down the road, my wife called. She was just checking on my plans for the day and how I slept. The conversation wasn't long. She told me she loved me, and we hung up. I paused to reflect on her words: "I love you." At that very moment, I felt her love as she said those magical words. What an amazing feeling to know that I am loved. Even more astounding is the fact that the God of all creation loves me even more... enough to sacrifice His Son.

1 John 4:10

This is love: not that we loved God, but that He loved us and sent His Son as an atoning sacrifice for our sins.

Notice the first part of this scripture: "not that we loved God." I remember when I didn't love God. I knew He was there, but the things of this world were more important. Despite my arrogant attitude and rejection of His presence, He still loved me enough to send His Son. Even though I denied Him many times, Jesus went to the cross for me... and you.

Romans 5:8

But God demonstrates His own love for us in this: While we were still sinners, Christ died for us.

Prayer: Lord, thanks and praise for your unlimited forgiveness. Thanks for your patience with my unrepentant heart. Thanks for your amazing grace and providing one of your greatest gifts, the opportunity to ask Jesus to be my Lord and Savior.

SATURDAY REFLECTIONS
Philippians 4:12–13

I know what it is to be in need,

And I know what it is to have plenty.

I have learned the secret of being content in any and every situation,

Whether well fed or hungry,

Whether living in plenty or in want.

I can do all things through Christ who strengthens me.

Lord, as I review the past week, I remember:

....

....

....

....

....

....

....

....

....

....

....

....

....

....

....

....

Psalm 25:4–5

Show me your ways, Lord,
Teach me your paths.
Guide me in your truth and teach me,
For you are God my Savior,
And my hope is in you all day long.

And my hope is in you all day long.

Prepare to worship and count your blessings.

....
....
....
....
....
....
....
....
....
....
....
....
....
....
....
....

Week #6

Monday: TGIM

Ephesians 5:18

Don't be drunk with wine, because that will ruin your life.

15–18 years old

I finally accepted the fact that my dad was an alcoholic. He wasn't mean or abusive, but he liked to argue and was quite obnoxious. My mom wouldn't have anything to do with him when he drank, unless she did too, and she definitely could not hold her booze very well. A few drinks, and she was looped. However, she drank very little, especially when my dad was trying to dry up. He would go six months hitting it hard and then lay off for six months and go back to church and teach Sunday school, and everyone thought he was the best.

My high school years were quite volatile, and when Dad was drinking, I would go out with my buddies because I had to get away. My friends would pick me up and joke about my dad drinking again. We all laughed, but deep down, it hurt.

My dad came to all my football games, and my parents would pick me up after the game most of the time. He didn't come to many of my basketball or baseball games, and I was okay with that because I wasn't sure what he might do. No, he wasn't a fighter, but I guess I was just embarrassed that people would see a drunk instead of seeing my real dad.

MONDAY
"Addiction: Part 1"

Ephesians 5:18

Don't be drunk with wine, because that will ruin your life.

I met with some friends whose son is an alcoholic. He recently lost his job, his house, and his wife to this dreaded disease. My heart goes out to them because I watched my dad slowly kill himself with this destructive addiction. My mom would get fed up and threaten him, and he would stop for weeks and even months, but he always returned to the bottle. He would teach Sunday school, which everyone loved, but after several months, he would disappear again. He studied the Bible and knew God's word, but he thought he could control his drinking. He could not understand or accept the fact that he could not have one drink.

My mom finally changed the locks and kicked him out of the house. He called me at college and asked me to meet him at a hotel. He said he was done with drinking and begged me to talk to my mom and convince her to take him back. I was young at the time and didn't realize I was enabling him to fall back into his old ways. I begged my mom, and she let him come home, but he never got help to assist him in conquering his dependency. He was just not strong enough on his own, which is true of most alcoholics. He needed counseling and a support team to fight the demon that constantly said, "Go ahead. You can have just one drink."

My dad retired at 64 years old and died of a heart attack at 65. His refusal to seek help killed him.

Proverbs 15:22

Refuse good advice and watch your plans fail; take good counsel and watch them succeed.

TUESDAY
"Addiction: Part 2"

Proverbs 13:10

Wisdom is found in those who take advice.

Just like my Dad, we are sometimes just not capable of solving our problems, and we must seek out Godly counsel. Everyone will go through difficult times that they can't resolve on their own.

Several years ago, I was confronted with a serious family crisis. Being the typical macho man, I kept saying, "I can handle this," but nothing seemed to work, and there didn't seem to be any answers. I prayed, and God humbled me and directed me to seek a Christian psychologist. This was one of best decisions I ever made. To this day, whenever there is a crisis of doubt or indecision, I will seek a professional who applies Godly principles. The Holy Bible is so full of wisdom, so why do we seek worldly answers and secular advice and neglect the help of counselors who know how to apply Biblical truths?

Romans 12:16

Don't be too proud... and don't think you know it all.

Proverbs 12:15

But the wise listen to advice

Why is it that we don't seek professional help? Are we too embarrassed or afraid someone will find out? As for me, I was just too proud. I thought, "I can handle this. I'm a big boy, and I don't need anyone's help." I even said I couldn't afford help, but I finally realized that I couldn't afford not to get help.

Proverbs 18:12

Before his downfall a man's heart is proud...

WEDNESDAY
Two-Minute Drill

Mark 11:25
And when you stand praying,
If you hold anything against anyone,
Forgive them, so that your Father in heaven
May forgive you your sins.

Are you holding any grudges?
Are there any members of your family you haven't forgiven?
Are there any business associates that were not fair?
The scripture says "anyone."
I don't see any exceptions, do you?
What did Jesus say at the cross while he was dying?

Luke 23:34
Father, forgive them, for they do not know what they are doing.

Maybe you even hold a grudge against yourself.
It's time to forgive!

Colossians 3:13
Make allowances for each other's faults,
And forgive anyone who offends you.
Remember, the Lord forgave you, so you must forgive others.

THURSDAY
"Addiction: Part 3"

Psalm 25:9

He guides the humble in what is right and teaches them His way.

I am so very thankful that God led me to a Christian psychologist. He helped me with many personal problems, including the anger dwelling inside over my Dad's alcoholism. Releasing some of those deep resentments took some time, but I finally forgave him.

My counselor also led me to the following scripture:

Ecclesiastes 4:9–10

Two people are better off than one, for they can help each other succeed. If one person falls, the other can reach out and help. But someone who falls alone is in real trouble.

Everyone needs someone to confide in and bare their heart and soul to. At the time I received this advice, I had many friends but no one to share my inner demons with. I reluctantly asked one of my business friends to start meeting early on Tuesday mornings to discuss God's word and His plan for us. It didn't take long before we were confiding our innermost thoughts and feelings. We started these meetings 25 years ago, and we never miss unless someone is on their deathbed or out of town.

If you don't have a close friend who you can call an accountability partner, find one! Eventually, your meetings will become an absolute priority. These weekly encounters allow you to verbalize your worldly and spiritual conflicts. God has answered many prayers during our search for Him on Tuesday mornings.

Proverbs 17:17

A friend loves at all times, and a brother is born for a time of adversity.

"Addiction: Part 4"

Ephesians 4:31

Get rid of all bitterness, rage and anger, brawling and slander, along with every form of malice.

I loved my dad, but he struggled with alcohol. There was no physical abuse, but because of his addiction, I was dealing with a lot of anger and rage. I disguised those emotions by ignoring the problem and pretending it didn't exist. I even joked about it with my buddies like it was an insignificant family situation. Internally, this was an expanding poison, and the Holy Spirit was prompting me to let it go. I remember reading the verse above, and I paused to look deep into my soul and how to confront the anger dwelling within. Then, I read the next verse:

Ephesians 4:32

Be kind and compassionate to one another, forgiving each other, just as in Christ God forgave you.

I never will forget the day I forgave him. What a remarkable feeling. I could feel the anger and rage leaving, almost like I exhaled those emotions out of my system. This was so easy, so why did it take so long? The devil knew he had a grip on something deep inside of me and that this cancer would continue to grow.

Whatever anger or bitterness issues you are dealing with today, just like the scripture says, *get rid of it*. Controversy with brothers, sisters, kids, parents, ex-husbands or wives, employment issues, whatever... Don't let it drag you down and destroy your joy because Satan wants you angry and bitter.

Proverbs 14:30

A heart at peace gives life to the body, but envy rots the bones.

SATURDAY REFLECTIONS
Philippians 4:12–13

I know what it is to be in need,

And I know what it is to have plenty.

I have learned the secret of being content in any and every situation,

Whether well fed or hungry,

Whether living in plenty or in want.

I can do all things through Christ who strengthens me.

Lord, as I review the past week, I remember:

....

....

....

....

....

....

....

....

....

....

....

....

....

....

....

....

SUNDAY
Psalm 5:7

But I, by your great love,
Can come into your house;
In reverence will I bow down
Toward your holy temple
Lead me, Lord, in your righteousness...

Lead me.

Prepare to worship and count your blessings.

....
....
....
....
....
....
....
....
....
....
....
....
....
....
....

Week #7
Monday: TGIM
Matthew 17:19
Why couldn't we drive it out?
15 and a half years old

I was almost at the legal driving age, and I was frustrated that no one would let me get behind the wheel. So, I decided to take things into my own hands. The 1961 Chevy had a keyed ignition on the steering column, and if you didn't turn the key all the way to lock, you would not need the key to start it again. Therefore, my mom always made sure she locked it all the way because although I was out of my harness from when I was 5 years old, I was still pretty sneaky.

My family watched television in the basement because it was cooler in the summer, and occasionally, everyone would go upstairs to the bathroom or to get something to drink. I made sure Mom and Dad's drinks were full and listened for their bathroom visits, and knew this was my chance. They were both comfortable and stable, so I nonchalantly went upstairs, rushed in the bathroom, flushed the toilet, and got the keys out of my mom's purse. Then, I quietly snuck outside and unlocked the ignition on the '61 Chevy. I then sprinted back inside, put the keys back, flushed the toilet again, and casually walked back down to the basement. What a plan... Phase one was a success, so it was then time for the CIA part of the mission. Fortunately, my parents slept upstairs on the second floor, and I was all alone on the first floor. I waited for them to go asleep and ever so quietly snuck out of the house and saddled up the six-cylinder rocket ship.

To be continued...

MONDAY
"Prayer"

2 Chronicles 30:27

And God heard them, for their prayer reached heaven, His holy dwelling place.

One day while at the grocery store, the pastor saw one of his members and said hello. He asked why he hadn't seen him in a while. The man responded with the following story: he had driven miles from civilization, and when he went to start his car, it would not turn over. There was nobody within miles, there was no cell phone service, and he had an important meeting to close a deal. The only choice he had was prayer.

He paused and asked God to start his car... no action. He prayed again, and still no action. Finally, he gave up and started walking to the nearest house. He missed his appointment and lost the deal. Infuriated by God's lack of response, he decided that he wasn't going back to church.

The pastor replied, "I certainly understand you being upset with the Lord. After all, you must pray four to five hours a day. The man answered that he didn't. Then, the pastor said, "Well, you must pray two to three hours a day then. Again, the main said, "no." "How about one hour a day?" No. "Maybe 10 minutes a day? No. "How about five minutes a day?" Still, the answer was no. Then, the pastor said, "The reason God didn't answer your prayer was because He didn't recognize your voice."

Lord, do you recognize my voice?

Romans 12:12

Be joyful in hope, patient in affliction, faithful in prayer.

TUESDAY
"Nehemiah"

Nehemiah's brother told him that his friends were in great trouble and the conditions of his hometown, Jerusalem, were appalling. The protective walls were crumbling, and the city was defenseless. Nehemiah responded as follows:

Nehemiah 1:4
When I heard these things, I sat down and wept.

How many times have you been devastated by some bad news? This news could be about loss of employment, a friend or loved one with cancer, marital problems, or a family conflict. Our world comes crashing down, and we search for strength and answers.

What do you do?

We are currently going through some stressful family problems. I analyzed the difficulties and decided on the action necessary. After many disputes and failed solutions, I finally drafted a letter to express my concern and my anger. Maybe they will get the message. Fortunately, my wife advised me not to send the letter.

What do I do now?

What did Nehemiah do after he sat down and wept?

Nehemiah 1:4
For some days I mourned and fasted and prayed before the God of heaven".

I finally realized that *I* had tried everything. *I* have been concentrating on how *I* could fix the problem. Sure, I prayed about it, but I thought *I* had the answers. I was really praying for a little spiritual boost so *I* could correct the issues *I* think are critical.

When am I going to realize that my solutions are not necessarily God's divine design? I need to learn that when I am confronted by life's complications, I should delay my reaction time and just slow down and...

Psalm 37:7
Be still before the Lord and wait patiently for Him.

WEDNESDAY
Two-Minute Drill

Joshua 23:16
If your violate the covenant of the Lord your God,
Which he commanded you,
And go and serve other Gods and bow down to them,
The Lord's anger will burn against you,
And you will quickly perish from the good land he has given you.

It only took one generation for the Israelites to forget these words.

Judges 2:11–12
Then the Israelites did evil in the sight of the Lord and served the Baals.
They forsook the Lord...

I know I have served other gods!
Money, possessions, power, prestige, greed, apathy, lust...
But after my seeking other Gods, there was no peace or happiness.
I didn't even like myself.
But Jesus still loved me enough to go to the cross for me.
Praise God!

John 3:16
For God so loved the world that He gave His one and only Son,
That whoever believes in Him shall not perish but have eternal life.

THURSDAY
"Class Reunion"

Isaiah 10:22

A remnant will return.

We had our fiftieth class reunion for Bardstown High School a few weekends ago. Before the event, one of my classmates who planned the celebration asked me if I would speak and deliver the prayer. I was honored and accepted immediately. The next day, I read this scripture in one of my morning devotionals:

Proverbs 17:6

Parents are the pride of their children.

My classmates and I were so privileged to have parents who put us ahead of themselves. My mom was a school teacher, my dad was a traveling insurance man, and neither one made much money. However, they always found the cash to buy me some new Converse or Bass Weejuns. There was never an abundance of toys at Christmastime, but there were always plenty of clothes to keep me in style.

They brought me to this great small town where almost all activities were within walking or biking distance. I remember every summer playing baseball all morning and riding my bike to the pool in the afternoon. I could walk to school and walk home after ball practice. A truly remarkable upbringing!

Psalm 126:3

The Lord has done great things for us, and we are filled with joy.

Prayer to our parents: We just want to thank you for all the sacrifices you made so we might have the opportunity to be successful in this world. We thank you for all the invaluable lessons, beliefs, values, and ethics you instilled in us. We know that many times, you had needs and that you set aside your own desires. We are sorry we never thanked you enough and never told you how important you were.

We were blessed to have you as parents.

We are filled with joy because of you.

We love you.

FRIDAY
"The Sea"

Genesis 1:9-10

And God said, "Let the water under the sky be gathered to one place…" And the gathered waters He called "seas."

My wife and I just returned from a cruise in the western Caribbean. I had been on ships before, but I had forgotten the vastness of the sea.

Just imagine: God spoke, and the oceans, rivers, and lakes appeared.

Psalm 95:5
The sea is his, for he made it.
Just imagine the power of hurricanes, typhoons, and tsunamis. However, God is…

Psalm 93:4
Mightier than the thunder of the great waters, mightier than the breakers of the <u>sea</u>—the Lord on high is mighty.
Another amazing thought:

Ecclesiastes 1:7
All streams feed into the sea, but the sea is never full.
Just imagine: one day, Jesus is coming, and He will conquer evil.

Habakkuk 2:14
The earth will be filled with the knowledge of the glory of the Lord as the waters cover the sea.
Just imagine: one day, our great God…

Zechariah 9:10
…will proclaim peace to the nations. His rule will extend from sea to sea and from the River to the ends of the earth.
Just imagine: all the times I have dishonored my Lord and despite all my sins, God loves me enough to forgive all my trespasses and…

Micah 7:19
Hurl all our iniquities into the depths of the sea.
Thank you, Lord, for your amazing grace.

SATURDAY REFLECTIONS
Philippians 4:12–13

I know what it is to be in need,

And I know what it is to have plenty.

I have learned the secret of being content in any and every situation,

Whether well fed or hungry,

Whether living in plenty or in want.

I can do all things through Christ who strengthens me.

Lord, as I review the past week, I remember:

....

....

....

....

....

....

....

....

....

....

....

....

....

....

....

....

....

SUNDAY
Psalm 11:4–5

The Lord is in His Holy temple;
The Lord is on His heavenly throne.
He observes everyone on earth;
His eyes examine them.
The Lord examines the righteous.

He examines the righteous.

Prepare to worship and count your blessings.

....
....
....
....
....
....
....
....
....
....
....
....
....
....

Week #8
Monday: TGIM
Matthew 17:19
Why couldn't we drive it out?
Part 2: The 1961 Chevy

I was afraid that if I started the car in the driveway, my parents might have heard the thunderous six-cylinder engine, so I decided to put the car in neutral and push it out of the driveway and into the street. I rocked it back and forth and pushed it as far into the street as I could. Then, I jumped in, started the engine, and took off to California (just kidding).

I decided to take some of the back roads out of town so nobody would recognize me. After all, it was close to midnight. All was going well, and after a leisurely exit from town, I decided it was time to go back home. On the way back, I passed a car, and when I scooted over, the tire went off the edge of the pavement. Of course, being the uneducated driver I was, I yanked it back rather abruptly. When it came back on the road, the car started to swerve back and forth and scared the... scared me badly.

I finally regained control, stopped and prayed, and thanked God for his mercy on my criminal behavior. It was definitely time to go home, and as I approached the driveway, I turned the lights out, sped up a little, shut the engine off, and quietly coasted to a halt. As I got out of the car and headed for the house, I saw my dad waiting for me (just kidding). If he had been there, I would not be writing this at this time. All went well, and I returned to my bed and swore I would never drive again.

To this day, my parents never knew this story and are gasping in heaven and waiting for my arrival.

I bet my mom is asking the Lord for that demon switch one more time.

MONDAY
"Jump!"

Matthew 18:3

Unless you change and become like little children, you will never enter the kingdom of heaven.

I remember my dad catching me as I *jumped* from various heights and distances as a child. I was a bold and fearless child, and as a 5-year-old, I attempted an impossible leap from a truck bumper to a tree limb. Unfortunately, I lost my grip and could not hold on, fell backward, and hit my head on a steel pipe that was used as a curb. I fractured my skull and lost the hearing in my left ear permanently due to nerve damage. Some of you reading this are saying, "I knew he had some brain damage."

Ten years ago, I remember another *jump* I made. I had some tremendous debts and had exhausted all avenues for repayment. I thought, "What now? Do I leave town, refuse to answer the phone, or file for bankruptcy?" I came home totally depressed, and my wife could feel the anxiety oozing from my body. We sat down, and after a long quiet period, she said, "We need to give this to the Lord." She quoted a scripture:

Psalm 55:22

Cast your cares on the Lord and He will sustain you...

Thirty years ago, I was in a similar situation as my football career was coming to an end. I sought the counsel of one of my Christian teammates and explained my dilemma. I mentioned multiple options, and he responded, "You forgot one!" Then, he spoke a remarkable two-word statement: "trust God." As I flashed back to those events, suddenly, a calm came over me, and I didn't care what the future held. If we had to move into a trailer, eat pork and beans, or drive a beat-up truck, we had each other, and most importantly, we had a God who would not desert us no matter what.

That day, my wife and I *jumped* into the loving arms of the living God.

1 Peter 5:7

Cast all your anxiety on Him because He cares for you.

Jeremiah 17:7

But blessed is the one who trusts in the Lord...

TUESDAY
"Waiting on the Lord"

2 Samuel 5:19

So David inquired of the Lord, "Shall I go and attack the Philistines? Will you hand them over to me?" The Lord replied to David, "Yes, go ahead. I will certainly hand them over to you."

King David, after receiving divine guidance from the Lord, had just won a battle against the Philistines, and his enemy was mounting another attack against the Israelites. Did David quickly gather his generals and plan his strategy? No. He paused, consulted the Lord again, and requested His advice.

2 Samuel 5:23–24

Once more the Philistines came up and spread out in the Valley of Rephaim; so David inquired of the Lord...

So many times, I have had an answer to prayer. Then, another situation will arise, and without hesitation, I proceed without prayer or seeking advice from the Lord.

Why do we forget to review things with God?

Is it because *we* think *we* are the ones responsible for success?

Is it our pride? Do we think, "God helped, but I did the work"?

Prayer: Lord, speak to my heart and mind, and help me realize you are the source, you are the power, and I am your vessel.

Psalm 40:1

I waited patiently for the Lord

Psalm 40:4

Blessed is the man who makes the Lord his trust...

Isaiah 40:31

Those who hope in the Lord will renew their strength. They will soar on wings like eagles; they will run and not grow weary, they will walk and not be faint.

WEDNESDAY
Two-Minute Drill

John 15:5
I am the vine; you are the branches.
If you remain in me and I in you, you will bear much fruit;
Apart from me you can do nothing.

Every day when we wake up, we have a choice to make.
Are we going to be part of the vine or not?
Are we too busy preparing for the world?
Are we too busy for God?
If so, we have declared our independence from the vine.
We are saying, "Lord I don't need you today. I can handle it."

Joshua 24:15
Then choose for yourselves this day whom you will serve.

Who will it be?

Joshua 24:15
As for me and my household, we will serve the Lord.

THURSDAY

"If You Love Me"

Romans 6:16

Whether you are slaves to sin, which leads to death, or to obedience, which leads to…?

My answer was life. The correct answer is righteousness. Why?

Many people believe that if they adhere to most of God's laws and as long as they are making a valiant effort, God will accept them into heaven. In Luke 11:37–53, Jesus visits with the Pharisees, and despite their strict obedience to the law, our Lord calls them hypocrites because of their hardened hearts. Jesus explains what our motivation for obedience should be.

John 14:15

If you love me, keep my commands.

When I first met my wife, we dated for an extended period. As we learned more about each other, our love increased (and it still does). As our love increased, the more we wanted to please each other. Our relationship to the Lord is no different. The more we search for Him, the more we learn to love Him. As our love expands, the more we desire to obey His commands and the more fulfilling our lives will be.

John 15:11

I have told you these things so that you will be filled with my joy. Yes, your joy will overflow!

I can only grow closer to my Lord by spending more time with Him. I know I must continually seek Him through His word, His church, Bible study, and fellowship with other Christians. We need to remember that:

Hebrews 11:6

He rewards those who earnestly seek him

FRIDAY
"The Roman Road"

The Romans were spectacular engineers and road builders. Many of their roads were built before the birth of Christ, and they still exist in parts of Europe, Asia, and Africa. The Roman Empire grew because of the construction of efficient roadways and to access their conquered neighbors.

These scriptures are from Paul's letter to the Romans.

The first three scriptures must be accepted into your heart and soul.

Romans 3:23

For all have sinned and fall short of the glory of God...

Romans 6:23a

For the wages of sin is death...

Romans 5:8

But God demonstrates His love for us in this: While we were still sinners, Christ died for us.

If we admit we are sinners and that God loves us, we may accept His gift.

Romans 6:23

But the gift of God is eternal life in Christ Jesus our Lord.

Romans 10:13

For whoever calls on the name of the Lord will be saved.

Romans 10:9–10

If you confess with your mouth that Jesus is Lord and believe in your heart that God raised Him from the dead, you will be saved. For with the heart one believes and is justified, and with the mouth one confesses and is saved.

Have you accepted Him as Lord and Savior?

SATURDAY REFLECTIONS
Philippians 4:12–13

I know what it is to be in need,

And I know what it is to have plenty.

I have learned the secret of being content in any and every situation,

Whether well fed or hungry,

Whether living in plenty or in want.

I can do all things through Christ who strengthens me.

Lord, as I review the past week, I remember:

....

....

....

....

....

....

....

....

....

....

....

....

....

....

....

SUNDAY
Psalm 13:5–6

But I trust in your unfailing love;
My heart rejoices in your salvation.
I will sing the Lord's praise,
For He has been good to me.

Rejoice.

Prepare to worship and count your blessings.

....

....

....

....

....

....

....

....

....

....

....

....

....

....

....

....

Monday: TGIM

2 Timothy 2:5

Anyone who competes as an athlete does not receive the victor's crown except by competing according to the rules.

16–22 years old

I played every sport: baseball, basketball, track, and of course, my favorite was football. As a freshman and sophomore in high school, I was pretty average, but as a junior, I grew to 6'2" and 190 pounds. As a senior, I then grew to 6'3 ½" and 205 pounds. I was a pretty good quarterback with a strong and somewhat accurate throwing arm, though my speed was average. I played linebacker and quarterback my senior year. We only had three seniors on the team, and the center I took snaps from was 5'8 and 150 pounds. We only won four games, but we beat our arch rival that was ranked in the top 25. This won the district and allowed us to play in the regional playoffs. Yes, our season had already been made, and we lost. But the next year, without me, the Bardstown Tigers won the state tournament.

I received a one-year scholarship to Louisville because I was still questionable. I weighed in at 6'3 1/2 and 208 pounds. They already had some big-name quarterbacks from the Louisville area, so I didn't get much of a chance to show off my arm strength and accuracy, but I enjoyed playing linebacker anyway. Freshman were not allowed to play varsity, but we had our own games, and I was obviously better than they thought because I soon received a four-year scholarship. Before spring practice of my freshman year, I had grown to 6'4 and 235 pounds. At that time in 1968, I was bigger than a lot of pro linebackers.

"Promises"

Joshua 1:9

The Lord God will be with you wherever you go.

What an awesome promise! Moses had just been buried and Joshua was leading the Israelites across Jordan to enter the Promised Land. Keep in mind that they wandered in the desert for 40 years because they did not trust the Lord their God. They witnessed all the plagues, the parting of the Red Sea, the destruction of Pharaoh's army, were fed with manna and quail, drank water from a rock, and yet, they rebelled and refused to believe God could defeat their opponents. Just like the Israelites, the Lord has blessed me. Then, shortly after, I have allowed the world to control my decisions and my actions. I can hear God speaking to me just like He did to the Israelites:

Numbers 14:11

How long will they refuse to believe me, in spite of all the miraculous signs I have performed among them?

Even after my God has rescued me, I have a tendency to take some of the credit. Why? Pride? Self-dependence? Then, as I studied God's word a little closer, I realized this world will absorb us unless we have a supernatural strength that is provided in God's Holy Word. God made Joshua a promise:

Joshua 1:9

The Lord your God will be with you wherever you go.

However, look at the preceding verse;

Joshua 1:8

Keep this Book of the Law always on your lips; meditate on it day and night, so that you may be careful to do everything written in it. Then you will be prosperous and successful.

Who is the first one to get squeezed out of my life? God. Why do I get too busy to start my day with the Creator of the universe?

If my desire is to truly have God with me wherever I go, then I must:

Meditate on it day and night.

TUESDAY
"Distractions"

1 Thessalonians 5:18

Give thanks in all circumstances…

I heard a great sermon at church a few weeks ago about the American people and how fortunate we are as a nation. But why do we continually want more and don't stop to reflect on our multitude of blessings? Will we ever be content? Our society is overwhelmed with desire, and as our preacher commented, we are:

CELEBRATING IN ACCUMULATION VS. CELEBRATING IN APPRECIATION

A buddy of mine goes to Africa ever two years to help out at the local orphanage. The kids there are so happy just to have food and a roof over their heads, and they continually praise God for His generosity. Residents must leave the facility at 18, find a job, and make room for others. One of the graduates was employed at the orphanage, and my friend saw him walking to work. He asked him where he was living, and he said that he lived two hours away. He walked four hours to and from work every day, and he didn't have any shoes.

Several days later, my buddy gave the boy a pair of new shoes, and his friend was overwhelmed and so very thankful for this special gift. As they talked, he asked him what he thought about America. He responded that it was the most amazing nation in the world and reviewed all the luxuries available to everyone. My friend asked him if he would like to go to the United Stated. He thought about it for a few seconds and finally responded, "No. I don't think so." "Why?" my friend asked. The ex-orphan replied, "Too many distractions!"

He did not want anything to interfere with his relationship to God. Nothing in the world was going to prevent him from spending time with the Lord.

Chronicles 28:9

If you seek Him, He will be found by you.

How about you? Do you have too many distractions?

Psalm 34:10

Those who seek the Lord lack no good thing.

WEDNESDAY

Two-Minute Drill

Nehemiah 1:2–3

Hanani, one of my brothers, came from Judah with some other men, and I questioned them about the Jewish remnant that survived the exile, and also about Jerusalem. They said to me, "Those who survived the exile and are back in the province are in great trouble and disgrace. The wall of Jerusalem is broken down, and its gates have been burned with fire."

Nehemiah has just been informed that his hometown of Jerusalem is defenseless against their enemies. He was very concerned about his friends and family being harmed by ruthless invaders.

What would you do if you knew your family had no protection?

When you are informed of a serious problem, what do you do?

What do you think Nehemiah did?

Nehemiah 1:4

When I heard these things, I sat down and wept.

For some days I mourned and fasted and prayed before the God of heaven.

FASTED AND PRAYED.

THURSDAY
"THIRSTY?"

John 4:14
But whoever drinks the water I give him will never thirst.
`

My wife and I were hiking in the Big South Fork National Forest on a cloudy but beautiful day. Midway through this adventure, the sun came out, the temperature increased, and we quickly realized we had depleted our water supply. With several miles to go, my wife (who is 100 pounds lighter than me) was doing fine, but I was dehydrating quickly. With my strength fading and my feet dragging, she spotted our truck in the parking lot. My spirits lifted because I knew we had plenty of water in the cooler. I never will forget sitting on the tailgate and drinking, pouring water on myself, and almost bathing in that cold water as I enjoyed one of the most refreshing moments of my life.

I reflected back on those moments as I read this scripture:

Psalm 42:1
As the deer pants for the streams of water, so my soul pants for you, my God.

I will not forget how thirsty I was that day in the forest.
Am I that thirsty for God?
Are you?

FRIDAY
"Thirsty? Part 2"

Revelation 7:16
Never again will they thirst.
Recently, we returned to the Big South Fork to revisit the Honey Loop Trail. This time, I packed five waters, and my wife had her own water supply. We arrived at the trailhead, and I commented about how different it looked three years ago. After hiking for two hours and not seeing any landmarks, we saw a sign that said: "Honey Loop Trail – 5 miles." Several miles later after climbing up and down rocky terrain and with only two bottles of water left, we finally came to one of the signature points of the trail, the Overlook.

We had been hiking for four and a half hours and had to climb two ladders and one stairway to get to the top. Weary and not sure what to do, a car pulled up, and a man and his wife walked over to the lookout. They commented that we looked pretty tired, and we told them we thought we had overlapped trails. We asked them how far it was to the Burnt Mill Bridge. When they told us that it was four miles, they could see the shock on our faces. We were dazed and not sure what to do, and then, amazingly, they asked, "Do you want a ride back?" I was soaking wet, but they reassured us they were in older open-air jeep and that we wouldn't hurt a thing. We piled in and headed back, and approximately a mile up the road, we spotted a sign that read, "Honey Loop Trailhead."

We had started at the wrong place and hiked almost 11 miles. We would have had to hike 4 miles back to the car. They dropped us off, and I watched as they returned up the gravel road. The lady had a bad knee and couldn't hike, and there was nothing else to see up this road. This had been a miraculous encounter, and I realized that these compassionate people were either angels or that God sent them to rescue us.

Luke 4:10
He will command His angels concerning you to guard you carefully.
If we had to walk another four more miles with limited water, we would have been in the hospital. Praise God He sent somebody! Thank you, Jesus!

Hebrews 13:2
Some people have entertained angels without knowing it.
We will not be going back to the Honey Loop Trail.

Proverbs 3:13
Blessed is the man who finds wisdom...

SATURDAY REFLECTIONS
Philippians 4:12–13

I know what it is to be in need,

And I know what it is to have plenty.

I have learned the secret of being content in any and every situation,

Whether well fed or hungry,

Whether living in plenty or in want.

I can do all things through Christ who strengthens me.

Lord, as I review the past week, I remember:

....

....

....

....

....

....

....

....

....

....

....

....

....

....

....

....

SUNDAY
Psalm 130:5

I wait for the Lord,
My whole being waits,
And in His word
I put my hope

In His word I put my hope.

Prepare to worship and count your blessings.

....
....
....
....
....
....
....
....
....
....
....
....
....
....
....

Week #10

Monday: TGIM

1 Timothy 4:8

For physical training is of some value…

College

My sophomore year, I started as one of the linebackers in a 5-2 defense. For our fifth game of the season, we played Cincinnati at Nippert Stadium. We watched their films and knew that their quarterback, Greg Cook, was good. He later started for the Cincinnati Bengals. I was going back on pass defense, and as I gained some depth, he threw back over the opposite direction from where I was going, so I turned quickly to make a play. As I turned, I felt my knee crunch, and instantly, I went down.

I went to the sidelines and recovered for a minute and got back into the game. A few plays later, I had collapsed again and was out for the game. The knee took several weeks of rehabilitation, but I came back and finished the season.

On the last game of the season, I was chasing a ball carrier and dove over someone trying to make a tackle. I landed on my shoulder, and I could feel it come out of place. As the doctors were coming onto the field, I moved it, and it went back into place. I wasn't quite sure what had just happened, and I couldn't explain it to the doctor. Normally, for dislocated shoulders, they strap you up for several weeks and allow the muscles to heal and move back in place. Unfortunately, since I didn't know exactly what happened, the treatment was just rest. But this injury would return with a vengeance.

During the off season, I played intramural basketball, and the knee collapsed several times. I went to the doctor and had it drained and worked on rehabilitating it, but it just wasn't right. Spring football practice was to begin soon, and the coaches had designed some agility drills for conditioning. As I was making a sharp turn, my knee locked up again. The only choice was surgery, and we scheduled it immediately. There was ligament damage, and the surgical procedure to repair the knee was called the "Slocum" process. Since it was late in the spring, the odds of me coming back for next season were not good, and eventually, I redshirted my junior season. The next football season, I worked hard on the knee and also helped the freshman coach during practice and at games. It was a long year, but the knee responded, and I gained some strength and speed until I was ready for spring ball.

MONDAY

"Feeling Down? Part 1"

Psalm 119:28

My soul is weary with sorrow; strengthen me according to your word.

Many times, I'll be struggling with a depressed attitude, so I'll turn on the Christian radio station. Miraculously, they always have something to lift my spirits.

Last week, I tuned into the show *Focus on the Family,* and as I listened to Kim Meeder's story, I was absolutely spellbound. She is an unbelievable communicator, and I was mesmerized by her passion. Her story began as 9-year-old who adored her parents. Her mom was beautiful, and Kim's desire was to grow up to be just like her. Her dad was her idol and her Superman too, and she envisioned him putting on his cape and rescuing the world.

One day before school was over, one of her dad's best friends unexpectedly picked her and her two sisters up. The three girls sat in the back seat, and nothing was said as they traveled the road to their grandparent's house. Kim knew something was terribly wrong as she watched tears run down her older sister's face. They arrived at the house full of people, and she remembers being able to feel the grief coming from within. As they entered the house, a close friend of the family was sobbing. She approached the girls and said, "I'm sorry. I don't know how to tell you this, but your father has just murdered your mother and has taken his own life. I'm sorry."

Nehemiah 1:4

When I heard these things, I sat down and wept.

TUESDAY

"Feeling Down? Part 2"

Psalm 34:4

I sought the Lord and He answered me...

In disbelief, Kim ran over to the woman and started hitting her and called her a liar. She then turned and bolted to the farm's orchard. She ran until she was exhausted and fell to the ground sobbing. At that moment, she said, "Jesus, help me. Jesus, help me. I need you now! I need you now!"

As she was telling the story about that awful moment in her life, she said, "At that time in my life, I didn't know who Jesus was. I think I only have a remembrance of going to church twice before that time, and all I knew is I think He's the guy on the cross and what I now know is that it doesn't matter who you are, how you were raised, what culture you were raised in, the truth of God's Word in Romans 10 is true today. Everyone who calls on the name of the Lord will be saved, and that salvation is as near as your lips and your heart. If you confess with your mouth that Jesus is Lord and believe in your heart that He is the Son of God, you will be saved."

Kim continued, "And what I now know is, as I cried out to the only One who could redeem this broken heart, that the Lord of all creation came down and crossed the expanse of heaven and knelt in the dirt beside a breaking child and took the hand that was reaching up to Him and my Jesus has never let go." She quoted the following scriptures:

Romans 10:13

Everyone who calls on the name of the Lord will be saved.

Psalm 34:18

The Lord is close to the brokenhearted and saves those who are crushed in spirit.

Whatever our circumstances, our God is always there!

*Focus on the Family Radio, Bringing Hope and Healing Through Rescued Horses, the Kim Meeder story (Part 1, 7-13-17)

WEDNESDAY
Two-Minute Drill

Psalm 119:176
I have strayed like a lost sheep.

Have you strayed?
We all have!
Romans 3:23
For all have sinned and fall short of the glory of God...

Why did we stray?
Because we weren't listening to the Shepherd.
Now, what happens?
1 John 1:9
If we confess ours sins,
He is faithful and just and will forgive us... from all unrighteousness.

Praise God for His forgiveness.

Romans 6:23
For the wages of sin is death,
But the gift of God is
Eternal life in Christ Jesus our Lord.

THURSDAY
"Reset Your Alarm Clock!"

Psalm 5:3

In the morning, Lord, you hear my voice…

Many days when I sign in at the YMCA, I am blessed to see a young woman named Maddie. She always has a radiant smile, and she lifts my spirits even when I am dreading my upcoming workout. She always has an unusual name for different days of the week. I asked her where she came up with this procedure, and she responded, "I taught elementary kids and Sunday school, and I always greeted them as they entered the room." Here are her designations:

Marvelous Monday, Terrific Tuesday, Whimsical Wednesday, Thrilling Thursday, Fantastic Friday, Super Saturday, and Spiritual Sunday.

How do you start your day? When your alarm clock goes off, do you begin dreading what is waiting for you at the office or plant? Or do you roll out of bed, set your feet on the floor, and pause and say, *"This is the day the Lord has made; let us rejoice and be glad in it" (Psalm 118:24)*

What's next? Put the coffee on, take a shower, grab a donut and a cup of caffeine, and head out the door. Here is another option: Set the alarm 5 to 10 minutes early and after rejoicing in the Lord, put the coffee on, take a shower, get dressed, and sit down for 10 minutes and enjoy your donut and coffee, and most importantly, spend 5 to 10 minutes with the Lord. Read your Bible or a short devotional or pray. Or, just be still and listen to what God wants to tell you. Your day will be different, and you will set your alarm early because you know God will speak to you.

Psalm 92:2

Proclaiming you love in the morning…

Ron Hutchcraft explains in his book, *Peaceful Living in a Stressful World*, "We're built to begin our day with our Creator. It started with Adam who met *"the Lord God as He was walking in the garden in the cool of the day" (Genesis 3:8).* Since then, men and women have been incomplete—whether they recognize it or not—without their morning walk with God.

Mark 1:35

Very early in the morning, while it was still dark, Jesus got up, left the house and went off to a solitary place, where He prayed.

FRIDAY
"Who Needs a Helmet?"

Ephesians 6:12

We are not fighting against flesh-and-blood enemies, but against evil rulers and authorities of the unseen world...

My grandson started playing full-contact football at an early age. He was so excited about wearing all the protective equipment until he put it on and could hardly walk, much less run. He was losing interest until his dad renamed the pads and helmet "his armor" so he would identify with the soldiers in his video games. Football is a rough sport that requires special equipment to protect the body from the opposing players. We must realize that the game of life has a serious opponent whose goal is to deceive us and not only damage our bodies but destroy our soul.

1 Peter 5:8

Your enemy the devil prowls around like a roaring lion looking for someone to devour.

Why do we play the game of life without wearing the proper equipment? Every morning, the devil is waiting at the doorstep, and his plan is to tempt us and prevent us from having a close relationship with the living God. Each day, we must prepare for battle by putting on our armor. We must take time with God by reading one of the 31 proverbs a day, reading a short devotional, taking five minutes to pray, thanking God for a new day and all our blessings, or meditating on his word, which is the sword of the Spirit (Ephesians 6:17).

Ephesians 6:11

Put on the full armor of God, so that you can make your stand against the devil's schemes.

During a professional football game, if you lose your helmet, you are required to go to the sidelines. Every day, we must remember that without our helmet (faith), we cannot play the game!

SATURDAY REFLECTIONS
Philippians 4:12–13

I know what it is to be in need,

And I know what it is to have plenty.

I have learned the secret of being content in any and every situation,

Whether well fed or hungry,

Whether living in plenty or in want.

I can do all things through Christ who strengthens me.

Lord, as I review the past week, I remember:

....

....

....

....

....

....

....

....

....

....

....

....

....

....

....

....

SUNDAY
Psalm 119:14–16

I rejoice in following your statutes
As one rejoices in great riches.
I meditate on your precepts
And consider your ways.
I delight in your decrees;
I will not neglect your word.

I will not neglect your word.

Prepare to worship and count your blessings.

....

....

....

....

....

....

....

....

....

....

....

....

....

Week #11

Monday: TGIM

1 Corinthians 9:26

Therefore I do not run like someone running aimlessly; I do not fight like a man beating the air.

College

Spring football practice arrived, and I was actually playing with some of the freshman I had helped coach the previous year. It felt so good to be back, and my knee felt absolutely great. I regained my starting position, had a blast, and enjoyed every minute. I had been out so long, and I realized how much I missed this game. We closed out spring practice with a scrimmage, and I finished with one of the hardest hits I ever delivered.

The offense faked a pass to the one side and then came back with a screen pass to the opposite side. I had chased the fake and then turned back to follow the screen pass. The back had proceeded straight up the field approximately 15 yards from the original line of scrimmage, and I was coming at almost a right angle at full speed. He never saw what was coming. I hit him so hard I actually think I blacked out for a split second. The contact lifted him off the ground and catapulted him 10 yards away into a heap. I remember Tom Jackson yelling and screaming as he watched the ball carrier elevate and finally come to rest. Coach Corso shook his head, and nobody was hurt.

All was well.

I was back!

MONDAY
"God's Gifts"

There are two amazing gifts God has made available to all.

Even though they are actually free, some choose not to accept them. I was one of those people. I thought I could control my own destiny without interference from the Lord. Eventually, I realized I was not capable of that, and I did not like the person I had become. All it took was a humble declaration to the Lord that I was not worthy, and would he accept me and take control of my life.

John 3:16

For God so loved the world that he gave his one and only son, that whoever believes in him will not perish but have eternal *life.*

That was the number one gift: *eternal* life.

The second gift happened almost simultaneously, and I was not even aware of it. I would soon recognize this remarkable gift because I started becoming more aware of some of my sinful actions. My language started to disturb me as well as my neglect and selfish attitudes toward my family. Yes, something unusual was inside of me.

Ephesians 1:13

When you believed, you were marked in Him with a seal, the promised Holy Spirit...

That was gift number two: the blessed *Holy Spirit.*

Nothing compares to these two extraordinary gifts.

Even more incredible? Both gifts are absolutely free.

All we have to do is ask... It's so simple.

Prayer: Lord, please forgive me and come into my life. My heart is yours.

TUESDAY

"Spiritual Exercise Is Non-Negotiable"

1 Timothy 4:7

Exercise daily in God—no spiritual flabbiness, please! Workouts in the gymnasium are useful, but a disciplined life in God is far more so, making you fit both for today and forever. (The Message)

How do we draw closer to our God?

2 Peter 3:18

But grow in the grace and knowledge of our Lord and Savior Jesus Christ. To him be glory both now and forever! Amen.

Our bodies need physical exercise, and in order for us to stay mentally sharp, our minds need exercise too.

Therefore, does our Spirit within us need spiritual exercise?

1 Corinthians 9:24–26

Do you not know that in a race all the runners run, but only one gets the prize? Run in such a way as to get the prize. Everyone who competes in the games goes into strict training. They do it to get a crown that will not last, but we do it to get a crown that will last forever. Therefore I do not run like someone running aimlessly; I do not fight like a boxer beating the air.

There is only one place to go for training!

1 Timothy 4:7

Have nothing to do with Godless myths and old wives' tales; rather, train yourself to be Godly.

2 Timothy 3:16

All Scripture is God-breathed and is useful for teaching, rebuking, correcting and training in righteousness...

Are you training?

WEDNESDAY
Two-Minute Drill

Joshua 23:16
If your violate the covenant of the Lord your God,
Which he commanded you,
And go and serve other Gods and bow down to them,
The Lord's anger will burn against you,
And you will quickly perish from the good land he has given you.

Our country is at a crossroads.
Yes, there are many Christians throughout our land,
But sometimes, we are not sure what to do.
Should we complain, gripe, sulk, or just become apathetic about everything?
We need to stand up and voice our opinions and vote,
But the most important thing we can do is...
Pray.

2 Chronicles 7:14
If my people, who are called by my name,
Will humble themselves and pray and
Seek my face and turn from their wicked ways,
Then I will hear from heaven and
I will forgive their sin and will heal their land.

THURSDAY
"How Do You Start Your Day?"

Psalm 59:16

But I will sing of your strength, in the morning I will sing of your love…

Psalm 143:8

Let the morning bring me word of your unfailing love, for I have put my trust in you. Show me the way I should go, for to you I entrust my life.

I started listening to the Christian radio station years ago. Most early mornings, I was on the road, and I always look forward to pastor LaVerne Butler of the Ninth & O Baptist Church. He was always so energetic, and he fired up my lethargic mornings with his opening line:

Psalm 118:24

This is the day the Lord has made; let us rejoice and be glad in it.

What a way to start the day! Shortly after you hear the alarm go off, or as you sit up on your bed, within a few minutes, give glory to our mighty God. Just imagine our God in heaven hearing your words as you get out of bed. Contemplate God's reaction and how much He appreciates being acknowledged. I can hear Him say:

"My precious child, I love you so. Thank you for acknowledging me. I look forward to being with you today."

Matthew 28:20

And surely I am with you always, to the very end of the age.

FRIDAY
"The Chase"

Proverbs 28:19

Those who works their land will have abundant food, but those who chase fantasies will have his fill of poverty.

From the time we are born, we continually receive food and information to develop our bodies and minds. We are trained to consume knowledge so that, ultimately, we will find a good job to become self-supporting. Employment usually results in a reasonable salary, and with the money we receive, hopefully, we will be able to purchase cars, homes, and many affordable conveniences. After we obtain these amenities, our society will classify us as "successful." This quest will continue because we are always *chasing* more of the "American dream."

In comparison, Christianity requires no *chasing* whatsoever. We do not have to do anything to earn God's Grace. Despite our sinful nature (Romans 3:23), this most precious of all gifts is absolutely free. Even more remarkable, all we have to do is...

Receive it.

John 1:12

Yet to all who did receive Him, to those who believed in His name, He gave the right to become children of God...

The choice is ours: keep *chasing* or receive God's amazing grace!

Prayer: Lord Jesus, I am so tired of *chasing*. I want you to come into my life and take control. Forgive my sins, and today, I receive you as my Lord and Savior. Amen.

SATURDAY REFLECTIONS
Philippians 4:12–13

I know what it is to be in need,

And I know what it is to have plenty.

I have learned the secret of being content in any and every situation,

Whether well fed or hungry,

Whether living in plenty or in want.

I can do all things through Christ who strengthens me.

Lord, as I review the past week, I remember:

....

....

....

....

....

....

....

....

....

....

....

....

....

....

....

....

....

SUNDAY
Psalm 119:33–35

Teach me, O Lord, the way of your decrees;
That I may follow it until the end.
Give me an understanding, so that I may keep your law
And obey it with all my heart.
Direct me in the path of your commands,
For there I find delight.

For there I find delight.

Prepare to worship and count your blessings.

....
....
....
....
....
....
....
....
....
....
....
....
....
....

Week #12

Monday: TGIM

1 Corinthians 9:24

Do you not know that in a race all runners run, but only one gets the prize? Run in such a way as to get the prize.

College

My junior football season arrived, and all went well, except I continued to have problems with my shoulder. The dislocation kept occurring and even started coming out while I was sleeping. I had to call the trainer over in the middle of the night once to put it back in place. I eventually started wearing a brace that restricted movement so my shoulder would not extend fully.

I prepared for my senior season and was elected captain of the team. What a great honor to be selected by your teammates to lead the team. Training camp began, and my shoulder seemed to be getting worse. Then, a couple of our offensive lineman got hurt, and Coach Corso called me into his office one day. He explained that we had plenty of linebackers and very few offensive lineman, and he needed me to help out and become a starting lineman. I accepted the challenge and left his office. After several minutes of contemplation, I remember returning to his office and sitting down and asking for another review of the situation. He said he did not have a choice and that this was what was best for the team and that he needed me to understand. This time, I grasped his decision and began my senior season as starting left offensive guard.

My senior season was fairly anticlimactic. There is only so much you can do at offensive guard. There were a few really good blocks but nothing spectacular, and we ended our season with a loss to Cincinnati. Fortunately, we did not have to review the films. My pass blocking was horrific, and I remember our quarterback, John Madeya, who was usually very unemotional, jumping my butt for letting my guy through. It was not a very pleasant goodbye as our season ended with no bowl games in sight. The football banquet went well, and I received recognition for being the captain and for being on the first team of the Missouri Valley Conference as an offensive lineman. This was more about politics because I was certainly not one of the best guards in the conference.

Shortly after the season, I had surgery on my shoulder. All went well, and rehab began, and I had planned on going to the pros as an undrafted linebacker.

MONDAY
"The Race"

Hebrews 12:1

Therefore, since we are surrounded by such a great cloud of witnesses... Let us run with endurance the race set out for us. Let us fix our eyes on Jesus...

We are in a race called "life." This is how I picture the competition:

I enter the stadium, and as I emerge from the tunnel onto the track, the crowd roars as my name is announced. There are so many people at the opposite end, and there are thousands of angels surrounding a colossal radiant figure. His gaze generates a warm feeling in my soul. Yes, it's God, and he is watching me race.

The starting pistol goes off, and as I head for the first turn, I see some people staring. Through some supernatural force, I recognize them. It's Abraham and Moses, and they are cheering for me. After the second turn, I see Daniel, Jeremiah, and Elisha shouting encouragement. A little further on, I notice David, Samuel, and Isaiah jumping up and down for me. As I reach the last turn, I am getting winded, but I see Ezekiel, Noah, and Joseph waving banners with my name. I am so close, but I am so tired. Then, I see a warm and irresistible glow coming from the finish line. Only a few yards to go, and I surge with a renewed energy as I see a pair of nailed, pierced hands reaching out to me. I stumble from exhaustion, and as I cross the finish line...

> I fall into the arms of my Jesus.

We are not alone. God and all His saints are cheering for us!

2 Chronicles 16:9

The eyes of the Lord search the whole earth in order to strengthen those whose hearts are fully committed to Him.

TUESDAY

"One Solitary Life"

Acts 17:26
From one man he made all the nations, that they should inhabit the whole earth; and he marked out their appointed times in history and the boundaries of their lands.

My dad and I had a long discussion about history and all the ramifications of actions of the people who preceded my generation. I was young, and of course, I disagreed with him and thought nothing of how the past affected my life or how it had any bearing on the future. That Christmas, he gave me a card that I still have to this day. Yes, it is worn and tattered, but I hold it dear to my heart. You may have read or heard it, but it should be repeated more often:

> *He was born in an obscure village. He worked in a carpenter shop until he was thirty. He then became an itinerant preacher. He never had a family or owned a house. He didn't go to college. He had no credentials but himself. He was thirty-three when the public turned against him. His friends ran away. He was turned over to his enemies and went through a mockery of a trial. He was nailed to a cross between two thieves. While he was dying, his executioners gambled for his clothing, the only property he had on earth. Nineteen centuries have come and gone, and today, He is the central figure of the human race. All the armies that ever marched, all the navies that ever sailed, all the parliaments that ever sat, and all the kings that ever reigned have not affected the life of man on this earth as much as that.........*
>
> ### ONE SOLITARY LIFE

John 3:15
Everyone who believes in Him may have eternal life.

John 3:16
For God so loved the world that He gave his one and only Son, that whoever believes in Him shall not perish but have eternal life.

Two-Minute Drill
Joseph

Genesis 37:2

Joseph, a young man of seventeen, was tending the flocks with his brothers, the sons of Bilhah and the sons of Zilpah, his father's wives, and he brought their father a bad report about them.

> Have you ever snitched on your brothers or sisters?
>
> Have you ever tattled on anyone?

Genesis 37:4

When his brothers saw that their father loved him more than any of them, they hated him and could not speak a kind word to him.

Have you ever had the feeling your parents loved your brother or sister more than you?

Genesis 37:28

So when the Midianite merchants came by, his brothers pulled Joseph up out of the cistern and sold him for twenty shekels of silver to the Ishmaelites, who took him to Egypt.

> How would you respond after you were sold into slavery?

Genesis 39:1

Potiphar, an Egyptian who was one of Pharaoh's officials, the captain of the guard, bought him from the Ishmaelites who had taken him from there.

> Joseph prospered and was put in charge of his household.

Genesis 39:6

With Joseph in charge, he [Potiphar] did not concern himself with anything except the food he ate.

> Life was good, but things were about to change!

THURSDAY

"Super Bowl: The Greatest Television Event of All Time"

Psalm 143:5

I remember the days of long ago; I meditate on all your works and consider what your hands have done.

What do you remember?

The unusual offensive play call and the interception?

The commercials?

The party you attended?

The halftime show?

Your team won? Your team lost?

Soon, it will be all forgotten. Maybe not for some fans, but for most of the world, the Super Bowl will have no bearing on their futures. Coaches and players may remember certain important plays, but for the most part, everything will soon be forgotten.

Our society is always looking for something new and fresh.

A new car,

A new house,

A new outfit, or golf clubs, or shoes, or video game.

And just like the Super Bowl, it fades away.

There is only one thing that never changes... **God!**

We search everywhere except the only place that never changes.

Malachi 3:6–7

"I the Lord do not change. Return to me, and I will return to you," says the Lord Almighty.

FRIDAY
"Treasures"

Hebrews 13:5
Keep your lives free from the love of money and be content with what you have...
If you had 10 cents and you were asked to give a penny to God, would you? Definitely.

If you had $1.00 and you were asked to give 10 cents to God, would you? Absolutely.

If you had $10.00 and you were asked to give $1.00 to God, would you? Maybe.

If you had $100.00 and you were asked to give $10.00 to God, would you? Doubtful.

God has blessed us so. All He asks is that we to set aside 10 percent for Him.

Deuteronomy 14:22
Be sure to set aside a tenth of all that your fields produce each year.

Genesis 14:20
Then Abram gave Him a tenth of everything.
We say, "But Lord, if I had more money, I would give more."

Ecclesiastes 5:10
Whoever loves money never has money enough; whoever loves wealth is never satisfied with their income.
When we stand before the judgement seat of God, will He ask us how much we saved or how much we gave?

2 Timothy 3:1–2
But mark this: there will be terrible times in the last days. People will be lovers of themselves, lovers of money...
We must continually ask ourselves, "Are we stewards for God or bankers for ourselves?"

Colossians 3:2
Set your minds on things above, not on earthly things.

SATURDAY REFLECTIONS
Philippians 4:12–13

I know what it is to be in need,

And I know what it is to have plenty.

I have learned the secret of being content in any and every situation,

Whether well fed or hungry,

Whether living in plenty or in want.

I can do all things through Christ who strengthens me.

Lord, as I review the past week, I remember:

....

....

....

....

....

....

....

....

....

....

....

....

....

....

....

....

Oh, how I love your law!
I meditate on it all day long.
Your commands are always with me
And make me wiser than my enemies.
I have more insight than all my teachers,
For I meditate on your statutes.

For I meditate on your statutes.

Prepare to worship and count your blessings.

....
....
....
....
....
....
....
....
....
....
....
....
....
....

Week #13
Monday: TGIM
Song of Solomon 7:6
How beautiful you are and how pleasing, my love, with your delights!
College

During the spring after my freshman football season, I fell in love. She was a Louisville girl who had attended Sacred Heart and then went to college at St. Catherine in Springfield, Kentucky. We met through some mutual friends in Bardstown, and the race was on. She was the only thing on my mind, and I almost flunked out of school because she was priority number one. I actually got mostly D's on my academic report at the end of my freshman year. My coach came and told me I was going to lose my scholarship if one of those grades did not change to a C. I made appointments to see all my professors, pleaded my ignorance, and asked if there was anything I could do to change the grade to a C. All of my professors had turned me down, and I had one last teacher to talk to. We met, and he really listened to me and allowed me to do some makeup work. If I completed it properly, he would reconsider. I worked hard, completed the assignment, and ultimately, he changed my grade to a C, and my scholarship remained intact.

God was really watching out for me throughout this ordeal.

I prayed continually during this trial and thanked Him for His response.

Shortly after, I forgot about His presence.

MONDAY
"Faith"

John 1:3
Through Him all things were made; without Him nothing was made that has been made.

After questioning a friend about the Christian faith, he challenged me to start reading the Bible. He suggested The Living Bible, a version similar to today's New Living Translation, which is written in today's vernacular. I had no clue where to start. He suggested the Gospel of John, and I was not disappointed. Here are a few highlights I remember:

John 1:4
In Him was life, and that life was the light of all mankind.
John 1:9
The true light that gives light to everyone was coming into the world.
John 1:12
Yet to all who did receive him, to those who believed in his name, He gave the right to become children of God.

Chapters 1 and 2 reference John the Baptist, Jesus's baptism, the first disciples, the first miracle, and the clearing of the temple. Then, the following verses in Chapter 3 really got my attention.

John 3:3
Very truly I tell you, no one can see the kingdom of God unless they are born again.
John 3:16
For God so loved the world that he gave his one and only Son, that whoever believes in him shall not perish but have eternal life.
John 3:36
Whoever believes in the Son has eternal life, but whoever rejects the son will not see life, for God's wrath remains on them.

As I reflect back on these verses, I am totally amazed by this remarkable book. **God's word** is the very source of our faith. **God's word** is the foundation of our judicial system. Without **God's word,** we would not know what to believe.

So why do you neglect reading **God's word**?

Joshua 1:6
Do not let this book of the law depart from your mouth, but you shall meditate on it day and night…

TUESDAY

"Prescriptions"

Colossians 3:23

Whatever you do, work at it with all your heart.

Just a few years ago, I was diagnosed with high blood pressure. At first, I thought that if I worked out more, it would go away. But according to my doctor, high blood pressure is part of the aging process. He prescribed the appropriate medicine, and I could tell the difference immediately. Occasionally, I would forget to take the medication, and I would feel the pressure increase, but it wasn't long before I never missed a day.

There is another prescription I must also take every day: God's word. Every day, I am forced to adhere to the world's standards, and I am not capable of fighting unless I am armed to battle satanic forces (Ephesians 6:12).

Colossians 3:16

Let the word of Christ dwell in you richly.

I used to believe that church on Sunday was the day to fill up my tank and that it would last me the rest of the week... wrong! I know I must allow God's word to penetrate my mind every day so I am equipped to combat the forces of evil. Not only do my daily devotionals prepare me for everyday life during the week, but they also psych me up for the only day of the week designated to gather together to worship the living God. Sunday is His time, and I am anxious to enter the sanctuary and praise His holy name. The songs come alive as I lift up the name of Jesus, and I know the sermon will be meaningful because God is going to speak to me through the minister. The message will be outstanding, but it will not be enough to last the whole week, and on Monday, I will return to God's word to maintain my spiritual strength. This will be an amazing week as the Lord prepares my heart for worship next Sunday.

Ephesians 6:17

Take the helmet of salvation and sword of the Spirit, which is the word of God.

Jeremiah 23:29

"Is not my word like a fire," declares the Lord, "and like a hammer that breaks a rock in pieces?"

WEDNESDAY
Two-Minute Drill

JOSEPH

Genesis 39:6–7

Now Joseph was well-built and handsome, and after a while his master's wife took notice of Joseph and said, "Come to bed with me!"

What would your answer be?

Genesis 39:9

"My master has withheld nothing from me except you, because you are his wife. How then could I do such a wicked thing and sin against God?"

Great answer, but the temptation would not go away.

Genesis 39:10

And though she spoke to Joseph day after day, he refused to go to bed with her or even be with her.

Day after day – so now, what do you do?

Genesis 39:11

One day he went into the house to attend to his duties and none of the household servants was inside. She caught him by his cloak and said, "Come to bed with me!" But he left his cloak in her hand and ran out of the house.

What would you do?

This is one of the most important parts of the story.

We will all be confronted by temptation.

Your sexy secretary or handsome boss makes a flirtatious remark.

What do you do?

A Facebook post invites you to a pornographic page.

What do you do?

You have to go to a meeting, and an attractive employee or coworker asks for ride.

What do you do?

RUN. NO EXCEPTIONS. RUN.

"The Meeting"

1 Corinthians 7:29
What I mean, brothers and sisters, is that the time is short.

I couldn't sleep last night because I was anxious about meeting my best friend in the morning. He had told me that he had something to tell me that was important. I woke up early in eager anticipation because our previous meetings had been so helpful. After our time together, I would always leave with some special knowledge or wisdom. With such uplifting results, I wondered why we didn't meet more often. Maybe we should, but I was and am extremely busy, and was not sure if I had time. If these meetings were so beneficial and lifted my spirits so much, I couldn't afford not to go. I will ask him today if we can start meeting every day because I know I need his influence in my life. Hopefully, he enjoys my company as much as I do his. I asked him that day, and here was his answer:

"I enjoy our time together, and it is so special every time we meet. I promise I will be here any time you want to get together. While I was on earth, I met with my Father early every morning as well as throughout the day, and His presence filled me continuously. I have been your Lord and Savior for a long time, but our meetings together have been somewhat erratic. I know you are busy, but I want to spend time with you every day. I love you so."

Hosea 10:12
For it is time to seek the Lord...

FRIDAY
"Who Are You?"

Matthew 16:13–16

He asked His disciples, "Who do people say the Son of Man is?" They replied, "Some say John the Baptist; others say Elijah; and still others, Jeremiah or one of the prophets." "But what about you?" he asked. "Who do you say I am?"

In his devotional book, *Uncommon Life,* Tony Dungy asks a unique spinoff of this question. During a team meeting, he asked his players this question: "Who are you?" Most of his players said they were professional athletes, but Tony pushed them beyond their current job status. If they were not a pro football player, who would they be?

This is a very profound question for you to ask yourself. Who are you? What would your answer be? Father, mother, husband, wife, businessperson, employee, housewife, Christian, child of God, disciple, student? This question may reveal interesting personal insights. Think about it... Who are you?

I am a flower quickly fading

Here today and gone tomorrow

A wave tossed in the ocean

A vapor in the wind

Still you hear me when I'm calling

Lord, you catch me when I'm falling

And you've told me who I am

I am yours

"Who am I" by Casting Crowns

John 1:21

They asked him, "Then who are you?"

SATURDAY REFLECTIONS
Philippians 4:12–13

I know what it is to be in need,

And I know what it is to have plenty.

I have learned the secret of being content in any and every situation,

Whether well fed or hungry,

Whether living in plenty or in want.

I can do all things through Christ who strengthens me.

Lord, as I review the past week, I remember:

....

....

....

....

....

....

....

....

....

....

....

....

....

....

....

SUNDAY
Psalm 119:103

How sweet are your words to my taste,
Sweeter than honey to my mouth!
I gain understanding from your precepts;
Therefore I hate every wrong path.
Your word is a lamp for my feet,
A light on my path,

Your word is a lamp for my feet,
A light on my path.

Prepare to worship and count your blessings.

....
....
....
....
....
....
....
....
....
....
....
....
....

Week #14
Monday: TGIM
Ecclesiastes 9:9
Enjoy life with your wife...
College

We dated for over a year, and during our romance, I went through knee surgery in the spring, and that summer, she met my parents. I was redshirted due to my knee surgery, and we were married in September and moved into the married student's dorm. Shortly after, she became pregnant, and our first child was on the way. I remember going to the hospital after my son was born, and several of my teammates came to see the baby. We were looking at my son, and as the nurse picked him up, he relieved himself as everyone watched. One of the players said, "That's Amos' kid alright."

We lived in the dorm for the next four years and struggled to make it financially, but our parents always helped us out. After my senior football season, I had surgery on my shoulder to correct the chronic dislocation. Not playing linebacker my senior season would probably eliminate me from the draft, and I had planned on attending training camp somewhere as an undrafted rookie.

Shockingly, I was drafted in the sixth round by the Minnesota Vikings.
What an honor and privilege and absolute surprise to be selected.

God was watching over me...

Again!

MONDAY
"Even If…"

Daniel 3:17

If we are thrown into the blazing furnace, the God we serve is able to save us from it, and He will deliver us from Your Majesty's hand.

There are some fantastic contemporary Christian singing groups today. Some of my favorite songs over the years include "The Revelation Song" by Phillips, Craig & Dean, "Oceans" by Hillsong United, "Blessed Be Your Name" by Matt Redman, and "I Can Only Imagine" by MercyMe. Today, MercyMe has a song called "Even If." The main chorus of this inspirational song goes:

"I know you're able and I know you can

Save through the fire with your mighty hand

But even if you don't

My hope is you alone…

I know the sorrow, and I know the hurt

Would all go away if you'd just say the word

But even if you don't

My hope is you alone"

In the third chapter of the book of Daniel, three Christian men stood up for their God. Even if they were thrown into the blazing furnace, they refused to serve or worship other gods. These three young men were not arrogant or condemning but, with a bold and loving heart, expressed their beliefs.

1 Corinthians 16:13

Be on guard; stand firm in the faith; be men of courage; be strong. Do everything in love.

Our society today and even some of our churches are suggesting we rationalize God's laws. There are no exceptions for disobedience, we must stand firm in our faith. Our country must return to the same beliefs of our Founding Fathers even though we may be criticized and persecuted. We must stand firm and restore our country to "In God We Trust." If we are thrown into the blazing furnace, we must trust that our God can save us from the fire, but…

Even if He does not, our hope is Him alone.

TUESDAY
"Reasons for Denial"

1 Timothy 2:3–4

...God our Savior, who wants everyone to be saved...

Reasons people refuse to invite Jesus Christ into their lives:

1. "With all the bad things I have done, God will never forgive me..." Wrong! Jesus forgave the thief on the cross.

Luke 23:43

And Jesus said to him, "I tell you the truth, today you will be with me in paradise."

Jesus forgave the adulterous woman.

John 8:11

"Then neither do I condemn you," Jesus declared. "Go now and leave your life of sin."

2. "I have to clean up my act first!" Wrong! No matter what you have done or what you are currently doing, God wants you just the way you are, no restrictions. All he wants is your heart.

Romans 10:10

For it is with your heart that you believe and are justified, and it is with your mouth that you profess your faith and are saved.

3. "I know some people who say they are Christians, and they seem very judgmental. They act like they are better than me."

Romans 14:10

You, then, why do you judge your brother or sister? Or why do treat them with contempt? For we will all stand before God's judgement seat.

We are representatives for the living God. Our behavior may determine someone's acceptance or rejection of our Savior.

"They will know we are Christians by our love."

–Fr. Peter Scholtes

WEDNESDAY
Two-Minute Drill

JOSEPH

Genesis 39:16–18

She kept the cloak beside her until his master came home. Then she told him this story: "That Hebrew slave you brought us came to me to make sport of me. But as soon as I screamed for help, he left his cloak beside me and ran out of the house."

Have you ever done the honorable thing and been blamed?

Genesis 39:19–20

When his master heard the story his wife told him, saying, "This is how your slave treated me," he burned with anger. Joseph's master took him and put him in prison...

Joseph honored God and got put in prison. Doesn't seem fair, does it?

Genesis 39:20–21

But while Joseph was there in the prison, the Lord was with him; he showed him kindness and granted him favor in the eyes of the prison warden.

God always honors the righteous... ALWAYS.

Psalm 34:15

The eyes of the Lord are on the righteous, and His ears

Are attentive to their cry.

Psalm 37:25

I was young and now I am old, yet I have never seen the

Righteous forsaken...

Psalm 55:22

Cast your cares on the Lord and He will sustain you;

He will never let the righteous fall.

Proverbs 15:29

The Lord is far from the wicked, but

He hears the prayer of the righteous.

God always honors the righteous... ALWAYS.

THURSDAY
"THE NEXT DAY"

Luke 24:40

He showed them His hands and feet. And while they still did not believe...

The disciples were still doubtful and refused to believe that Jesus had returned from the grave. They remained skeptical until they finally saw their Savior in person. Even then, they were hesitant to be convinced that He was alive.

Acts 1:3

He appeared to them over a period of forty days...

The risen Christ did not make just one appearance but several. This was so the disciples could again have physical contact with the Savior of the world and also so they could trust that He truly was the Messiah.

Acts 1:5

In a few days you will be baptized with the Holy Spirit.

Before his death, Jesus mentioned the "counselor" and compared the Holy Spirit to streams of living water. The disciples were oblivious to this explosive power that would saturate their very souls.

Acts 2:4

All of them were filled with the Holy Spirit...

Then, just as Jesus had promised, God would bestow on mankind one of His greatest gifts. The truly devoted followers of Jesus, the ones who had decided to commit their lives to God, were filled with the Holy Spirit.

Jesus's death and resurrection occurred so we, just like the disciples, would have the same opportunity to receive the "Spirit of Truth," the blessed Holy Spirit. No, you don't have to become a missionary, sell everything, join the church, change your name, or quit cussing or drinking. You don't have to correct all the things you have done wrong or are still doing wrong. God wants us just the way we are, and through the mighty power of the indwelling Holy Spirit, He will direct the changes. All we have to do is ask Him to take control of our lives and show us the way.

Romans 10:9–10

If you confess with your mouth that Jesus is Lord and believe in your heart that God raised Him from the dead, you will be saved.

FRIDAY

"Do You Believe?"

For many years, I would have told you I *believed* in Jesus Christ and that He was God's Son. This *belief* was just another piece of information stored in my mind. I was shocked to read the following verse:

James 2:19

"You <u>believe</u> that there is one God. Good! Even the demons believe that— and shudder."

Wow! How am I different than the demons? Even Satan recognized the fact that Jesus was the Son of God. As Jesus was tempted in the desert, Satan attempted to persuade Jesus into compromising his supernatural power. The devil said to him, "If you are the Son of God, tell these stones to become bread" (Matthew 4:3).

Nicodemus, one of the Pharisees and a religious man, came to our Lord and *believed* that Jesus was a "teacher who has come from God." Jesus declared, "I tell you the truth, no one can see the kingdom of God unless he is born again" and then reiterated "you should not be surprised at my saying, 'you must be born again.'" (John 3:2 and 3:7).

So, what is this born-again experience?

If I told you I was a trained jet pilot, you could nod your head and agree with me. But until you step on the plane and risk your life on a flight with me, you really don't *believe* in me. To be born again, we must climb aboard God's plane of grace, risk our very souls, and trust the Lord with all our hearts (Romans 10:9–10). We need to realize that we are hopeless sinners (Romans 3:23) and ask Jesus to take control of our lives. By truly *believing* that Jesus is our Lord and Savior, a whole new life will begin, and therefore, we are…

BORN AGAIN!

2 Corinthians 5:17

Therefore, if anyone is in Christ, the new creation has come: The old has gone, the new is here!

SATURDAY REFLECTIONS
Philippians 4:12–13

I know what it is to be in need,

And I know what it is to have plenty.

I have learned the secret of being content in any and every situation,

Whether well fed or hungry,

Whether living in plenty or in want.

I can do all things through Christ who strengthens me.

Lord, as I review the past week, I remember:

....

....

....

....

....

....

....

....

....

....

....

....

....

....

....

....

SUNDAY
Psalm 119:171–174

May my lips overflow with praise,
For you teach me your decrees.
May my tongue sing of your word,
For all your commands are righteous.
May your hand be ready to help me,
For I have chosen your precepts.
I long for your salvation, Lord,
And your law gives me delight.

Your law gives me delight.

Prepare to worship and count your blessings.

....

....

....

....

....

....

....

....

....

....

....

....

Week #15

Monday: TGIM

2 Timothy 1:7

For the Spirit God gave us does not make us timid, but gives us power, love, and self-discipline.

NFL

I remember preparing for training camp and working on my shoulder as well as my legs. I lifted weights and ran the 11 flights of stairs in the married student dormitory many, many times. That summer, we moved to Jackson Mississippi to stay with my wife's parents. They had a three-bedroom townhouse, and if I did not make the team, I would return there and determine my future plans.

Fortunately, I did make the team, and my wife had to drive from Jackson to Minneapolis with a four-year-old. I was extremely blessed to meet a former Navy Seal while I was working out at the YMCA. We lifted weights together, and we would usually play full-court basketball for two hours at a time.

Then, one day, he asked me if I wanted to jog with him in the afternoon. I said sure and met him at his house around 5 p.m. We started jogging, and I asked him how far we were going. I was used to running two to three miles, but then he told me that we were going to run six miles. He was 5'8 and 175 pounds, and I was 6'4 and 235 pounds. I told him I had to carry a lot more weight than he did. He called me a sissy, and the challenge began. We talked and time went by, and he finally informed me that the end was nearing. I surprised myself and sprinted the last 200 yards. This was my routine the rest of the summer, and I went to camp in great shape.

Training camp arrived, and the first day was picture day and a light practice. The coaches told 80 guys to circle up to begin the exercises. I noticed that the veterans were jacking around, but the rookies were giving it everything they had. They had us do some extremely difficult drills, and I noticed that the veterans were kidding around while I was busting a gut. We finally finished, and I caught my breath to go into some linebacker drills—basically cutting and catching the ball. This was not a problem, but if I knew that if I had to go through those exercises again, I was going to die. I thought about it all night and prayed for divine intervention. The next day, the linebackers started off in some extensive stretching drills. No sweat. I knew I could make it! From there, we went into up downs. There were many, many up downs, but again, this was not a problem.

This was the place for me!

MONDAY

"Are You Ready for Some More Football?"

Matthew 22:37

Jesus replied: "Love the Lord your God with all your heart and with all your soul and with all your mind."

Shortly after attending my first training camp with the Vikings in 1972, my linebacker coach handed me the defensive playbook. I almost went into shock because this was the largest collection of alignments, formations, blitzes, passes, and run coverages I had ever seen. There was no way I could digest all this information, especially in a short period of time. Fortunately, I received some help from some of the other rookies as well as a few veterans. This was a slow process of repetitious review, and eventually, my body was reacting to the mental signals ingrained in my subconscious.

Even today when I coach middle school football, the same principles hold true. Constant repetition is mandatory, and running the plays over and over is the only learning mechanism that works. Memorizing is one thing, but application in a split second is another.

Our spiritual life is no different. We all make mistakes, and we are all looking for answers on how to correct our weaknesses. The Bible, the greatest book in the history of mankind, was given to us as a playbook for living a joy-filled life. If we neglect this book, our minds and bodies will return to our sinful ways prescribed by the world. We are not capable of fighting without absorbing the power of God's holy instruction manual.

2 Timothy 3:16–17

All scripture is God-breathed and is useful for teaching, rebuking, correcting and training in righteousness, so that the servant of God may be thoroughly equipped for every good work.

Are you prepared for the schemes of the devil?

TUESDAY
"Expand Your Mind"

2 Peter 3:18

But grow in the grace and knowledge of our Lord and Savior Jesus Christ.

Why do pro football players spend long hours reviewing and studying films every week and then designing new plays and modifying defenses? Why do good cooks constantly read and research in order to find new ingredients and new recipes? Why are we constantly absorbing more information about computers and smart phones? To expand our minds!!!!!

Therefore in order to expand our mind about spiritual things, where do you go?....................**God's word, the Bible**

Years ago, a friend told me to start reading the Bible, and I accused him of having a mental disorder. All those "thees" and "thous" and stories about Charlton Heston, Moses, and Ben-Hur, and who was going to translate for me? I was told to try the Living Bible (which is paraphrased) and to start with the Gospel of John. I thoroughly enjoyed it and actually understood this version of the Bible because it read like a novel.

Here's a suggestion for those of you who are not sure where to start or are looking for a plan. Not only is this one of the greatest inventions ever, but it's also free. Go to your computer or smartphone, and get a Bible app. There are so many super-new translations. Find the one you like, and then look at the various reading plans, videos, audios, and the myriad of fantastic authors that are absolutely free! I recently helped my granddaughter search for devotionals for teenagers.

Here is a project for you: Go to your Bible app, look up the following scripture, and fill in the blanks. Review the same verse in several different translations, and see which one you like best. God bless.

Hebrews 4:12

For the word of God is living and _____. Sharper than any double-edged _____, it penetrates even to dividing _____ and _____, joints and _____; it judges the _____ and _____ of the heart.

WEDNESDAY
Two-Minute Drill

JOSEPH

Genesis 40:23

The warden paid no attention to anything under Joseph's care, because the Lord was with Joseph and gave him success in whatever he did.

Psalm 37:4–7

Delight yourself in the Lord,

And He will give you the desires of your heart.

Commit your way to the Lord; trust in Him and He will do this:

He will make your righteous reward shine like the dawn,

Your vindication like the noonday sun.

Genesis 41:1

When two full years had passed, Pharaoh had a dream…

Genesis 41:14

So Pharaoh sent for Joseph, and he was quickly brought from the dungeon.

Joseph had been a slave for Potiphar for 13 years and had been imprisoned for at least two years before he was called to interpret Pharaoh's dream.

Are you that patient?

But the Lord was with him. (Genesis 40:20)

The eyes of the Lord are on the righteous. (Psalm 34:15)

A man's wisdom gives him patience. (Proverbs 19:11)

Do you have some important decisions to make?

Wait on the Lord: be of good courage, and he shall strengthen your heart. (Psalm 27:14)

I waited patiently for the Lord; He turned to me and heard my cry. (Psalm 40:1)

Do you feel rushed?

Psalm 130:5

I wait for the Lord, my whole being waits, and in His word I put my hope.

WAIT!

THURSDAY
"I Can't"

John 5:6

When Jesus saw him lying there and learned he had been in this condition for a long time, he asked him, "Do you want to get well?"

Many times, I am anxious to give my kids or friends advice, though I truly think my understanding of the situation and my Godly wisdom through prayer could really help. However, if they really don't think they need help, I am probably wasting my time.

John 5:8

Then Jesus said to him, "Get up! Pick up your mat and walk."

The healing at the pool is a perfect example of someone who wanted help. This man had been an invalid for 38 years, and he now had a decision. Jesus healed him, but it was his choice to move, or since he had been disabled for 38 years, to say, "I can't." The crippled man picked up his mat and walked.

Some people listen to advice and say, "I can't," but they really mean, "I won't." One friend of mine smokes, and several members of his family have died from lung cancer. He says, "I can't," but he really means, "I won't." Another close friend has multiple health problems and potential diabetes, but he refuses to quit drinking soft drinks, will not drink water, and will not exercise. He says, "I can't," but he really means, "I won't."

Likewise, I have my own vices. I could stop, but I say, "I won't."

Prayer: Merciful God, I want to help people, and I know I can fix them... WRONG. Only you can help the situation and speak to me on how to respond to people. Slow me down to receive your wisdom and your guidance and not search for earthly answers. Help me to review my own inadequacies and the areas in which I am saying, "I won't."

"Eternity"

Luke 10:25

On one occasion an expert in the law stood up to test Jesus. "Teacher, he asked, "what must I do to inherit eternal life?"

If you were driving down the road and you suddenly saw an 18-wheeler coming directly at you, there would be no time to brake, turn, or avoid what was about to happen. Yes, you would be killed in a horrendous traffic accident.

What would be next? Heaven? Hell? Purgatory? Limbo?

Where will you spend eternity? Are you absolutely positive?

What is God's desire for everyone on earth?

Matthew 18:14

In the same way your Father in heaven is not willing that any *of these little ones should perish.*

God wants *everyone* to join Him in heaven, and that's why he sent Jesus.

Romans 6:23

For the wages of sin is death, but the gift of God is eternal life in Christ Jesus our Lord.

We have two options on earth: Accept or reject. Receive Christ as our Lord and Savior, or deny him.

John 3:36

Whoever believes in the Son has eternal life, but whoever rejects the Son will not see life…

Are you sure where you will spend eternity?

1 John 5:11–12

And this is the testimony: God has given us eternal life, and this life is in his Son. Whoever has the Son has life; whoever does not have the Son of God does not have life.

SATURDAY REFLECTIONS
Philippians 4:12–13

I know what it is to be in need,

And I know what it is to have plenty.

I have learned the secret of being content in any and every situation,

Whether well fed or hungry,

Whether living in plenty or in want.

I can do all things through Christ who strengthens me.

Lord, as I review the past week, I remember:

....

....

....

....

....

....

....

....

....

....

....

....

....

....

....

Psalm 27:4

One thing I ask of the Lord,
This only do I seek:
That I may dwell in the house of the Lord
All the days of my life,
To gaze on the beauty of the Lord
And to seek Him in His temple.

SEEK HIM.

Prepare to worship and count your blessings.

....

....

....

....

....

....

....

....

....

....

....

....

....

....

....

Week #16
Monday: TGIM
Psalm 28:7
My heart leaps for joy, and with my song I praise Him.
NFL

I made it through training camp. As we returned to Minneapolis, I was still on the team, and the last cut was fast approaching. That day came, and I was on pins and needles. Would I be called into the office? Because if so, that meant I received my walking papers. We started our meetings, and I noticed the linebacker I was competing against was not there, and then at practice, he was missing too. In other words, I had made the team! What a fantastic day! I could not wait to call my wife and give her the good news. This was unbelievable! A country bumpkin from Bardstown, Kentucky was going to play professional football. No way... Get out of town!

The season began, and I did not see much action except on special teams, but that was okay because I was still trying to figure everything out. The defenses were complicated, and there was no room for errors. If I went the wrong way on pass coverage, then someone was going to be wide open. We did not just make a single call in the huddle but we "play the defense called," which meant you had to know what the scouting report had designated for each alignment.

When I first saw the scouting report in training camp, I was totally lost even though it was an abbreviated version for rookies like me. It was one page, but it would soon grow to two and three pages and all the various calls to be made. Play the defense, play the blitz, play the pass coverage for each and every formation... all dictated by the tendencies analyzed prior to our game. This was the most comprehensive memory requirement I had ever come across, and my football future depended on my ability to recall all this stored information.

Fortunately, my previous education had trained my brain to respond, and it wasn't long before I could recall the scouting report. I saw several really good athletes put on waivers specifically because they could not understand and comprehend the system. I did not play much in year one, and our season was a disaster. We had seven wins and seven loses. Bud Grant, our head coach, told everybody that they had better be ready for training camp next year.

Are you ready for some football?!

MONDAY
"Spreading the Gospel"

Matthew 5:16

Let your light shine before others, that they may see your good deeds and glorify your Father in heaven.

After making the team and completing my first year in professional football, there was still a tremendous void in my life. Fortunately, during training camp of my rookie year, my roommate was Jeff Siemon, the number one draft choice for the Vikings in 1972. As I examined and experienced his friendship, I knew there was something different about him, and I wanted whatever he had. He invited me to attend chapel service, and his attitude and demeanor eventually led me to our team church service in Oakland, California, where I accepted Christ as my Lord and Savior.

2 Corinthians 9:2

And your enthusiasm has stirred most of them to action.

The devil wants us to believe our actions and personal testimony don't matter. We try to be a witness and don't feel we have an effect on the world around us. How did the disciples feel as they went from town to town? I am sure they were exhilarated to baptize and see conversions, but many times, they were run out of town. They couldn't possibly imagine their ministry would be responsible for Christianity becoming the number one religion in the world with 2.6 billion Christians. Just 12 men with a passion for Jesus!

Philippians 2:15–16

You will shine among them like the stars in the sky as you hold firmly to the word of life.

Just like the disciples, we have no idea who watches our actions or who absorbs our message. Just as I observed Jeff Siemon, we are on display to our family, friends, and the entire world.

The big question is… What do they see?

We must not demand results but let our light shine, spread the gospel, and let God do the work.

TUESDAY
"The Sword of the Spirit"

Matthew 6:9
Our Father who are in heaven, hallowed be your name.
Most everyone recognizes the Lord's Prayer, and many have memorized it through repetition while growing up. God's word is powerful and can reroute our evil thoughts and can definitely change our actions. If you have problem with selfishness, greed, anger, lust, worry, or any other sinful thoughts, then scripture can be your sword of the Spirit to fight the demonic forces we battle every day. Why do you think Jesus quoted scripture when he was confronted by the devil in Matthew 4:1–11? Here are just a few examples:

Anger: Ephesians 4:26
Do not let the sun go down while you are still angry.
My wife and I have had disagreements, and feelings were hurt. Although I am strong-willed, I always remember this scripture from Ephesians. *Don't go to bed angry!* Anger can possess our entire spirits, and God warns us about its harmful effects.

Humility: Philippians 2:3
In humility value others above yourselves.
When I start feeling superior to others, this scripture pops into my mind and helps me remember that we are all equal in the eyes of God. Whether a beggar on the street or a CEO of a major corporation, God loves all of us the same.

Communication: Proverbs 12:18
Reckless words pierce like a sword, but the tongue of the wise brings healing.
Most people are aware of their imperfections, so the question is, "Do you really want to correct your weakness?" Whatever temptations you face, look up the word online at "Blue Letter Bible" or in the concordance in your Bible. Find the appropriate scripture, write it down on a note card, and keep it handy so you will be equipped to fight our satanic enemies (1 Peter 1:13).

WEDNESDAY
Two-Minute Drill

JOSEPH

Joseph interpreted Pharaoh's dream. The ruler of Egypt was impressed with the prediction, and then...

Genesis 41:37–40

The plan seemed good to Pharaoh and to all his officials. So Pharaoh asked them, "Can we find anyone like this man, one in whom is the spirit of God?" Then Pharaoh said to Joseph, "Since God has made all this known to you, there is no one so discerning and wise as you. You shall be in charge of my palace, and all my people are to submit to your orders. Only with respect to the throne will I be greater than you." So Pharaoh said to Joseph, "I hereby put you in charge of the whole land of Egypt."

Is our God a miraculous God?

Joseph left prison one day, and the next day, he became vice president of one of the strongest countries in the world.

Genesis 41:46

Joseph was thirty years old when he entered the service of Pharaoh king of Egypt.

Joseph was 17 years old when he was sold into slavery.

And then, he was the number two man in charge of Egypt!

Is God good or what?

Genesis 41:44

Then Pharaoh said to Joseph, "I am Pharaoh, but without your word no one will lift hand or foot in all Egypt."

Talk about going from the outhouse to the penthouse!

Psalm 37:5–6

Commit your way to the Lord; trust in Him and he will do this: He will make your righteousness reward shine like the dawn, your vindication like the noonday sun.

THURSDAY
"Can You Hear God?

John 8:47
Whoever belongs to God hears what God says. The reason you do not hear is you do not belong to God.

John 10:4
He goes on ahead of them, and His sheep follow Him because they know His voice.

God spoke to the prophets and heroes of the Old Testament, but does He speak today? What was different then from now?

TIME!

The ancients spent time with God every day. Adam, Noah, and Enoch walked with God. Daniel prayed three times a day. Isaiah, Jeremiah, and Ezekiel were continually on their knees praying. David was constantly writing his thoughts as evidenced by the Psalms. The most important person in the New Testament, Jesus, would disappear in the mornings to have a quiet time with the God of the universe (I think Jesus did this every day).

Do you have time for God?

On Sundays?

Occasionally?

Every day?

2 Chronicles 15:2
If you seek Him, He will be found by you.

God speaks. The big question is... Do you have time?

FRIDAY
"Success"

Psalm 49:18

In this life they consider themselves fortunate and are applauded for their success.

From the time we are able to walk, we are all being groomed to be successful according to the world's standards. If we obtain success, we are told that it will lead to fame, hopefully, fortune, and of course, money. We think that these things will solve all our problems and our temporary unhappiness.

I was very fortunate at an early age to reach the pinnacle of my dreams and aspirations. I also obtained a certain degree of wealth and notoriety, but despite my accomplishments, something was missing. There was a tremendous void.

"Where do I go from here?" I wondered. "Will a bigger contract satisfy me? What is missing?" I noticed that several of my friends had an unusual peace that seemed ever-present. Where did they get this unmistakable joyful attitude? One of my teammates asked me to attend chapel service, so I decided to check it out. I would discreetly sit in the back, but through some supernatural force, the big questions and doubts I had were discussed, and my reasons for disbelief disappeared. I grew up in a small-town church and was familiar with the historical Jesus and who he was and what he did. I even assumed I was a Christian.

But after attending two years of chapel services, I was challenged by one of our speakers to commit my life to Jesus. How do I ask him to come into my life? I just prayed:

Lord, I have been running from you a long time, and I don't like who I am. I've done bad things. Please forgive me. I'm not sure if I am saying the right words, but please come in and take over my life because I want to live for you and not me.

Mark 8:36

What shall it profit a man, if he shall gain the whole world, and lose his own soul?

SATURDAY REFLECTIONS
Philippians 4:12–13

I know what it is to be in need,
And I know what it is to have plenty.
I have learned the secret of being content in any and every situation,
Whether well fed or hungry,
Whether living in plenty or in want.
I can do all things through Christ who strengthens me.

Lord, as I review the past week, I remember:

....

....

....

....

....

....

....

....

....

....

....

....

....

....

....

....

Psalm 27:1

The Lord is my light and my salvation—whom shall I fear?
The Lord is the stronghold of my life—of whom shall I be afraid?

Of whom shall I be afraid?

Prepare to worship and count your blessings.

....
....
....
....
....
....
....
....
....
....
....
....
....
....
....
....
....
....

Monday: TGIM

John 3:16

For God so loved the world that He gave His one and only Son, that whoever believes in Him shall not perish but have eternal life.

NFL

I left out one of the most important points of my rookie season and my initial arrival at training camp. We stayed in a non-air-conditioned dormitory, and who of all people would be my roommate but Jeff Siemon, the number one draft choice? I received this news before meeting him and anticipated that he would be some California flower child with long hair who smoked dope. I was totally shocked when he arrived with short hair and a very mannerly person.

Jeff was very easy going, read his Bible and didn't cuss. No way could he be a wild and crazy middle linebacker in the NFL. Wrong! Once I saw him in action, there was no question why he was number one. But his actions off the field seemed a little strange. He would always hang out with the veterans that were similar personalities. There was something different about Jeff and I could not figure it out.

When the exhibition season began, Jeff asked me to come to chapel service on the mornings of our games. I would slide in the room and sit in the back and just listen. I was too shy to ask the big questions I had, but through some supernatural force, all were asked and all had legitimate answers.

Question #1: If God is so good, why is there so much evil in the world? Answer: God put man on earth in perfect form and gave him everything, and man chose to disobey God. That's when sin came into the world.

Question #2: I came from a small town and knew the people in town who were doing bad things. Then I would see them in church on Sundays. Seems a little hypocritical, doesn't it? Answer: I realized I wasn't perfect either, and if church wasn't for sinners, then who was it for?

Question #3: I was watching my son as he worked on a puzzle and realized how blessed I was to be his father. I couldn't sacrifice him for anything, but God did! **He sacrificed His perfectly innocent Son for me.**

MONDAY
"The Shepherd"

Psalm 23:1–2

The Lord is my shepherd, I shall not want. He makes me lie down in green pastures, He leads me beside the quiet waters.

Verse 1: *The Lord is my shepherd, I shall not want.*

Shepherds guard and protect the sheep and will go to any length to insure their safety. If just one sheep is lost, he will search diligently and thoroughly to find it. The shepherd will provide food and shelter and every necessity.

The Lord is our shepherd, and He will not desert us no matter what we do. We are continually wandering, but no matter how far we stray, He will always take us back. He knows our desires and will give us what we need, not what we want.

Verse 2: *He makes me lie down in green pastures.*

Imagine a sunny day and a field bursting with wild flowers and glistening emerald green grass. As you walk through this unbelievable meadow, you decide to lie down and feel the warmth of your surroundings. As you look up at the amazing blue sky, you spread your arms and legs back and forth like you're making a snow angel, and you can feel the very peace and presence of God. The great "I AM" is here.

Verse 3: *He leads me beside the quiet waters.*

I can imagine holding my wife's hand as we walk beside the quiet waters of a mountain brook. The tranquil and gentle flow of water is soothing as it ripples across the rocks and boulders. I am reminded of Psalm 42:1–2: "As the deer pants for the streams of water... My soul thirsts for God, for the living God." I gently squeeze her hand, and the calming water alerts me to the realization that streams of living water flow within us.

We are one, and God is with us.

TUESDAY
"Restoration"

Psalm 23:3

He restores *my soul.*

We have all been through some tough times, and a variety of trials await us. The challenges ahead will be strenuous physically, mentally, emotionally, and spiritually. Several years ago, the economy collapsed, and my business did too. Times were difficult, but I knew God was there. Through those moments of depression and feeling that all was lost, God provided one of His many remarkable gifts: hope.

Romans 15:13

May the God of hope fill you with all joy and peace as you trust in him, so that you may overflow with hope by the power of the Holy Spirit.

Jeremiah 29:11

"For I know the plans I have for you," declares the Lord, "plans to prosper you and not to harm you, plans to give you hope and a future."

As I look back, I truly thank the Lord for those trials because I learned to trust Him. We have grown so much closer, and I wouldn't change any of the past. What I found is so much better than what I lost. At the time, I didn't think I needed those trials, but as I look back, I know He truly did *restore my soul.*

1 Peter 5:10

And the God of all grace…. will himself restore *you and make you strong, firm and steadfast.*

Psalm 51:12

Restore *me to the joy of your salvation…*

WEDNESDAY

Two-Minute Drill

JOSEPH

When Joseph was summoned from prison to interpret Pharaoh's dream, the King of Egypt said:

Genesis 41:15

"I have heard it said of you that when you hear a dream you can interpret it."

Despite being in prison and looking for a way out of jail, it never crossed Joseph's mind to try to manipulate the situation, and he responded:

Genesis 41:16

"I cannot do it," Joseph replied to Pharaoh, "but God will give Pharaoh the answer he desires."

> Have you ever been in a serious predicament?
>
> And would you have done anything to escape? Anything?
>
> Did you pause and consult the Lord?

Joseph gave God the glory and proceeded to interpret Pharaoh's dream:

Genesis 41:25–27

Then Joseph said to Pharaoh, "The dreams of Pharaoh are one and the same. God has revealed to Pharaoh what he is about to do. The seven good cows are seven years, and the seven good heads of grain are seven years; it is one and the same dream. The seven lean, ugly cows that came up afterward are seven years, and so are the seven worthless heads of grain scorched by the east wind: They are seven years of famine."

After evaluating Joseph's interpretation, Pharaoh responded;

Genesis 41:39

"Since God has made all this known to you, there is no one so discerning and wise as you. You shall be in charge of my palace, and all my people are to submit to your orders. Only in respect to the throne will I be greater than you."

> Joseph gave God the glory, and he was rewarded.
>
> Do you give God the glory, or do you take it?

133

THURSDAY
"The Path"

Psalm 23:3

He guides me along the right paths for his name's sake.

On an excursion through the Mammoth Cave, a guide impressed us with his extensive knowledge about this fascinating cavern. Not only was he extremely informative, but I felt he knew every step of the way and that I could trust him with my life. Our God is no different. He just wants us to follow him and listen to His words as we travel through this adventure we call life. His textbook is called the Bible, and the knowledge within this miraculous book will highlight the right path so we may avoid any disastrous calamity.

Proverbs 15:10

Stern discipline awaits anyone who leaves the path...

Only when we disobey this holy manual will we suffer the consequences. Keep in mind that we are no different than significant characters in the Bible. Abraham, Moses, King David, Peter, and Paul all strayed off the path, but after confession and repentance, our God provided his endless amazing grace (1 John 1:9).

The world distracts us, and we all wander off course. But praise God, our Lord waits patiently for our return to the path of righteousness.

Isaiah 58:11

The Lord will guide you always; He will satisfy your needs...

John 16:13

When the Spirit of truth comes, He will guide you into all truth.

FRIDAY
"Stand"

Psalm 23:4

Even though I walk through the valley of the shadow of death, I will fear no evil, for you are with me...

David, too young to be a soldier, was instructed by his father to take some food to his brothers who were at war with the Philistines. As he traveled to their camp, he stopped at the battle lines and heard the Philistine champion, Goliath, shout his defiance. Goliath was nine feet tall and weighed 450 to 500 pounds. He carried a shield weighing 150 pounds.

After hearing and seeing this gigantic man, the Israelite army "ran from him in great fear" (1 Samuel 17:24). However, David's response was, "who is this pagan Philistine anyway, that he is allowed to defy the armies of the living God?" (1 Samuel 17:26) Although David was just a young shepherd boy inexperienced in war, nobody was going to curse and offend his God. He responded, "Let no one lose heart on account of this Philistine; your servant will go and fight him" (1 Samuel 17:32).

Our nation is always preparing for elections. We will have a chance to stand up against "those who defy the living God." We can nonchalantly stand by and have another apathetic response as in previous elections. Or, we can say, "I don't care how big the giant is. No matter what the odds, we can and will make a difference. Why are we electing people who do not represent Godly principles?"

We must voice our opinions and speak out and defend our mighty God.

Isaiah 7:9

If you do not stand firm in your faith, you will not stand at all.

SATURDAY REFLECTIONS
Philippians 4:12–13

I know what it is to be in need,

And I know what it is to have plenty.

I have learned the secret of being content in any and every situation,

Whether well fed or hungry,

Whether living in plenty or in want.

I can do all things through Christ who strengthens me.

Lord, as I review the past week, I remember:

....

....

....

....

....

....

....

....

....

....

....

....

....

....

....

SUNDAY
Psalm 23:1–3

The Lord is my shepherd, I lack nothing.
He makes me lie down in green pastures,
He leads me beside quiet waters,
He refreshes my soul.

HE REFRESHES MY SOUL.

Prepare to worship and count your blessings.

....
....
....
....
....
....
....
....
....
....
....
....
....
....
....
....

Week #18

Monday: TGIM

Revelation 3:20

Here I am! I stand at the door and knock. If anyone hears my voice and opens the door, I will come in and eat with that person, and they with me.

NFL

I had a lot of questions in my first season in the NFL. I made the team and had a great salary and good friends, but most noticeably, playing pro ball was not as fulfilling as I expected. Something was missing, and I could not figure it out. During the off-season, I remember reading a phrase that I didn't know the origin of: "What shall it profit a man if he gains the whole world and loses his own soul?" I had everything the world had to offer, and I was still not completely satisfied.

Prior to my second training camp, my wife and I had many conversations with some girls at our apartment complex about Christianity. We had lots of questions, but we didn't talk about anything monumental before I left for training camp. A few weeks later at training camp, I called my wife, and she said she was with those girls at the swimming pool. She had accepted Jesus Christ as her Lord and Savior. This sparked my interest, and I became more assertive in chapel service because I was seeking some answers.

We started exhibition season, and things were going well. I had no fear of not making the team, but I was still searching. Our last exhibition game was against the Oakland Raiders in California, and the Sunday morning of the game, I went to the most remarkable chapel service I would ever attend. The speaker was actually a friend of Jeff Siemon, and he was a rather small fellow who was appropriately named Jim Stump. He had a great message, and when he came to the end of his talk, he mentioned this process of asking Jesus to be your Lord and Savior. It seemed so simple, and I was so tired of being the person I had become. I realized how selfish I had been and how I had neglected my family. Jim said a prayer that went something like this, "Today you can ask Jesus to become your Lord and Savior by confessing your sins and simply asking Him to take control of your life. All you have to do is ask, and He promised in His word He would come in."

I asked that day in Oakland, California.

MONDAY

"Reflections from the Tomb"

Matthew 27:65

Make the tomb as secure as you know how.

I was in the tomb for more than a third of my life. Satan had sealed the entrance, and my life was dark because I wasn't sure about my purpose. I had all the worldly pleasures: money, success, and a certain amount of fame and notoriety, but something was missing. Several of my teammates had a special kind of joy and peace, and they seemed so confident about their reason for existence. They talked about Jesus like He was their friend. I followed them to chapel service and sat in the back row listening and evaluating. One of the guys gave me a Living Bible and told me to start with the Gospel of John. I remember when I began to read the first chapter:

John 1:5

His life is the light that shines in through the darkness—and the darkness can never extinguish it.

I reflected on this statement and realized that the darkness in my life could be overcome, not just temporarily, but forever. As I continued to read, I had to pause again.

John 1:12

But to all who received him, he gave the right to become children of God. All they needed to do was to trust him to save them.

Wow! I thought I was His child, but all my buddies had some kind of special relationship with God. It seemed that they could talk to Him, like He was their dad.

After months of examination, I finally understood that I didn't have to stay in the tomb because Jesus went to the cross so I could escape the darkness. Jesus came back from the dead and removed that boulder from the entrance, and the light of the almighty God penetrated my soul. I remember the day He carried me out of the tomb and whispered, "I have watched you struggle, and I am so glad you asked me to come into your life. I love you so much."

1 John 5:11

God has given us eternal life, and this life is in his Son.

"What's Your Game Plan?"

1 John 1:7
The blood of Jesus Christ, his Son cleanses us from all sin.
Within 24 hours of most games in the NFL, the players meet with the coaches to review the "game film." The plays have been dissected, and your personal game history is about to be displayed to the entire offensive or defensive squad. Your good plays are noted quickly, and the bad plays seemed to be discussed forever. Your mistakes are discussed so you may become a better and more complete team player.

As my life apart from Christ unfolded, every day was a "game film" of my sinful actions. Why did I do that? I knew it was not right, but I did it anyway. Fortunately, God was revealing to me that I was not capable of fighting my sinful desires without his power. Ultimately, I said, "Lord I can't do this on my own. Would you come into my life, take control, and be my Lord and Savior?" At that very moment, the Holy Spirit entered my very soul and he promised to be my helper and counselor.

John 14:26
But the counselor, the Holy Spirit, whom the Father will send in my name, he will teach you all things and will remind you of all that I have said to you.
The Holy Spirit makes me aware and advises me on how to avoid and prevent sinful mistakes. The "counselor" also reminds me of my unrepentant sin so I can confess and restore my closeness to my God.

1 John 1:9
If we confess our sins, he is faithful and just and will forgive us our sins and purify us from all unrighteousness.
No matter what I have done, if I express my heartfelt remorse and repentance, my God totally forgives me and assures me that my guilty feelings should be released.

Psalm 103:12
As far as the east is from the west, so far has he removed our transgressions from us.
John 8:32
"...The truth will set you free"

WEDNESDAY
Two-Minute Drill

JOSEPH

Genesis 41:47–49

During the seven years of abundance the land produced plentifully. Joseph collected all the food produced in those seven years of abundance in Egypt and stored it in cities... Joseph stored up huge quantities of grain, like the sand of the sea; it was so much that he stopped keeping records because it was beyond measure.

Many times in my life, I have been very successful,

But I didn't store up much, and when the famine came,

I was not prepared.

Are you?

People say the more you make, the more you spend.

Do you think that is true?

During those times of monetary increase,

I did not give back to the Lord proportionately.

God blessed me, and He is the first one I neglect.

Why do I so easily forget the most important principle?

GOD OWNS EVERYTHING.

THURSDAY
"Quiet Time"

Luke 5:16

Jesus often withdrew to the wilderness for prayer.

Hypothetical situation: You have an appointment with Jesus to discuss several life situations. During the meeting, your phone suddenly rings. Do you tell the Lord to excuse you for a minute and take the call or send the call to voicemail?

Early one morning, I was looking forward to spending time with the Lord. I showered and dressed first and then remembered that I needed to call my plumber to remind him about an upcoming job. After preparing my coffee and protein smoothie, I sat down to have my quiet time with the Lord. Within seconds, my electrician called, and a long discussion followed. Back to my readings, and then, my Facebook phone signal went off and required my attention. This pattern continued, and after I finished my quiet time, I couldn't remember what I read except that Max Lucado had discussed weeds growing in my garden. I realized that my time with God was overrun by the weeds of the world and drowned the impact of God's Holy Word on my life.

Mark 1:35

Very early in the morning, while it was still dark, Jesus got up, left the house and went off to a solitary place...

This was God's time, and I failed to dedicate to Him the significance He deserves. My appointment with Jesus was interrupted by the world. If I don't set aside a specific quiet time, then I will continue with countless distractions that deflect the Holy Spirit's counsel. Why should God speak to me if I am not focused on Him?

Luke 4:42

At daybreak, Jesus went out to a solitary place.

If Jesus spent time totally alone with God, what should I do?

FRIDAY

"Overwhelmed"

Job 30:15

Terror overwhelms me; my dignity is driven away as by the wind, my safety vanishes like a cloud. And now my life ebbs away; days of suffering grip me.

As I read the trials of Job, I reflected on my own hard times and my conversations with God.

Hey, Lord. This is Amos down here. Things are extremely tough. How do you expect me to survive? There are so many temptations and so many struggles. Then, I got really frustrated and very upset and said, "Why don't you come down here and experience what I am going through?"

Then, I paused for a few minutes and apologized for my anger. Then, I heard him say, "That's why I sent my Son! He went through everything you have and did not sin. Then, He died for you... Then, He sent the Holy Spirit to help you overcome. He is with you always... Even now! Listen to Him!"

Hebrews 4:15

For we do not have a high priest who is unable to sympathize with our weakness, but we have one who has been tempted in every way, just as we are—yet was without sin.

SATURDAY REFLECTIONS
Philippians 4:12–13

I know what it is to be in need,

And I know what it is to have plenty.

I have learned the secret of being content in any and every situation,

Whether well fed or hungry,

Whether living in plenty or in want.

I can do all things through Christ who strengthens me.

Lord, as I review the past week, I remember:

....

....

....

....

....

....

....

....

....

....

....

....

....

....

....

....

Even though I walk through the
Valley of the shadow of death,
I will fear no evil,
For you are with me...

For you are with me.

Prepare to worship and count your blessings.

....
....
....
....
....
....
....
....
....
....
....
....
....
....
....
....

TGIM

Ephesians 1:13

And you also were included in Christ when you heard the message of truth, the gospel of your salvation. When you believed, you were marked in Him with a seal, the promised Holy Spirit...

NFL

That day in Oakland, California, I asked Jesus to be my Lord and Savior, and I will never forget leaving that conference room and going back to my room. As I walked back to the room, the long corridor seemed 100 miles long, and I was waiting for something to happen—for lights to flash or someone to congratulate me for this monumental decision. Nothing happened, but I know from that moment on, my life changed for the better.

I know that day the Holy Spirit came to dwell in my very soul. There was not an overwhelming feeling of God's presence, but gradually, something inside was telling me about things in my life that needed to be changed. I realized that my language was offensive and wondered what my family thought of some of the words I spoke. I realized that going out with the boys and bar hopping with the single guys was not what I should be doing. God did not put all my faults on a list and burn them into my brain, but I just seemed to be more aware of the things I knew offended my Lord.

This process did not happen overnight, but it took months and even years to eliminate some of my more drastic habits. Today, I am more aware of the Holy Spirit as He urges me to review some of my actions and thought patterns. I am still a work in progress and always will be!

MONDAY

"Holy Spirit"

John 20:22

And with that he breathed on them and said, "Receive the Holy Spirit."

When you accept Jesus Christ as your Lord and Savior, one of the most miraculous moments of your life has just occurred. You have received one of God's most precious gifts: the Holy Spirit. Here is the way I visualize this spectacular event:

God is sitting on His throne in heaven, and he is surrounded by thousands of angels. Standing beside Him are Jesus and the Holy Spirit (three in one: Father, Son, and Holy Spirit). He is looking down on earth, and He knows you are searching and contemplating giving your life to the Lord. God feels your apprehension as you try to make this monumental decision. You hesitate, not quite sure what God wants from you. You remember someone saying He doesn't want anything, all He wants is your heart. You know that you cannot continue living like this. Your conscience keeps telling you that there has to be a better way. You finally decide to ask Jesus to take control and commit your life to His leadership and not yours. You pray, "Lord, I am yours…"

At that precise moment, thousands of angels burst into the most joyful and ecstatic hallelujah chorus ever heard. The jubilant singing of countless celestial beings resonates throughout the eternal spiritual realms and echoes throughout the universe.

Just imagine, all of heaven is rejoicing just for *you*! (Luke 15:7)

Then, God turns His head toward the Holy Spirit standing beside Him, and He nods His approval. In a split second, the Holy Spirit extends His arm toward earth, and He points his finger directly at you. Instantaneously, you are filled with the gift of the Holy Spirit, and God's supernatural and mighty power has become an integral part of your life.

Acts 2:17

"In the last days," God says, "I will pour out my Spirit on all people."

Acts 2:21

And everyone who calls on the name of the Lord will be saved.

TUESDAY

"You Have the Holy Spirit... Now What?"

Ephesians 1:13

When you believed, you were marked in him with a seal, the promised Holy Spirit...

I was at a chapel service in Oakland, California, when I asked Jesus Christ to be my Lord and Savior. Immediately following the meeting, I left the conference room at the hotel, and I remember walking down the empty corridor. Nothing spectacular happened, but I know that was the day my life changed and the Holy Spirit entered my heart.

It wasn't long before I became more aware of things in my life that needed to change. Curse words seemed to exit my mouth frequently, and I knew this was not a good habit. I slowly began to erase the obscene words from my vocabulary. When I slipped, I cringed because I didn't want to offend my Lord. The Spirit was at work.

Romans 8:6

The mind governed by the flesh is death, but the mind governed by the Spirit is life and peace.

There have been many more corrections since that day, and there will continue to be more because I am so imperfect. The good news is that *Jesus is living in me* through the power of the Holy Spirit. God's desire is for me to eliminate all my bitterness, anger, and other acts of the flesh (Galatians 5:19). I must continually come before my God and ask him to make me aware of my deficiencies so I can cleanse myself from all unrighteousness (1 John 1:9).

Sometimes, I refuse to listen to the Spirit. If I continually deny his voice, I will soon feel my joy slipping away. He will never leave me, but his power is diminished, and my peace will erode until I attempt to correct my sin.

God's ultimate goal is for me to fully enjoy his precious gifts.

Galatians 5:22

The fruit of the Spirit is love, joy, peace, patience, kindness, goodness, faithfulness, gentleness, and self-control.

Two-Minute Drill

JOSEPH

Genesis 41:56–57

When the famine had spread over the whole country, Joseph opened all the storehouses and sold grain to the Egyptians, for the famine was severe throughout Egypt. And all the countries came to Egypt to buy grain from Joseph, because the famine was severe everywhere.

Jacob, Joseph's father, had been told by his brothers over 10 years ago that his son had been killed by a wild animal when he actually was sold into slavery.

Genesis 42:1–2

When Jacob learned that there was grain in Egypt, he said to his sons, "Why do you keep looking at each other? Listen," he went on, "I have heard there is grain in Egypt. Go down there and buy some for us so that we will live and not die."

Ten of Joseph's brothers went to Egypt to purchase some grain. They encountered Joseph, but since Pharaoh had given him his signet ring, dressed him in fine robes, and put a gold chain around his neck, his brothers did not have a clue that the vice president of Egypt was the brother they had sold into slavery.

So, imagine you were Joseph and more than a decade later, you were confronted by the same brothers who threw you in a pit and then sold you into slavery.

How would you react? Are you a person who seeks revenge?

Genesis 42:7

As soon as Joseph saw his brothers, he recognized them, had them imprisoned, and then had them executed... **(Just kidding).**

...He recognized them, but he pretended to be a stranger and spoke harshly to them. "Where do you come from?" he asked. "From the land of Canaan," they replied, "to buy food."

Joseph was slave for 13 years and in prison for two more years, and somebody was going to pay!

What would you do?

THURSDAY
"Are You Hiding?"

John 16:13

But when He, the Spirit of truth, comes, he will guide you into all the truth.

After Jesus was arrested, the disciples virtually disappeared. We read very little of their appearance at the trial, crucifixion, or the burial. Not until Mary Magdalene discovered the empty tomb do we hear about any of the disciples.

Why were they hiding? They experienced the miracles and walked with the most remarkable man on earth and then went into seclusion. Throughout my life, I saw many remarkable pieces of evidence for this man called Jesus, but I was in hiding too. I refused his invitation to be part of his kingdom because the world was more important to me. Just like the disciples, it was time to come out of hiding.

John 20:19–22

...When the disciples were together with the doors locked... Jesus came and stood among them and said "peace be with you...." And with that he breathed on them and said, "Receive the Holy Spirit."

With this amazing gift, the disciples were instantaneously transformed, and the planet would never be the same. We have the same opportunity to receive the Holy Spirit. All we have to do is ask.

Ephesians 1:13

And when you believed in Christ, he identified you as his own by giving you the Holy Spirit, whom he promised long ago.

Ask yourself, "Am I hiding?"

If so, all you have to do is believe and accept Jesus as your Lord and Savior.

Revelation 3:20

Here I am! I stand at the door and knock. If anyone hears my voice and opens the door, I will come in and eat with him, and they with me.

All you have to do is ask!

FRIDAY
"If You Love Me"

Romans 6:16

Whether you are slaves to sin, which leads to death, or to obedience, which leads to…?

My answer was life. The correct answer is righteousness… why?

Many people believe that if they adhere to most of God's laws and as long as they are making a valiant effort, God will accept them into heaven. In Luke 11:37–53, Jesus visits with the Pharisees, and despite their strict obedience to the law, our Lord calls them hypocrites because of their hardened hearts. Jesus explains what our motivation for obedience should be:

John 14:15

"If you love me, you will obey what I command."

When I first met my wife, we dated for an extended period, and as we learned more about each other, our love increased (and still does). As our love increased, the more we wanted to please each other. Our relationship to the Lord is no different. The more we search for Him, the more we learn to love Him. As our love expands, the more we desire to obey His commands, and the more fulfilling our lives will be.

John 15:11

I have told you these things so that you will be filled with my joy. Yes, your joy will overflow!

I can only grow closer to my Lord by spending more time with Him! I know I must continually seek Him through His word, His church, Bible study, and fellowship with other Christians and remember…

Hebrews 11:6

He rewards those who earnestly seek him.

SATURDAY REFLECTIONS
Philippians 4:12–13

I know what it is to be in need,

And I know what it is to have plenty.

I have learned the secret of being content in any and every situation,

Whether well fed or hungry,

Whether living in plenty or in want.

I can do all things through Christ who strengthens me.

Lord, as I review the past week, I remember:

....

....

....

....

....

....

....

....

....

....

....

....

....

....

....

SUNDAY

Psalm 23:6

Surely your goodness and love will follow me
All the days of my life,
And I will dwell in the house of the Lord
Forever.

FOREVER

Prepare to worship and count your blessings.

....

....

....

....

....

....

....

....

....

....

....

....

....

....

Week #20
Monday: TGIM
Genesis 27:20
"The Lord your God gave me success," he replied.

I played a lot more in season two, and the Vikings went undefeated through exhibition season and the first nine games of the regular season. During the season, I had three interceptions and against the Packers I had a fumble recovery and returned it for a touchdown. I remember those interceptions so vividly. One was against Kenny Stabler in our last exhibition game. In the regular season, I picked off one against Roger Staubach, Jim Plunkett, and Dan Pastorini.

The one against the Oilers and Pastorini was a thing of beauty. I cut in front of the running back, made the interception and headed for the sidelines. Pastorini was going to cut me off at the pass, but I faked in and went out and stiff-armed him, and headed to the goal line. I could see the end zone, but during my prolonged fake on Pastorini, the running back I cut in front of recovered and caught me from behind. If only Doug Sutherland (yes, you Doug!) had blocked him, I would have scored.

We continued winning through the season and the playoffs, and my first Super Bowl was about to happen. Unfortunately the Vikings never played well in any of my three Super Bowls. The offense always seemed to struggle, and you have to keep your opponent's off the field because they wouldn't be there if they were not capable of scoring points.

All in all, a very disappointing performance in each of my three Super Bowls, but being part of all the hype, press coverage, and various events connected to the game was an amazing experience. I also received three awesome National Football Conference championship rings for being there too.

One last comment regarding the Super Bowls: I was traded to the Seattle Seahawks after the 1976 Super Bowl, and the Vikings have not been back to the Super Bowl since I left! You do the math.

MONDAY
"Ezekiel"

Ezekiel 36:26

I will give you a new heart and put a new spirit in you.

A few years ago, if you asked me who Ezekiel was, I would have told you he was a character in a science fiction movie. At that time, I would not even think about reading the Old Testament because I did not understand why these historical writings were relevant to today's world. Fortunately, God led me to a comprehensive bible study called "DC." Through that learning experience, I finally got a better grasp on how and why the Old Testament was written. Sometime in the future, we will discuss the amazing first 39 books of the Bible, but today, the scripture above speaks to me.

This verse was written over 2,500 years ago, 500 years before Jesus. This is God's promise to us, and He never reneges on His word. Everyone on this earth has a chance to start over and put the past behind... everybody! We are all sinners, and yet, God still loves us enough to allow us to know Him more intimately and bless us with a whole new heart and spirit.

God continues to tell us through His prophet Ezekiel why we need a new heart and spirit.

Ezekiel 36:25

I will cleanse you from all your impurities and from all your idols.

Ezekiel 36:26–27

I will remove from you your heart of stone and give you a heart of flesh. And I will put my Spirit in you...

TUESDAY
"A Whale of a Tale"

Jonah 1:11–12

The sea was getting rougher and rougher. So they asked him, "What should we do to you to make the sea calm down for us?" "Pick me up and throw me into the sea," he replied, "and it will become calm."

Some say the Bible is a fictional storybook because there are so many miraculous occurrences: Moses parting the Red Sea (Exodus 14:13–18), David as a young boy defeating a nine-foot giant with a sling (1 Samuel 17:45–50), and an angel from God wiping out 186,000 Assyrians (2 Kings 19:35). Jonah and the whale also creates a certain amount of skepticism.

Jonah 1:15–17

Then the sailors picked Jonah up and threw him into the raging sea.... Now the Lord had arranged for a great fish to swallow Jonah. And Jonah was inside the fish for three days and three nights.

While watching television, I noticed the story of Jonah and the whale on the History Channel. The commentators reviewed the plight of Jonah as he was thrown off the boat into the turbulent waters. The professors all agreed being swallowed by a fish was preposterous, and their final conclusion was... are you ready for this? He was rescued by the first submarine (in 612 BC)!

Do you believe in the story of Jonah and the whale?

Do you believe in Jesus?

Do you believe and trust what Jesus said?

Matthew 12:40

"For as Jonah was three days and three nights in the belly of a huge fish, so the Son of Man will be three nights in the heart of the earth."

So, is the book of Jonah 1. Just a symbolic story, 2. A rescue by a submarine, or 3. GOD'S HOLY WORD?

2 Timothy 3:16

All scripture is given by inspiration of God...

Two-Minute Drill

JOSEPH

Joseph's brothers had no idea that this was the same brother they had sold into slavery more than a decade ago. They could not recognize him because Egyptian rulers shaved all their hair, their faces were decorated, and they wore a headdress in addition to long robes.

Joseph spoke harshly to his brothers but sold them grain for their return home. He forced them to return home without their brother Simeon and requested that they return with Benjamin, the youngest brother... How long would the grain last?

Genesis 43:1–2

Now the famine was still severe in the land. So when they had eaten all the grain they had brought from Egypt, their father said to them, "Go back and buy us a little more food."

Jacob, the father, reluctantly allowed all the brothers to return, including Benjamin. Upon arrival back in Egypt, they brought multiple gifts from Canaan for Joseph. After negotiating for more grain, Joseph prepared a banquet for the entire group.

Genesis 43:29–30

As he looked about and saw his brother Benjamin, his own mother's son, he asked, "Is this your youngest brother, the one you told me about?" And he said, "God be gracious to you, my son." Deeply moved at the sight of his brother, Joseph hurried out and looked for a place to weep. He went into his private room and wept there.

Haven't you been hurt before? How did you react to the violators?

Joseph had played the charade long enough!

Genesis 45:1–3

Then Joseph could no longer control himself.... Joseph said to his brothers, "I am Joseph! Is my father still living?" But his brothers were not able to answer him, because they were terrified at his presence.

If you sold your brother into slavery, assumed he was dead for 15 years, and suddenly he appeared before you, what would you do?

THURSDAY
"The Word of God"

2 Timothy 3:16
All Scripture is inspired by God. (NLT)
Everyone needs to find a Bible translation that they can understand and enjoy. I originally studied a version similar to the New Living Translation, but whatever Bible you end up with, God will speak to you through His Everlasting Word.

After reviewing Ephesians 4:29–32 (NIV), I used the Bible app to compare this verse to a translation called "The Message."

The following is my question and answer session with myself:

Ephesians 4:29a
Watch the way you talk. Let nothing foul or dirty come out of your mouth. (The Message)
What should I do?

Ephesians 4:29b
Say only what helps, each word a gift.
Why?

This next verse is powerful, so please pause and read slowly. Then, reread it and let it penetrate into the very depths of your soul.

Ephesians 4:30
Don't grieve God. Don't break his heart. His Holy Spirit, moving and breathing in you, is the most intimate part of your life, making you fit for himself. Don't take such a gift for granted.
How do I do this?

Ephesians 4:31
Make a clean break with all cutting, backbiting, profane talk. Be gentle with one another, sensitive.
What else can I do?

Ephesians 4:32
Forgive one another as quickly and thoroughly as God in Christ forgave you.
Proverbs 30:5
Every word of God is flawless. (NIV)
Proverbs 30:5
Every promise of God proves true. (MSG)

FRIDAY
"Who Are You Listening To?"

John 7:38
"Whoever believes in me, as the Scripture has said, streams of living water will flow from within him."

What is the number one selling book of all time?

The Bible, hands down. Not even a close runner-up.
Slowly read and review the following scripture:

2 Timothy 3:16
All scripture is inspired by God and is useful to teach us what is true and to make us realize what is wrong in our lives. (New Living Translation)

No wonder it is number one. It was inspired by God.

"It corrects us when we are wrong & teaches us to do what is right."

The Bible is our guidebook for life.

"God uses it to prepare and equip his people to do every good work."

So why do we rationalize the Bible's truths?

The world wants to change the rules, but every society and civilization that has violated the rules set forth in the Bible is no longer in existence.

Who will you listen to?

SATURDAY REFLECTIONS
Philippians 4:12–13

I know what it is to be in need,

And I know what it is to have plenty.

I have learned the secret of being content in any and every situation,

Whether well fed or hungry,

Whether living in plenty or in want.

I can do all things through Christ who strengthens me.

Lord, as I review the past week, I remember:

....

....

....

....

....

....

....

....

....

....

....

....

....

....

Psalm 8:1 and 8:9

Oh Lord, our Lord, how majestic
Is your name in all the earth!
Oh Lord, our Lord how majestic
Is your name in all the earth!

HOW MAJESTIC IS YOUR NAME IN ALL THE EARTH

Prepare to worship and count your blessings.

....
....
....
....
....
....
....
....
....
....
....
....
....
....

#21

Monday: TGIM

Psalm 10:4

In his pride the wicked man does not seek him; in all his thoughts there is no room for God.

Prior to the 1977 football season, I wrote a letter to the head coach for the Vikings, Bud Grant, regarding my desire to play the outside linebacker on the right side of the defense. My playing time had been very limited, and I thought I could outplay my fellow linebacker.

Once at training camp, I could tell that this was not going to happen and that I would be backing up the middle and the left side linebacker positions. I was not happy, and my play during exhibition season was less than exemplary. Ultimately, I was traded to the Seattle Seahawks just prior to the last exhibition game. Although I hated to leave the Vikings, this was the opportunity I had waited for. I played a little in the last exhibition game, and then, during our first game of the season, we would play the Cincinnati Bengals at Riverfront Stadium. I did not start, but during the first quarter of the game, the head coach told me to replace the right-side linebacker on the next series. This was the big break I had been praying for.

Prior to going into the game on defense, I was on the punt coverage special team. I headed down the field for punt coverage, got rid of the blocker, and I watched as the punt receiver caught the ball. He started across the field, and I was going to head him off at the pass. I had a good angle on him, and he was not going to get around me, and then, suddenly, he turned up the field trying to go inside of me. I went to put on the brakes, and when I tried to stop quickly, I felt my knee collapse. I immediately went to the ground. Out for the season! All the pieces of the puzzle had come together, and this is not what I had planned. God had provided this opportunity, and now not only was I out of the game, but my season was over.

This can't be happening!

MONDAY

"Why Do We Have an Old Testament and a New Testament?" Part 1

2 Corinthians 3:14

But their minds were made dull, for to this day the same veil remains when the old covenant is read. It has not been removed, because only in Christ is it taken away.

I first starting reading the Living Bible just prior to my conversion in 1974. For years, I mostly read the New Testament, and I struggled with the Old Testament. When I did read various parts of the Old Testament, I wondered why God wrote this portion and even questioned why He remained loyal to the Israelites. I was fortunate to take part in a two-year Bible study called DC (Discipleship Curriculum) that opened my eyes to the magnificence of the Old Testament.

From the beginning, our God was a loving and forgiving God. He bestowed on man the perfect environment, and man chose to disobey His commands, and sin entered the world. Also, in the garden, He provided a way for man to redeem himself.

Genesis 3:15

And I will put enmity between you and the woman, and between your offspring and hers, he will crush your head, and you will strike his heel.

As you read from Noah, Moses, Judges, Kings, Chronicles, and through the prophets, one thing is evident: Man began to follow and trust God, and our God provided all their needs, but they always stray and worship other Gods.

Deuteronomy 29:26

They went off and worshiped other Gods and bowed down to them...

What Gods are you worshipping? Money, prestige, power, beauty?

TUESDAY

"Why Do We Have an Old Testament and a New Testament?" Part 2

2 John 1:6

And this is love: that we walk in obedience...

The book of Joshua is a great example of God's devoted people following Him for a while then turning to other Gods. Joshua and his tribesman became one of the fiercest groups of fighting men in history. God was with them and allowed them to conquer many kings and kingdoms, and most of that time, they were greatly outnumbered. After they defeated all their opponents and settled and occupied the land the Lord had blessed them with and provided for them, they were devoted to God for one generation, and then:

Judges 2:10

After that whole generation had been gathered to their ancestors, another generation grew up who knew neither the Lord nor what he had done for Israel.

Are you telling your kids about your God and what He has done?

The book of Judges is another great example of the multiple times our living God provided for His children until they eventually pursued other Gods.

Judges 3:12

Again the Israelites did evil in the sight of the Lord.

Kings and Chronicles again emphasize the disobedience of the Israelites. King Solomon was blessed with wisdom and tremendous wealth and followed the Lord until he violated one of the Lord's commands:

1 Kings 11:2

The Lord had told the Israelites, "You must not intermarry with them [foreign women], because they will surely turn your hearts after their Gods.

1 Kings 11:4

As Solomon grew old, his wives turned his heart after other Gods, and his heart was not fully devoted to the Lord his God...

God gives us rules to follow. If we don't, there will be consequences.

Are there any rules you are not following?

Two-Minute Drill

JOSEPH
Genesis 45:4–7

Then Joseph said to his brothers, "Come close to me." When they had done so, he said, "I am your brother Joseph, the one you sold into Egypt! And now, do not be distressed and do not be angry with yourselves for selling me here, because it was to save lives that God sent me ahead of you. For two years now there has been famine in the land, and for the next five years there will be no plowing and reaping. But God sent me ahead of you to preserve for you a remnant on earth and to save your lives by a great deliverance."

After all the trials and tribulations, Joseph recognized God's almighty hand.

Genesis 45:8

"So then, it was not you who sent me here, but God. He made me father to Pharaoh, Lord of his entire household and ruler of all Egypt."

God's plan... not mine!

Have you been through the fire too?

Can you look back and see the plan God had for you?

Or are you burned too badly?

Genesis 45:16–18

When the news reached Pharaoh's palace that Joseph's brothers had come, Pharaoh and all his officials were pleased. Pharaoh said to Joseph, "Tell your brothers, 'Do this: Load your animals and return to the land of Canaan, and bring our father and your families back to me. I will give you the best of the land of Egypt and you can enjoy the fat of the land."

Joseph had persevered slavery and imprisonment and realized that his destiny was all planned by the Creator of the Universe.

God has a plan!

Do you trust Him?

THURSDAY

"Why Do We Have an Old Testament and a New Testament?" Part 3

Psalm 138:4

May all the Kings of the earth praise you, Lord,

Several kings returned the people to be a Godly nation and tore down the Asherah poles and the statutes of Baal, but their successor would put all the ungodly images back in place.

As you review 1 and 2 Kings and 1 and 2 Chronicles, you will consistently see this common characteristic of the kings: "They did evil in the sight of the Lord."

Then, there would be good kings.

Hezekiah was a great king who honored God and restored Judah by purifying the temple and made many other outstanding accomplishments. He was followed by his son Manasseh.

2 Chronicles 33:1–3

Manasseh was 12 years old when he became king, and he reigned in Jerusalem fifty-five years. He did evil in the eyes of the Lord, following the detestable practices of the nations the Lord had driven out before the Israelites.

There are many great stories of God's grace as His people embraced His power and mighty love, including David and Goliath (1 Samuel 17:1–4), Elijah and the prophets of Baal (1 Kings 18:16–46), Elisha being surrounded by a hostile army (2 Kings 18:8–23, Hezekiah and the angel of the Lord putting 186,000 troops to death (2 Kings 19:1–37), and Jehoshaphat defeating an army without using any weapons (2 Chronicles 20:1–30). These are awesome examples of God's amazing love, compassion, and His great power to respond to His people's obedience.

Psalm 34:15

The eyes of the Lord are on the righteous, and his ears are attentive to their cry.

Psalm 55:22

Cast your cares on the Lord and He will sustain you; he will never let the righteous be shaken.

FRIDAY
"Why Do We Have an Old Testament and a New Testament?" Part 4

Psalm 115:9

O Israel, trust in the Lord! He is their help and shield.

As I mentioned in day one of this week, for years, I could not imagine why God would continually save these sinful people called Israelites. I finally realized that I am one of those people. I tried to obey most of the rules but could never be successful. Jesus told the Pharisees that obedience to the law was not our ticket to heaven.

Matthew 23:27–28

"Woe to you, teachers of the law and Pharisees, you hypocrites! You are like whitewashed tombs, which look beautiful on the outside but on the inside are full of the bones of the dead and everything unclean. In the same way, on the outside you appear to people as righteous but on the inside you are full of hypocrisy and wickedness.

We cannot be saved by strict obedience to the law, and we cannot receive salvation by doing good works. All the good deeds you do will not save you.

Ephesians 2:8–9

For it is by grace you have been saved, through faith—and this not from yourselves, it is the gift of God—not by works, so that no one can boast.

Jesus came and not only died for our sins and our redemption but was resurrected so we may know that we can have eternal life. Prior to His departure, He assured us He would send the Holy Spirit.

John 14:26

But the Advocate, the Holy Spirit, whom the Father will send in my name will teach you all things and will remind you of everything I have said to you.

Without Jesus and the Holy Spirit, we have no hope!

SATURDAY REFLECTIONS
Philippians 4:12–13

I know what it is to be in need,

And I know what it is to have plenty.

I have learned the secret of being content in any and every situation,

Whether well fed or hungry,

Whether living in plenty or in want.

I can do all things through Christ who strengthens me.

Lord, as I review the past week, I remember:

....

....

....

....

....

....

....

....

....

....

....

....

....

....

....

....

....

SUNDAY
Psalm 5:3

In the morning Lord, you hear my voice;
In the morning I lay my requests before you
And wait expectantly.

WAIT

Prepare to worship and count your blessings.

....
....
....
....
....
....
....
....
....
....
....
....
....
....
....
....
....

Week #22
Monday: TGIM
Colossians 3:23

Whatever you do, work at it with all your heart, as working for the Lord, not for human masters...

I worked extremely hard during rehabilitation so I could play the following year. During training camp, my knee had some swelling, but I continued to practice. The first few days were mostly checking our speed and endurance. I was the fastest on the quarter mile sprint at the end of practice due to my distance training. I was really focused on playing the right outside position, and on the first day of contact drills, I worked primarily at that position.

But then, it happened. They have a drill they call "the hamburger drill," which lines up an offensive player against a defensive one and a single ball carrier. I was anxious to go against one of the tight ends, and the head coach called out my name. I was ready to show my stuff, but then he called out one of the offensive centers who usually goes against the middle linebackers. I had trimmed my weight down to 225 pounds so I could be quicker on the outside, but I was not mentally prepared to go against a 280-pound center versus a 230 pound tight end.

I was disappointed and my attitude showed as I was pushed backward by my opponent. My effort was somewhat lackadaisical and I was ready to go to the back of the line and wait my turn to go against the tight ends, but the head coach said, "Again." We lined back up, and I tried to improve my demeanor, but it was too late, and I was pushed back again by the center. My attitude had basically destroyed my future with the Seahawks. My knee had already made me a high risk, but this performance had sealed my doom. Instead of being my normally very aggressive self, I let the hamburger drill accent my selfish desire to play the position I wanted to play instead of being excited to perform wherever they wanted me to play.

I had forgotten about this drill by our first exhibition game and was anxious to prove myself to be a valuable asset to the team, but I soon realized my plans were not the coach's plan.

MONDAY
"Old Testament vs. New Testament" Summary

Romans 15:4

For everything that was written in the past was written to teach us, so that through the endurance taught in the Scriptures and the encouragement they provide we might have hope.

The Old Testament was written to emphasize that man without Jesus and the Holy Spirit is not capable of obedience. Jesus is the only way.

John 14:6

Jesus answered, "I am the way, the truth, and the life. No one comes to the Father except through me."

The Old Testament is the story of man and his total failure to follow the law. If we did not have this valuable book, we would not see the need for a Savior. If we just had the New Testament, our sinful nature would not believe what Jesus told the Pharisees about obedience to the law. The Jewish nation is evidence of that today. Following the laws of the Old Testament will not provide eternal life. Only by accepting Jesus as our Lord and Savior are we blessed with 2 priceless gifts:

John 3:16

For God so loved the world that he gave his one and only Son, that whoever believes in Him shall not perish but have eternal life.

Ephesians 1:13

And you also were included in Christ when you heard the word of truth, the gospel of your salvation. When you believed, you were marked in him with a seal, the promised Holy Spirit...

TUESDAY

"The Plank"

Luke 6:41

"Why do you look at the speck of sawdust in your brother's eye and pay no attention to the plank in your own eye?"

I was walking into the mall yesterday, and as I approached the entrance, I noticed two young men (teenagers?) just ahead of me. They had earbuds in, shirt tails out, and jeans falling down below their rear ends. My immediate evaluation was not good: two punk kids looking for trouble. I should proceed with caution. I wasn't very far behind them, and the first young man went in. Then, the second young man saw me coming and held the door open for me, and his buddy held the next door open too. I thanked them both, and they were very polite and soft-spoken as they said, "you're welcome." Not what I expected as I passed by holding my wallet.

Why was I so judgmental? Would Jesus have looked at them the same way?

How many times have I totally evaluated someone just by their appearance? I have been with bikers, prison inmates, and ex-drug addicts who all have a heart for God, so how can I predetermine anything? I know I need to adjust my eyes and take time to see the heart. While pulling the plank out of my eye, I can evaluate my own heart.

Luke 6:37

"Do not judge, and you will not be judged. Do not condemn, and you will not be condemned."

Prayer: Thank you, Lord, for loving me despite my sin. I was doing a lot of things worse than wearing my jeans too low, and you accepted me into your kingdom. Praise God!

WEDNESDAY
Two-Minute Drill

Revelation 2:18–19

These are the words of the Son of God, whose eyes are like the blazing fire and whose feet are like the burnished bronze. I know your deeds, your love and faith, your service and perseverance, and that you are now doing more than you did at first.

This scripture provokes a serious self-evaluation.

Am I doing more than I did when I first met Jesus?

Do I trust God more now?

Do I have more responsibility for serving God?

Am I really listening to God?

Colossians 3:16

Let the word of Christ dwell in you richly...

Does God's word dwell in you richly?

Colossians 3:17

And whatever you do, whether in word or deed, do it all in the name of the Lord Jesus, giving thanks to God the Father through him

THURSDAY
"Are You the Judge?"

Matthew 7:1–2

"Do not judge, or you too will be judged. For in the same way you judge others, you will be judged, and with the measure you use, it will be measured to you."

One of my big hang-ups as a young boy growing up in a small town was seeing people at church whose activities during the week were not representative of God's people. They seemed hypocritical to me. I always thought, "What are they doing here?" It took me a long time before I realized that even I was not worthy of being there, but God still loved me despite my transgressions. If church isn't for sinners, then who is it for?

I know I am old school, but I also have a problem with people's attire when they go to God's house. I still roll my eyes when I see sandals and cutoffs, but I try to stop and remind myself how unworthy I am and praise God that they came to worship the Creator of the universe. Who am I to judge them?

Luke 6:41

"Why do you look at the speck of sawdust in your brother's eye and pay no attention to the plank in your own eye?"

A man came forward to accept the Lord and commit his life to God, and he was wearing jeans and tennis shoes as he approached the minister. As he walked to the front of the church, I caught myself with the plank in my eye. He was making the most important decision of his life, and I was focused on his clothes. Jeans, shorts, sandals, or pajamas… What difference does it make?

Prayer: Lord, despite my appearance, I was so dirty and so filthy inside, and yet, you accepted me. I didn't have to change anything but my heart. Thanks and praise for your loving kindness and grace.

FRIDAY

"Flashback"

Romans 3:23

For all have sinned and fall short of the glory of God.

I knew I wasn't living like God wanted me to, but I continued my quest for self-satisfaction. I did not understand why some of my fellow players seemed to have a unique joy and peace. After countless hours of introspection, I decided to ask my teammate, "How do I get what you have?" He answered me with the story of Nicodemus, a wealthy and religious man who asked Jesus, "What must I do to be saved?"

John 3:3

In reply Jesus declared, "I tell you the truth, no one can see the kingdom of God unless he is born again."

Just like Nicodemus, I asked, "How can a man be born when he is old?"

My teammate responded with this verse:

Romans 10:9

That if you confess with your mouth "Jesus is Lord," and believe in your heart that God raised him from the dead, you will be saved.

I pondered all this and wasn't sure what to do. I knew intellectually who Jesus was and believed He was the Son of God, but my heart was hesitant. Do I really want to commit my life to God? The next week, I read the book of Romans, and the night before our chapel service in Oakland, California, I read the following:

Romans 10:10

For it is with your heart that you believe and are justified, and it is with your mouth that you confess and are saved.

At chapel service the next day when the speaker finished his talk, he said, "If anyone wants to ask Jesus Christ to be his Lord and Savior, all you have to do is ask Him to come into your life." It was time, and I gave my heart to Jesus. Have you?

175

SATURDAY REFLECTIONS
Philippians 4:12–13

I know what it is to be in need,

And I know what it is to have plenty.

I have learned the secret of being content in any and every situation,

Whether well fed or hungry,

Whether living in plenty or in want.

I can do all things through Christ who strengthens me.

Lord, as I review the past week, I remember:

....

....

....

....

....

....

....

....

....

....

....

....

....

....

....

....

....

SUNDAY

Psalm 9:1–2

I will praise you, Lord, with all my heart;
I will tell of all the marvelous things you have done.
I will be filled with joy because of you.
I will sing praises to your name, O Most High.

O Most High

Prepare to worship and count your blessings.

....
....
....
....
....
....
....
....
....
....
....
....
....
....
....

Week #23

Monday: TGIM

Isaiah 26:4

Trust in the Lord forever, for the Lord, the Lord himself, is the Rock eternal.

I did not play in the first exhibition game and not in the second or third game either. I asked my linebacker coach why I hadn't played, but he had no answer. Obviously, he had been given orders to hold me back and restrict my playing time. I was not sure what to do and went to see my teammate Norm Evans, a former All-Pro lineman with the Miami Dolphins. I sat with Norm and explained my dilemma and reviewed my options: 1. Leave camp and hope another team would pick me up, 2. Leave camp and go to the Canadian football league, or 3. Go talk to the head coach. After explaining my options, Norm said, "You forgot one other possibility." I assumed he had a terrific idea to suggest that would solve my problem. His answer was, "Trust God." I paused and picked myself up off the floor (just kidding) and realized what a phenomenal answer that was. I had searched, worried, and stressed out looking for my solution and had forgotten about my God.

Philippians 4:6–7

Do not be anxious about anything, but in every situation, by prayer and petition, with thanksgiving, present your requests to God. And the peace of God, which transcends all understanding, will guard your hearts and minds in Christ Jesus.

I felt that peace after I absorbed Norm's answer, and a calm came over me like I had never felt before. We prayed and praised God, and I left that room on a mission.

Sometimes, we turn things over to God and assume He will handle it, but I was determined to work harder than I have ever worked before and to prove myself on the practice field. I had some great practices the next three weeks but still was not put in the game. I assumed they were keeping me for security measures in case someone got hurt, but I continued to work and practice as if I were a starter. Ultimately, I was called to the coach's office prior to the first game and relieved from my contract. Basically, I was called in by the head coach and told, "You're fired." Although I was not happy with the treatment I received, everything was pleasant, and I still maintained the same peace as the day I left Norm's room. I knew God had a plan, and I was prepared for the answer, whatever it might be.

MONDAY
"Trust and Obedience" Part 1

Throughout my football career, I was first string until I was drafted by the Minnesota Vikings. For five years, I played on special teams and was an on and off starter replacing injured teammates. One of those years, I was part of a special pass defense and was fortunate enough to have three interceptions during one season. At times, I was frustrated, but I knew God put me there to be part of the team. The coach for the Seattle Seahawks, a former Minnesota line coach, traded for me to replace one of the linebackers. I felt God's presence as my opportunity approached, but unfortunately, my knee collapsed on a punt return in the first game of the season against the Cincinnati Bengals, and I was out for the season.

The next year, after extensive rehab, the knee did not respond, and the odds of making the team were doubtful. During the exhibition season, I'll never forget meeting with one of my Christian brothers on the team and sharing my fears. We prayed together, and I turned it over to God. Many times in the past, I have turned things over to God, but in reality, I was still hanging on. However, this time, I committed to work as hard as I could to make the team, and my faithful teammate and I prayed and repeated the following scripture:

Philippians 4:6–7

Do not be anxious about anything, but in every situation, by prayer and petition, with thanksgiving, present your requests to God. And the peace of God, which transcends all understanding, will guard your hearts and minds in Christ Jesus.

I never will forget that day as I left his room and a supernatural calm fell over me. I had left my worries in that room and put my future in the hands of the Lord. Regardless of the outcome, I was prepared to be content and accept God's future plans for me. We all have problems in which we have not totally trusted God with the outcome. We all want our prayers answered in the way we imagine, but that is not necessarily God's plan. We must ask ourselves:

Am I truly ready to accept God's response to my prayers?

Matthew 6:9–10

Our Father who art in heaven, hallowed be thy name,

Your kingdom come, your will be done...

TUESDAY
"Trust and Obedience" Part 2

Proverbs 3:5–6

Trust in the Lord with all your heart and lean not on your own understanding; in all your ways acknowledge him, and…

Yesterday's devotional was about trusting God and the tough decision I had to make as it related to my job and future employment. My friend and I prayed, and I sincerely trusted God and turned the problem over to him. I promised Him I would work harder than ever before, and if they were going to get rid of me, then it wasn't going to be because I was lazy or had a bad attitude.

However, sometimes, we turn things over to God and expect Him to do all the work. In my situation, I could work enthusiastically or become angry, bitter, and resentful. Other examples: If you are trying to stop drinking, you should not hang out with your buddies at the local pub. If you are trying to lose weight, don't walk into a Krispy Kreme for coffee. We need to be proactive, positive, and persevere while we are waiting on the Lord's answer.

Also, in order to really trust God, we also need to spend more time with Him on a daily basis. If we don't, the world will slip in, and we will force God out. Why should God help us if we don't have time for Him?

I love the following quote: "Every day, I wake up, I picture myself as an empty cup, and I am going to fill that cup with Jesus!"

If you really trust Him……..*"He will direct your paths."*

WEDNESDAY
Two-Minute Drill

Joshua 6:2–5

Then the Lord said to Joshua, "See, I have delivered Jericho into your hands, along with its king and fighting men. March around the city once with all the armed men. Do this for six days. Have seven priests carry trumpets of rams' horns in front of the ark. On the seventh day, march around the city seven times, with the priests blowing the trumpets. When you hear them sound a long blast on the trumpets, have all the people give a loud shout; then the wall of the city will collapse and the army will go up, everyone straight in."

Walk around the walls for seven days and then shout!

What would you do?

Most of us will not be asked to do something this unbelievable.

However God does ask us to do certain things.

Matthew 22:37–39

Love the Lord you God with all your heart

And with all your soul and with all your mind...

Love your neighbor as yourself

THURSDAY
"Trust and Obedience" Part 3

1 Corinthians 3:9
We are God's fellow workers.

My last three weeks of being a professional football player was one of the most significant times in my life. I decided to give every ounce of energy and not reflect on the past. I visualized an enormous football stadium, and nobody was there but my Creator. The Lord was observing my performance and evaluating my attitude and enthusiasm. Regardless of my opinion of my boss (head coach), I was not going to neglect my practice time before the Lord.

Colossians 3:23–24
Whatever you do, work at it with all your heart, as working for the Lord, not for human masters, since you know that you receive an inheritance from the Lord as a reward. It is the Lord Christ you are serving.

Whatever your job status, whether you are the second in command or the lowest seniority employee, you are "working for the Lord, not human masters." I have a friend from Africa who works as a busboy in a restaurant. He always has a smile and continually comments, "God is so good."

Ephesians 6:7–8
Serve wholeheartedly, as if you were serving the Lord, not people, because you know the Lord will reward each one for whatever good they do…

Many parents have kids on athletic teams who are not first string. So what? Your child may never be a starter, but it's more important that they are part of a team. They may never own their own business and may be working for someone the rest of their life so, "work for the Lord, not human masters." My role as a second string linebacker with the Vikings was to be enthusiastic and motivate my teammates to excel even if it restricted my personal playing time.

Galatians 1:10
Am I now trying to win the approval of human beings, or of God?

FRIDAY
"Trust and Obedience" Part 4

1 Peter 5:7

Cast all your anxiety on Him...

Several weeks after meeting and praying with my teammate, I had cast all my concerns to the Lord, and I was pleased with my efforts while competing for my position. I listened to the coaches and tried to exceed their expectations on every drill, scrimmage, and sprint. This continued for the next three exhibition games (which I never played). The week before the first regular season game, I was called to the head coach's office. I knew what was coming and repeated Philippians 4:6–7 to myself: Don't be anxious, pray, give thanks, and a peace that transcends all understanding will be yours in Christ Jesus. I think I actually smiled as I was told I was being waived (fired).

It was time to go home and evaluate the circumstances because I hadn't played in any of the previous exhibition games, so it was doubtful that any other teams would pick me up. I decided after five games that if no one hired me, it was time to focus on my building career that I had started two years earlier. God blessed me and has provided for me so bountifully since that day, and I know He did so because I completely trusted Him with my future. Since then, there have been trials, and many times, I completely ignored the Lord's guidance and attempted to resolve complicated issues and make decisions by myself. Eventually, I realized the error of my ways, and I have reflected back on scripture:

Psalm 40:4

Blessed is the man who makes the Lord his trust...

How can I prevent distractions from the world? Only by spending time with the Lord on a daily basis and consulting *the decision maker*, who is never wrong. To quote Charles Stanley, "The basic foundation to faith is this: trust God more than you trust yourself."

Proverbs 3:6

In all your ways acknowledge Him, and He will make your paths straight.

SATURDAY REFLECTIONS
Philippians 4:12–13

I know what it is to be in need,

And I know what it is to have plenty.

I have learned the secret of being content in any and every situation,

Whether well fed or hungry,

Whether living in plenty or in want.

I can do all things through Christ who strengthens me.

Lord, as I review the past week, I remember:

....

....

....

....

....

....

....

....

....

....

....

....

....

....

....

SUNDAY
Psalm 143:8

Let the morning bring me word of your unfailing love,
For I have put my trust in you.
Show me the way I should go,
For to you I entrust my life.

For to you I entrust my life.

Prepare to worship and count your blessings.

....

....

....

....

....

....

....

....

....

....

....

....

....

....

....

Week #24

Monday: TGIM

Luke 6:48

He is like a man building a house...

I returned home to my wife and kids and decided to wait five games to see if another team would pick me up, but since I did not play a down during exhibition season, the odds were pretty slim. If the head coach for Seattle was contacted, I doubt if he would say anything good, so basically, I had been blackballed out of the NFL. I continued to stay in shape and waited, but after five games and no phone calls, it was time to earn another living for my family.

Three years earlier, I had purchased a house from a builder who I got to know, and then, the next year, we formed a partnership and actually built a couple of homes in the previous off season. The company we formed had agreed to build six houses so I could be educated and steered in the right direction. The lead superintendent who also supervised my own personal house was Al Lochner. Al and I became close friends, and we traveled together to my job sites as well as the other houses he was building separately for my partners. This was definitely a hands-on experience from the ground up. Some days, I would help the framers, shovel sand, and dig ditches, and other days, I would just hang out with the subcontractor on the job and ask a million questions. Al's demeanor on the job and his concern and care for all the subcontractors as well as the homeowners taught me some invaluable lessons.

One of the first houses I started after football was a typical two-story house on a great cul-de-sac lot. I was always looking to do something a little different, and I selected a black and white brick that was on sale. After the brick mason finished, I was skeptical—no, scared—that I had made the wrong decision. This was going to be my first source of income from my new job, and I was worried—no, panicked. This continued to plague me for several weeks until I remembered my visit with Norm Evans and the most important lesson of my life: Trust God. I prayed and asked for forgiveness for my doubt and turned it over to the Lord. I can still feel the unbelievable stress release and how my joy was restored. A few weeks passed, and I was still so pumped. Before long, the house sold. I was so very thankful and amazed at God's goodness and protection.

MONDAY

"How to Spend Time with the God of the Universe"

1 Timothy 4:7

Train yourself to be Godly.

Sometimes, it is tough getting up in the morning, but just like everything else in life… Just do it. However, if you know that our God is going to speak to you, you won't be able to sleep. God does speak through His Word, but when you are just starting, the Bible can be a challenging book.

When I made a commitment to spend five minutes a day, every day, with the Lord, I did not know where to begin. All I had was a King James Version, which seemed a little stiff, but someone told me about the Living Bible. At that time, I understood it so much better than the other translations I had read. There are other translations like The Message, New Living Translation, and of course, the New International Version. I was also told to start in the Gospel of John and then read the other Gospels.

After reading the New Testament for several months, I started just randomly opening the Bible, exploring the scripture, and trying to relate it to everyday living. This soon became boring, and I knew I needed something else. I went to the Christian bookstore and browsed around the devotional section. I found a small book by Max Lucado that seemed short and brief but still gave his interpretation of the scripture. This was perfect and gave me a daily guideline and direction. Max's writings were so simple yet so provocative and made me stop and reflect on how to follow Jesus and become a better man. I still have that original tattered version, and each page had a small area at the bottom to write down my thoughts.

I currently read devotionals by Max Lucado and Charles Stanley every day. These writings have provided so many answers to prayer, and it's absolutely amazing how God responds through their insights. God speaks if……

2 Chronicles 15:2

If you seek Him, He will be found by you…

TUESDAY

"What's Missing?"

John 20:19

When the disciples were together, with the doors locked for fear of the Jewish leaders, Jesus came and stood among them…

The disciples watched Jesus as He performed countless miracles for three years. Despite being there and witnessing these events, when Jesus was arrested in the garden, they went into hiding. Peter watched from close by, but eventually, he denied knowing Jesus three times. Even after hearing from Mary Magdalene that she had seen the Lord, they were still in hiding. Why were they so scared? What was missing?

As I grew up, I recognized that Jesus was a great teacher, prophet, healer, and the Son of God. What was missing? The Holy Spirit!

Acts 2:1–4

When the Day of Pentecost came…. All of them were filled with the Holy Spirit.

Jesus promised this special gift before He was crucified.

John 14:26

The Advocate, the Holy Spirit… will teach you all things and will remind you of everything I have said to you.

After the disciples were filled with the Spirit of Truth from the Mighty Advocate, they spread the Gospel throughout the world and, ultimately, all would be martyred but one who was exiled to Patmos.

After several years in hiding, I accepted Jesus Christ as my Lord and Savior. When I committed my life to Him, I was blessed with the same gift the disciples received: the Holy Spirit!

Ephesians 1:13

When you believed, you were marked in Him with a seal, the promised Holy Spirit…

If you are not sure if you have received the Holy Spirit, all you have to do is open your heart and ask Jesus Christ to be your Lord and Savior.

Romans 10:9

If you confess with your mouth, "Jesus is Lord," and believe in your heart that God raised Him from the dead, you will be saved.

WEDNESDAY

Two-Minute Drill

Ephesians 4:1

As a prisoner for the Lord, then, I urge you to live a life worthy of the calling you have received.

Have you received the call?

Romans 10:13

Everyone who calls on the name of the Lord will be saved.

How do you call?

Romans 10:9

If you confess with your mouth that Jesus is Lord, and believe in your heart that God raised Him from the dead, you will be saved.

What happens if I don't make the call?

1 John 5:11–12

And this is the testimony: God has given us eternal life, and this life is in his son. Whoever has the Son has life; whoever does not have the Son of God does not have life.

WHOEVER HAS THE SON HAS LIFE;
WHOEVER DOES NOT HAVE THE SON OF GOD DOES NOT HAVE LIFE.

THURSDAY
"God's Workmanship"

Ephesians 2:10

We are God's workmanship, created in Christ Jesus to do good works which God prepared in advance for us to do.

I coached my son's football team through his early years, and upon his entrance to high school, I retired. Four years later, as college approached, I was asked to return, and I accepted. The league had suffered management problems, and I only had 20 players and could barely compete. After several years of losing and no new personnel in sight, I contemplated quitting. Then, something remarkable happened. I decided to pray and search God's word for the answer. I found the scripture above and realized God had a plan prepared and that it was up to me to seek his answer.

The football season ended in October, and as the holidays approached, I was still undecided but praying for God's guidance. The week of Christmas, one of my players unexpectedly showed up at my office. He was so excited to see me and to give me a present. I opened the package, and it was a very expensive NFL memoir book with many of my old Viking teammates. Needless to say, I was speechless, and then I opened the front cover. It said, "Thanks coach, for the best year of my life."

There was no question what God wanted me to do, and I continue to coach to this day. The experiences I have had have been phenomenal. Under our name in God's mind is a list of things he wants each of us to do, just like the scripture above states. If we don't search and find his plan, we will miss the monumental blessing he will bestow upon each of us. If you are currently serving God in some capacity and not enjoying the experience, then you need to regroup and determine if it is God's plan or yours. God promised us an abundant life (John 10:10 KJV) and joy (Galatians 5:22). However, it is up to us to really seek Him through his word and prayer to find the special place he wants to apply our individual talents and gifts.

Acts 2:28

You have made known to me the paths of life; you will fill me with your joy in your presence.

Isaiah 65:14

My servants will sing out of the joy of their hearts...

FRIDAY
"Are You Prepared?"

1 Peter 1:13

Therefore, prepare your minds for action...

I was blessed to speak to a group of coaches at the Nike clinic luncheon. The Fellowship of Christian Athletes asked me to share my faith walk and how I found the Lord. I have had so many great experiences: three Super Bowls, a great team, awesome coaches, and fantastic comradery. These were all monumental moments, but nothing compares to the chapel service in Oakland, California, when I asked Jesus Christ to be my Lord and Savior.

There have been many trials since that day. Some were extremely tough, and several made me quite angry at my God. Although I did not understand at the time, each one was necessary for me to learn to trust the Lord and not the world.

Proverbs 3:5–6

Trust in the Lord with all your heart and lean not on your own understanding; in all your ways submit to him, and he will make your paths straight.

Athletics and my walk with God have some striking similarities. There is a tremendous amount of conditioning and training required to produce a complete player and team. Dedication and discipline are required to compete.

Our spiritual lives are no different. Without training, we are not ready for combat against the toughest opponent will we ever face: Satan (1 Peter 5:8). Without spiritual preparation and awareness of God's word, we cannot fight against these unseen but deadly forces.

Ephesians 6:12

For our struggle is not against flesh and blood, but against the rulers, against the authorities, against the powers of this dark world and against the spiritual forces of evil in the heavenly realms.

Spiritual exercise is mandatory!

191

SATURDAY REFLECTIONS
Philippians 4:12–13

I know what it is to be in need,

And I know what it is to have plenty.

I have learned the secret of being content in any and every situation,

Whether well fed or hungry,

Whether living in plenty or in want.

I can do all things through Christ who strengthens me.

Lord, as I review the past week, I remember:

....

....

....

....

....

....

....

....

....

....

....

....

....

....

....

....

SUNDAY
Psalm 148:1–5
Praise the Lord.

Praise the Lord from the heavens;

Praise Him in the heights above.

Praise Him, all His angels;

Praise Him, all His heavenly hosts.

Praise Him, sun and moon;

Praise Him, all you shining stars.

Praise Him, you highest heavens and you waters above the skies.

Let them praise the name of the Lord,

For at his command they were created...

PRAISE HIM

FOR AT HIS COMMAND THEY WERE CREATED

Prepare to worship and count your blessings.

....

....

....

....

....

....

....

....

....

....

....

....

Week #25
Monday: TGIM
Proverbs 17:17
A friend loves at all times, and a brother is born for a time of adversity.

I continued with my partners for six houses to get in the Home Builders Association, and then, we amicably decided to end our partnership as a new section of a very successful development was just being opened to builders. Fortunately, my ex-partners had been very involved with this organization, and we decided to merge our request for lots. Since we had large volume, we would receive a more favorable selection. After we selected the lots as a team, we then divided the lots equally. This was the launching pad for Amos Martin Construction Company. God was surely with me and gave me some good ideas and an unbelievable education on how to build a house and how to treat my subcontractors and my clients.

My business continued to grow, and we were building 25 to 30 homes a year. As the business grew, I obviously needed some help and hired a book keeper/secretary and a foreman to watch over jobs. The economy was bursting at the seams. Al and I had remained in touch, and one day, he called and wanted to get together. He came into the office and explained that he had a falling out with my ex-partners and was looking for a job. I could not believe my ears. Here was the guy who taught me the building business, and he was asking me for a job. Of course I asked him, "When do you want to start?"

What a blessing to have this man on my team.

Not just my building team but my life support team.

MONDAY

"Thanks"

Psalm 7:17

I will give thanks to the Lord because of His righteousness; I will sing the praises of the name of the Lord Most High.

I was reflecting on all my blessings: my wife, my kids and grandkids, my friends, my job, my shower head that I repaired to spray harder, my house, my yard, my car, my relatives, my power drill, my church, my past, my future, and so many more. Then, I paused and realized there was a time in my life that the reason I appreciated all my blessings was because *I* had earned them. Now, I am thankful for everything because God opened my heart and gave me a whole new perspective through my Savior Jesus Christ!

1 Corinthians 15:57

But thanks be to God! He gives us the victory through our Lord Jesus Christ.

Many times in my life, I thought I was a pretty good person. I actually thought I was worthy of His mercy, but I now know that I have not done anything to deserve His amazing grace!

"Amazing grace, how sweet the sound that saved a wretch like me."

2 Corinthians 9:14–15

Their hearts will go out to you, because of the surpassing grace God has given you. Thanks be to God for his indescribable gift

I have had so many blessings and so few trials, so why do I let the problems dominate my mind?

1 Thessalonians 5:18

Rejoice always, pray continually, give thanks in all circumstances; for this God's will for you in Christ Jesus.

TUESDAY

"Super Bowl: The Greatest Game Ever?"

Matthew 16:25–26

For whoever wants to save their life will lose it, but whoever loses their life for me will find it. What good will it be for someone to gain the whole world, yet forfeits their soul?

My life as a young man revolved around football and becoming a professional athlete. After being drafted by the Vikings, the thought of being in a Super Bowl was always on my mind. It's hard to believe I played in three Super Bowls and have three National Football Conference Championship rings (yes, we did lose all three games).

Memories? Yes. Exhilarating? Yes. Significant? Yes.

On second thought, is it really significant in comparison to the other extraordinary moments in my life?

Does it compare to experiencing my grandchildren's births? Or when they look at me and say, "I love you Papaw?" Just to have them sitting in my arms and feeling their happiness and joy is overwhelming. Is there any comparison between a grandchild's love and the greatest sporting event in the world?

Those National Football Conference Championship rings represent the most important event of my football career. No, not the Super Bowl, but the fact that football brought me to the cross and an awareness of the greatest story ever told. Without the Lord, I am not capable of loving anybody the way I should. Without Jesus in my life, I will not become the man God wants me to be.

Revelations 3:20

Look, I am standing at the door and knocking. If anyone listens to my voice and opens the door, I will come in and eat with him, and he will eat with me.

Praise God I opened the door.

196

WEDNESDAY
Two-Minute Drill

Hebrews 4:12
For the word of God is living and active.
Sharper than any double-edged sword,
It penetrates even to dividing soul and spirit, joints and marrow;
It judges the thoughts and attitudes of the heart.

The word of God:

IT'S LIVING
IT'S ACTIVE
IT PENETRATES
IT JUDGES

Having problems and looking for answers?

GOD'S HOLY WORD

2 Timothy 3:16
All scripture is inspired by God
And is useful for teaching, rebuking, correcting
And training in righteousness,
So that the man of God may be
Thoroughly equipped for every good work.

THURSDAY

"Will You Pray for Our Government?"

1 Timothy 2:1

I urge, then, first of all, that petitions, prayers, intercession and thanksgiving be made for all people—for kings and all those in authority…

Paul wrote this in the first century when the Roman government was controlled by the neurotic dictator Nero. I may not have agreed with the policies of the previous administration, but I did pray for them. Government officials need divine wisdom and not ugly and disparaging remarks. We can express our disagreement without being so condescending. Do you ever recall Jesus publicly criticizing the Roman government? After being questioned by the Pharisees about paying taxes, Jesus said, "Give to Caesar what is Caesar's!"

It makes no difference if you are Republican, Democrat, or Independent, we are called to pray and support our government regardless of our political allegiance. We can't change the President or any other elected officials until the next election, so just imagine how God would react if the entire country would pray for the current authorities and the *United* States of America.

Romans 13:1

Let everyone be subject to the governing authorities, for there is no authority except that which God has established. The authorities that exist have been established by God.

Prayer: Lord, we give you all the praise for allowing us to live in this great country. Please provide divine guidance and wisdom for all our government officials regardless of their political parties.

FRIDAY
"God's Plan or Mine?"

Proverbs 16:3

Commit to the Lord whatever you do, and He will establish your plans.

God's plan, not mine, will provide the maximum joy in my life.

Jeremiah 29:11

For I know the plans I have for you... Plans to prosper you and not to harm you. Plans to give you hope and a future.

How do I determine God's plan for my life?

Every close relationship you have is dictated by the quality time you spend with the person. If they live in a distant city, you must communicate by phone, email, letter, Facebook, etc. Haven't you heard someone say, "We used to be close, but we lost track of each other and we just grew apart"? You cannot maintain that closeness without some form of fellowship.

A relationship with God is no different.

He wants to be my closest friend and help me plan my daily activities as well as my entire future. The only way for me to advance my relationship with the God of all creation is by spending more time with Him. Not just on Sundays, but every day.

1 Corinthians 2:9

"What no eye has seen, what no ear has heard, and what no human mind has conceived"—the things God has prepared for those who love him—

Hebrews 11:6

He rewards those who earnestly seek him.

SATURDAY REFLECTIONS
Philippians 4:12–13

I know what it is to be in need,

And I know what it is to have plenty.

I have learned the secret of being content in any and every situation,

Whether well fed or hungry,

Whether living in plenty or in want.

I can do all things through Christ who strengthens me.

Lord, as I review the past week, I remember:

....

....

....

....

....

....

....

....

....

....

....

....

....

....

....

....

SUNDAY
Psalm 150:1–6
Praise the Lord.

Praise God in his sanctuary;

Praise him in his mighty heavens.

Praise him for his acts of power;

Praise him for his surpassing greatness.

Praise him with the sounding of the trumpet,

Praise him with the harp and lyre,

Praise him with timbrel and dancing,

Praise him with the strings and pipe,

Praise him with the clash of cymbals,

Praise him with resounding cymbals.

Let everything that has breath praise the Lord.

Praise the Lord

Praise the Lord

Prepare to worship and count your blessings.

....

....

....

....

....

....

....

....

....

....

Proverbs 27:9 (NLT)
The heartfelt counsel of a friend is as sweet as perfume and incense.

The business continued to grow, and we expanded into developing and selling lots as well as patio homes. It wasn't long until my son graduated from college. He had worked for me in the summer, and I wanted him to choose his career direction. I told him he had no obligation to work with me. What a glorious day when he said he wanted to continue with me. The business thrived, and we built our personal house that backed up to a lake with our own swimming pool. Life was good. Then, unexpectedly, my wife and I had some serious marital problems. She had been seeing a counselor, and then we saw one together, but some very traumatic situations occurred. My world was falling apart.

I still remember the day everything exploded, and I left home with a broken heart. I did not know where to go. I drove around forever and eventually bought some beer and tried to drown my sorrows. After a while, I decided to call the psychologist we were seeing. He answered, and said he would see me. We talked and reviewed everything, and then he asked a question I will never forget: "Do you have a friend you can talk to about this?" I thought for a minute, and as I skimmed through my list of my friends, I realized I couldn't share any of this with them. There wasn't anybody I could talk to and share my innermost feelings.

I was an ex-pro football player, and I thought I could do it all.

I never thought I would need anybody like I needed someone then.

MONDAY
"How to Fight" Part 1

1 Peter 5:8

Stay alert! Watch out for your great enemy, the devil. He prowls around like a roaring lion, looking for someone to devour. Stand firm against him, and be strong in your faith.

How do we endure satanic attacks that persuade us to do something we know is against God's law?

What did Jesus do? He fought Satan with Scripture.

Matthew 4:3–4

The tempter came to him and said, "If you are the Son of God, tell these stones to become bread." Jesus answered, "It is written: 'Man shall not live on bread alone, but on every word that comes from the mouth of God.'"

On Satan's third and last temptation, Jesus retaliated again with Scripture and said,

Matthew 4:10

"Away from me, Satan! For it is written: 'Worship the Lord your God, and serve Him only.'"

Why can't we do the same? We can. God's word will fight for us.

Whatever problem you are facing, God's word is alive, and it penetrates and judges the heart (Hebrews 4:12). God's holy word will fight for you. Find scriptures that relate to the specific temptation you are confronting. Write them down on a small piece of paper or index card and keep it with you. When Satan approaches, use God's mighty weapons to fight the temptation. Remember...

Ephesians 4:27

And do not give the devil foothold.

TUESDAY
"How to Fight" Part 2

If you are looking for some scriptures for various temptations, I have a few suggestions:

When I am frustrated and about to lose my temper:

Proverbs 25:28

Like a city whose walls are broken down is a man who does not control his temper.

Galatians 5:22–23

But the fruit of the spirit is love, joy, peace, patience... and self-control.

When I meet someone and immediately determine who they are:

Matthew 7:1

Do not judge, or you too will be judged.

When I abuse my body with food, drink, or lack of exercise:

1 Corinthians 3:16

Don't you know that you yourselves are God's temple and that God's spirit dwells in your midst?

When my eyes deceive me:

Job 31:1

I made a covenant with my eyes not to look lustfully at a young woman.

1 John 2:16

The lust of the flesh, the lust of the eyes... comes not from the Father but from the world.

WEDNESDAY
Two-Minute Drill

Psalm 63:1
'O God, you are my God; I earnestly search for you
Are you seeking God?

Jeremiah 29:13
You will seek me and find me when you seek me with all your heart.
What will happen if I seek you with all my heart?

Psalm 119:2
Blessed are they that... seek him with the whole heart.
Are you sure I can find you?

Proverbs 8:17
I love those who love me, and those who seek me find me.
Despite all my sins, can I still come to you?

Hebrews 11:6
Without faith it is impossible to please God...
Because anyone who comes to Him must believe that He exists and that He rewards those who earnestly seek Him.

HE REWARDS THOSE WHO EARNESTLY SEEK HIM.

THURSDAY
"How to Fight" Part 3

When I worry:

Matthew 6:25–27

"Therefore I tell you, do not worry about your life…. Who of you by worrying can add a single hour to your life?"

Philippians 4:6–7

Do not be anxious about anything, but in every situation, by prayer and petition, with thanksgiving, present your requests to God. And the peace of God, which transcends all understanding, will guard your hearts and your minds in Christ Jesus.

When I doubt:

James 1:6

But when you ask, you must believe and not doubt, because the one who doubts is like a wave of the sea, blown and tossed by the wind.

When I don't trust God:

Psalm 84:12

Lord Almighty, blessed is the one who trusts in you.

Proverbs 16:20

Whoever gives heed to instruction prospers, and blessed is the one who trusts in the Lord.

Proverbs 28:25

He who trusts in the Lord will prosper.

Proverbs 3:5–6

Trust in the Lord with all your heart, and lean not on your own understanding; in all your ways acknowledge Him, and He shall direct your paths.

FRIDAY
"1 Thessalonians 5:23"

May God Himself, the God of peace, sanctify you through and through. May your whole spirit, soul and body, be kept blameless at the coming of our Lord Jesus Christ.

Another definition of "sanctify"? *"Set the person apart for the use intended by its designer."*

The first question is: Who is the designer?

GOD.

The next question is: "Am I set apart for my intended use?"

Here is a quote from Rick Warren's bestselling book, *The Purpose Driven Life: What on Earth Am I Here For?*

"You cannot fulfill God's purposes for your life while focusing on your own plans."

God has a plan for each of us, and it is our responsibility to find our "intended use." God's plan will be revealed as we search His word (Jeremiah 29:13) and are continually praying (1 Thess. 5:17) for His divine direction.

Jeremiah 29:11
"For I know the plans I have for you," declares the Lord, "plans to prosper you and not to harm you, plans to give you hope and a future."

SATURDAY REFLECTIONS
Philippians 4:12–13

I know what it is to be in need,

And I know what it is to have plenty.

I have learned the secret of being content in any and every situation,

Whether well fed or hungry,

Whether living in plenty or in want.

I can do all things through Christ who strengthens me.

Lord, as I review the past week, I remember:

....

....

....

....

....

....

....

....

....

....

....

....

....

....

....

....

SUNDAY

Psalm 37:4–7

Delight yourself in the Lord,

And he will give you the desires of your heart.

Commit your way to the Lord;

Trust in him, and he will act.

He will bring forth your righteousness as the light,

And your justice as the noonday.

Be still before the Lord and wait patiently for him...

WAIT.

Prepare to worship and count your blessings.

....

....

....

....

....

....

....

....

....

....

....

....

....

....

....

....

Week #27
Monday: TGIM

Proverbs 27:17 (NLT)
As iron sharpens iron, so a friend sharpens a friend.

My wife and I separated, and we both went to individual counselors until we thought we were ready to see a new impartial counselor. During this time, I decided to form a closer relationship with one of my current buddies. I asked Al if he wanted to meet for breakfast once a week to talk about work, etc. Of course, I never did tell Al my objective, but after getting together a few times, we both realized how much we needed to verbalize our feelings. We had been friends for a long time but had never opened up and discussed some of the personal issues going on in our lives. We started at 6:30 on Tuesday mornings and began the quest for a closer relationship. This time became indispensable to both of us, and we would not miss a meeting unless we were out of town or on our deathbed.

Al helped me through this tough time in my life, and we continued to meet on Tuesdays and Fridays and had a Bible study on Thursdays. It is hard to believe our initial meeting was almost 30 years ago. That is a lot of meetings, but we have both been through some tough times. We knew we could share our hearts with each other.

Also during this time, I had another friend from my high school days, Dave Ritchie, who was always there too. Dave and I usually met on Friday afternoons after work, and I can't thank him enough for being there too. Both of these men are so very important to me, and we formed a relationship that every man needs. Macho men are not really that tough because they are struggling inside and need someone they can share their hearts with. If you don't have someone you can tell your deepest secrets to, then find someone ASAP. It will take some time, but I can tell you that after 30 years of sharing my soul with my best friends, they have been irreplaceable, and we all know how much we need each other.

"Accountability"

Proverbs 17:17

A friend loves at all times, and a brother is born for a time of adversity.

During a very traumatic time in my life, I went to see a psychologist for advice and guidance. I had visited him before for some generic problems, but this time, some devastating events had occurred, and I did not know where to turn. We discussed things, and then, he asked a very disturbing question: "Do you have any friends you can talk to about this?" I was speechless. I had a lot of buddies, but I didn't have a close friend that I could share these very personal problems with.

After evaluating this question for several days, I reluctantly asked one of my friends (a business associate) if he would be interested in getting together once a week. We began slowly, but we both immediately knew this was what we needed. We learned our time together was not about giving advice, but sometimes, we had to put our worries and fears into words, and we just needed someone to listen. Men are the worst about being macho, and our society tells us that we have to be tough and hold everything in. Baloney! God put us on this earth to have fellowship (1 John 1:7). We must share each other's lives—not just the good stuff, but even the demons within our soul.

My best friend and I started meeting every Tuesday morning almost 30 years ago, and unless we are out of town or on our deathbed, we are not going to miss a meeting. I can truly say this has been one of the most rewarding experiences of my life.

I am so very blessed to have someone on this earth I know I can count on, but I know I have a spiritual best friend in Jesus. He wants to know my inner feelings, and He doesn't just want to meet on Tuesdays. He wants to meet every day so I can focus on His plans, not mine. He also wants to know how much I love Him. After all, He loved me all the way to the cross.

John 15:13

Greater love has no one than this: to lay down one's life for one's friends.

TUESDAY

"Who's Training?"

1 Corinthians 9:25

Everyone who competes in the games goes into strict training

If we say we know God, then let's step up our efforts and prove it. Do you want Him to speak? If so, it is going to take a serious commitment. You are going to have to make a dedicated sacrifice. It's going to be hard work, and you will lose some sleep from this regimen, but it's going to be worth it. I know it is asking lot, but please contemplate this extreme request.

Here are the steps of this demanding training program:

1. Set your alarm to wake up 5 to 10 minutes early.
2. Designate a specific place to concentrate.
3. Here is the rest of the workout from a Max Lucado devotional called *Just Like Jesus:*

"The second tool you need is an open Bible. God speaks through His word. The first step in reading the Bible is to ask God to help you understand it… Don't go to the scripture looking for your own idea; go searching for God's.

There is a third tool… Not only do we need a regular time and an open Bible, we also need a listening heart… If you want to be just like Jesus, let God have you. Spend time listening for Him until you receive your lesson for the day— then apply it."

When my alarm goes off in the morning, I am anxious to start my day with the living God. There are millions of people in the world, and the God of all creation wants to speak to me. If I don't have time to listen to Him, then I cannot be the man God wants me to be.

It's all about Him. If not, then it's all about me.

2 Timothy 3:16 (NLT)

All Scripture is inspired by God and is useful to teach us what is true and to make us realize what is wrong in our lives.

WEDNESDAY
Two-Minute Drill

1 Corinthians 10:13

No temptation has seized you except what is common to man.

Temptations happen to everybody.

The waitress gave me back too much money.

My secretary asked if I could take her home.

I was scrolling through Facebook, and a very sexual picture appeared.

My boss treated me unfairly, and I want to get him back.

The waitress asked me if I was happily married.

I'll do anything to make more money.

1 Corinthians 10:13

And God is faithful; He will not let you be tempted beyond what you can bear. But when you are tempted, He will provide an escape, so that you can stand up under it.

So, what do I do?

Tell the waitress she made a mistake.

You promised your wife you would never be in a car with another woman.

Go on to the next Facebook page and thank God for protecting you.

Forgive your boss, and do not harbor any resentment

Tell her you are blessed with an amazing wife.

Ask yourself, "Why do I need more money?"

1 Timothy 6:10

For the love of money is a root of all kinds of evil. Some people, eager for money, have wandered from the faith and pierced themselves with many griefs.

THURSDAY
"Trouble Praying?" Part 1

1 Thessalonians 5:16–17

Be joyful always; pray continually...

I continually struggle with prayer. I am so easily distracted as my thoughts shift to business, weather, golf, etc. I know the devil will do anything to divert my attention, so I needed a sequence to keep me focused. I require structure to keep me on task, and the organizational tool that helped me is the acronym ACTS.

"A" is for adoration. I would open my prayer with praise and exaltation for the living God. Psalms 145 through 150 are great scriptures to concentrate on the grandeur of our Lord.

Psalm 145:3

Great is the Lord and most worthy of praise; His greatness no one can fathom.

"C" is for confession. I need to review my sins and ask my Lord to make me cognizant of any grievances so I can repent and restore fellowship. We all have the tendency to ignore our sinful actions.

1 John 1:9

If we confess our sins, he is faithful and just and will forgive us our sins and purify us from all unrighteousness.

"T" is for thanksgiving. I need to express my thanks for all the blessings in my life as well as the trials and how they have allowed me to grow closer to my God. Everybody has difficulties, but our blessings far outnumber our problems.

1 Thessalonians 5:17

Give thanks in all circumstances...

"S" is for supplication. This is a tough one for me because I am an action person, and it is hard to sit and be quiet and wait for the Lord.

Psalm 37:7

Be still before the Lord and wait patiently for Him...

Jesus withdrew and took time to be with God............Shouldn't we?

FRIDAY
"Trouble Praying" Part 2

Psalm 54:2

Hear my prayer, O God; listen to the words of my mouth.

I participated in a two-year Bible study called Thoroughly Equipped (DC). There were multiple workbooks that required daily reading, answering thought-provoking questions, and memorization. After several months of dedication to the program, I had become saturated in studying God's Holy Word, but I felt that something was missing. Several days of introspection went by, and suddenly, I realized I had neglected my prayer life.

Colossians 4:2

Devote yourselves to prayer, being watchful and thankful.

I returned to my "ACTS" formula, but my mind continued to wander. I found a small book by Bill Hybels, and he had a similar problem that prevented him from concentrated prayer. His solution was so simple: Write your prayers. Think about it. If your pen is not moving, you are not praying. No writing… no prayer. Your mind cannot be on business, kids, family, etc. if your pen is moving. Sometimes, I scribble words that are not legible, but I know I am praying.

Thessalonian 5:16–17

Rejoice evermore. Pray without ceasing.

We usually go to church on Saturday nights, and on Sunday morning after my devotional time, I journal and print my prayers so I can review my notes in the future. This has been a great resource to review my past thoughts, concerns, worries, frustrations, and joys. Every time I go back, I am amazed at how my God always heard me… *always*!

2 Chronicles 30:27

And God heard them, for their prayer reached heaven, his holy dwelling place.

SATURDAY REFLECTIONS
Philippians 4:12–13

I know what it is to be in need,
And I know what it is to have plenty.
I have learned the secret of being content in any and every situation,
Whether well fed or hungry,
Whether living in plenty or in want.
I can do all things through Christ who strengthens me.

Lord, as I review the past week, I remember:

....
....
....
....
....
....
....
....
....
....
....
....
....
....
....
....

SUNDAY

Psalm 5:1–3

Listen to my words, Lord,

Consider my lament.

Hear my cry for help,

My King and my God,

For to you I pray.

In the morning, Lord, you hear my voice;

In the morning I lay my requests before you

And wait expectantly.

WAIT EXPECTANTLY.

Prepare to worship and count your blessings.

....

....

....

....

....

....

....

....

....

....

....

....

....

....

Matthew 19:3

They asked, "Is it lawful for a man to divorce his wife for any and every reason?"

Our counseling went on for several months, and during those first few months, I was very angry, drank a lot, and did a lot of things I shouldn't have done. But eventually, I realized the error of my ways, and we began to see a neutral counselor. After several weeks of seeing him, we were reunited, and I moved back into the house with my family. I wish I could tell you everything returned to normal, but we separated again.

During the second separation, my counselor and I discussed what the separation was all about. He had discussed this previously in the first separation, but I was too angry to listen.

Separation is a time of healing but also a time to draw closer to God. This time, I decided to focus on my relationship with my Jesus, and I began spending a concentrated time with Him every morning. I had neglected my study time in God's word, so I focused on how I could grow closer to the Lord and become the man of God he wanted me to be. My relationship with my wife never was the same, and I remember drafting a letter with multiple items that I thought we needed to work on and improve. She responded very negatively and disagreed with many of those items, and after reading her return correspondence, I basically gave up. I convinced myself that I didn't want to continue living like this. Even after 20 years of marriage, I was still a young man, and I could not picture another 20 like the last two or three years.

I filed for divorce, and after a year of disputing finances...

I was a single man.

MONDAY
"Too Busy?"

Isaiah 26:9
...in the morning, my spirit longs for you.

Everybody is busy, and you probably have several errands or a checklist you must complete every day. Most people write their appointments down and have reminder alarms on their smartphones or highlights on their notepad. Psalms (NLT) says, "All our busy rushing ends in nothing." With all the planning we do, the first one left out is God.

I finally decided to put God on my calendar. If I can arrange all the other meetings I have, then an appointment with God should be priority number one. To arrange the meeting with God, I needed a time and a place. How about lunch? Too hectic and to noisy. Late at night? Too tired and too little focus. I knew it needed to be quiet, so really, the best time for me was first thing in the morning before the kids got up. I figured I could sacrifice a little sleep time and squeeze God into my busy day.

I started with a pretty simple devotional book. I read the scripture and even looked it up in the Bible to see what the circumstances were surrounding this verse. I was amazed how interesting my limited adventure into God's word had become. It felt like God was actually speaking to me. I proceeded with the author's input, and again, there was another remarkable application for me. How did God know I needed to hear those words?

I am not saying that every time I sit down with the Lord, I have a major revelation, but I know His word is absorbed by my very soul and stored for future reference. I also know that if my Jesus, the Savior of the world, needed time with the God of the universe, then so do I.

Mark 1:31
Very early in the morning, while it was still dark, Jesus got up, left the house and went off to a solitary place, where He prayed.

Is God on your calendar? Every day?

219

TUESDAY
"Sin"

Hebrew 12:1

Since we are surrounded by such a great cloud of witnesses, let us throw off everything that hinders and the sin that so easily entangles. And let us run with perseverance the race marked out for us...

Several years ago, in Sunday school class, I had a disagreement with the teacher and most of the class regarding sin and the Holy Spirit. Everyone was of the opinion that sin has no effect on the Holy Spirit within us. Some thought I was saying the Holy Spirit leaves us if we are involved in sin, but that was far from the truth.

Upon accepting Jesus Christ as Lord and Savior, everyone is blessed with the gift of the Holy Spirit.

Ephesians 1:13

Having believed, you were sealed with the Holy Spirit of promise...

The Holy Spirit within our souls is there to encourage, boost, protect, and warn us about our relationship with the living God. The Spirit's desire is for us to grow closer to the living God, and when anything interferes with this process, he is hoping to let us know.

Jesus said, "But the Counselor, the Holy Spirit whom the father will send in my name, will teach you all things and remind you of everything I have said to you."

Ephesians 4:30

Do not grieve the Holy Spirit of God...

WEDNESDAY
Two-Minute Drill

Ephesians 2:10
'For we are God's workmanship,
Created in Christ Jesus to do good works,
Which God prepared in advance as our way of life.

The first question you have to ask yourself:
Have you been created in Christ Jesus?

2 Corinthians 5:17
'Therefore, if anyone is in Christ,
He is a new creation;
The old things have passed away; behold, the new has come into being!'

After we become a new creation, we must search for our good works. Not just anything, but the one God has specifically designed for you.
What good works are you doing for God?
Are you enjoying them?
If not, you must continue your search because He has prepared a plan just for you, and this is where you receive the greatest joy.

John 10:10
I am come that they may have life,
And that they might have it more abundantly.

THURSDAY
"The Greatest Commandment"

Matthew 22:36–37

"Teacher, which is the greatest commandment in the Law?"

Jesus replied: "Love the Lord your God with all your heart and with all your soul and with all your mind."

It is difficult to conceptualize loving someone with all your heart, soul, and mind. How much do your love your parents, spouse, brothers, sisters, or children? Quite a lot, so this probably qualifies. The reason you can comprehend that much love for siblings and family is because you can actually feel and touch them.

On the other hand, we can't touch God or Jesus. So, one of the first ways for me to establish a relationship with God was to accept Him with my mind. I had to have some knowledge about who He was and what He did before I would be truly convinced. It took me quite a while to prove to myself the validity of the Bible and Jesus, and I still had some doubts and skepticism. But as I continued to explore God's word, it was evident that I was not the man he wanted me to be. I realized there is an *eternal* difference between believing in my mind who Jesus is and actually accepting Him as my Lord and Savior. So, after years of struggling with the things of this world, my life was miraculously transformed when I asked Jesus into my heart.

What about you? Mind or heart?

Romans 10:10

For it is with your heart that you believe and are justified, and it is with your mouth that you profess your faith and are saved.

FRIDAY

"Judgement Day"

Matthew 12:36

Everyone will have to give account on the day of judgment for every empty word they have spoken.

As I read this scripture, I began to contemplate my destination when my life comes to a conclusion. What happens next?

Our time on this earth is so limited and so brief. Our minds cannot begin to comprehend our short lifespan on earth in comparison to eternity. According to God's word, I will "Give an account of every empty word I have spoken." All the disgusting words that have come out of my mouth will be revealed. That, quite frankly, scares me and makes me feel ashamed that I could say such things. What about the times I actually cursed my God? Occasionally, in moments of anger, I hear people use the Lord's name in vain, and I know in the past, I did too.

I can imagine standing before the Judgment Seat of God, and right before me, my evil words are flashed. How could I have been so heartless?

As I fall to my knees before the living God, the tears run down my cheeks because of my shameful performance. How could I hurt Him so badly with my mouth? Then, my Jesus steps forward, reaches out His hand, wipes my tears from my face, then helps me up and says, *"Because you know Me, you are forgiven!"*

Prayer: Lord, you know my heart and forgive my sins and cleanse me from all unrighteousness. Let me not say or do anything that offends you. Thanks and praise for your forgiveness for my many trespasses.

SATURDAY REFLECTIONS
Philippians 4:12–13

I know what it is to be in need,

And I know what it is to have plenty.

I have learned the secret of being content in any and every situation,

Whether well fed or hungry,

Whether living in plenty or in want.

I can do all things through Christ who strengthens me.

Lord, as I review the past week, I remember:

....

....

....

....

....

....

....

....

....

....

....

....

....

....

....

SUNDAY

Psalm 96:1–4

Sing to the Lord a new song;

Sing to the Lord, all the earth.

Sing to the Lord, praise His name;

Proclaim His salvation day after day.

Declare His glory among the nations,

His marvelous deeds among all peoples.

For great is the Lord and most worthy of praise.

GREAT IS THE LORD AND MOST WORTHY OF PRAISE.

Prepare to worship and count your blessings.

....

....

....

....

....

....

....

....

....

....

....

....

....

....

....

....

Week #29

Monday: TGIM

Genesis 34:3

But then he fell in love with her, and he tried to win her affection with tender words.

The settlement almost destroyed everything I had worked for, but I told the Lord I was going to do the best I could do, and if the business failed, so be it. Fortunately, several opportunities came my way, and I started expanding into developing land, selling lots, and building patio homes. Business was booming, and the banks were lending money.

One of the developers I was buying lots from wanted to help out the Younger Women's Club by participating in a show house to benefit their organization. We arranged a meeting at my office, and the developer brought his secretary, Kathy Compton, with him. I had not met her before, and after the meeting ended, I was talking to several of the women's club members, and she left before I had a chance to talk to her. I assumed she was not interested, but I couldn't get her out of my mind and eventually asked her to meet and have a cup of coffee and dinner. This would be the first of many dates, and I told her my priority was my kids, who were 16, 18, and 21 at the time and that their request would supersede anything we as a couple wanted to do.

She was very understanding, and we continued to date for five years. During that time, we had only one serious argument. I finally proposed and gave her a beautiful zirconia diamond right before Christmas in 1994. (Yes, I told her it was a fake.) We were married on December 9, 1995 and didn't have much money, so we decided to hold off on an expensive honeymoon and went to Cincinnati for a few days. I had traded for an older two-story house not too far from work, and the painters were working there while we were gone. When we came back, they were not quite through, so we went to the movie theatre to kill the afternoon. We still talk about seeing *Jumanji* with Robin Williams that day, and we have watched it several times since.

MONDAY

"Are You Marked?"

1 Corinthians 12:13

We were all given the one Spirit to drink.

I remember standing at the altar anxiously awaiting my bride-to-be. Shortly after the wedding music began, she appeared in her radiant white gown. As she approached, I could not believe that God had blessed me with this beautiful woman. She truly was a gift from God, and I felt so undeserving.

How did I deserve for my Savior to die for me? I haven't done anything worth His sacrifice on the cross. Despite my sin and unworthiness, He died for me. Then, after the Resurrection, He sent back to Earth the Mighty Counselor, the Holy Spirit.

John 14:16–17

I will ask the Father, and He will give you another advocate to help you and be with you forever—the Spirit of truth.

This Holy Spirit is available to everyone, but unfortunately, many refuse or do not know how to accept this remarkable gift. As my bride-to-be made her way to the altar, we had to complete the ceremony by saying our vows and committing our lives to one another. Our relationship to God through Jesus Christ is no different. We can admit that Jesus lived, died, and was resurrected, but until we commit our lives to Him, He is just another fact in our minds. We are not capable of living the life God wants for us without the Holy Spirit. The Old Testament is proof of life without the Spirit. People continually turned away from God because they did not have Jesus or the Holy Spirit.

Nicodemus had everything the world had to offer. He was a wealthy and religious man who came to Jesus and asked Him, "What must I do to be saved?" Jesus told him, "You must be born again" (John 3:1–22).

Romans 8:9

And if anyone does not have the Spirit of Christ, they do not belong to Christ.

Prayer: Lord Jesus, today, this day, I want you to come into my heart and take control. Forgive my sins and take my life and allow me to receive the gift of your Holy Spirit to lead and guide me forever.

TUESDAY

"How Much Do You Love Your Spouse?"

Ephesians 5:33
Each man must love his wife as he loves himself.

The first step in loving my wife more is by putting God first. I cannot be in control... God must be. I tried being in control for many years, and not only was I unsuccessful, but I realized I was totally incapable. If God is not on the throne of my life, then I am!

I knew I must relinquish control by accepting Jesus as my Lord and Savior. Upon acceptance, the Holy Spirit entered my soul, and he prompts me to spend time with my God. Time... quality time. I had trouble just opening the Bible and staying focused while reading, so I went to the bookstore and found several devotionals to help me concentrate. Authors like Max Lucado (short and simple), Tony Dungy (sports), and Charles Stanley (heavier). Each one relates Scripture to everyday life, and God speaks through His word.

Hebrews 4:12
The Word of God is alive and active... it penetrates... it judges the thoughts and attitudes of the heart.

His word helps me maintain God's position on the throne of my life. I know that without feeding each day on His word, I will usurp His authority and place myself at the helm again. How can I put my wife before my wants and desires? How can I consistently think of her first before myself? By drawing closer to the living God! He will make me aware of her needs as well as my deficiencies in loving her as he would.

Ephesians 5:28
He who loves his wife loves himself.

228

Two-Minute Drill

The book of Philippians has always been one of my favorites. The apostle Paul wrote this while in prison primarily to thank the Philippians for their support of his ministry while incarcerated.

Philippians 1:14

Because of my chains, most of the brothers and sisters have become confident in the Lord and dare all the more to proclaim the gospel without fear.

Philippians 2:3

Do nothing out of selfish ambition or vain conceit, but in humility consider others as more important than yourselves.

Philippians 3:8

What is more, I consider everything a loss compared to the surpassing excellence of knowing Christ Jesus my Lord, for whom I have lost all things.

Philippians 4:4–7

Rejoice in the Lord always. I will say it again: Rejoice! Let your gentleness be evident to all. The Lord is near. Do not be anxious about anything, but in every situation, by prayer and petition, with thanksgiving, present your request to God. And the peace of God, which transcends all understanding, will guard your hearts and your minds in Christ Jesus.

Philippians 4:11

I am not saying this because I am in need, for I have learned to be content whatever the circumstances.

Philippians 4:13

I can do all this through him who gives me strength.

EVERYTHING

THURSDAY
"Miraculous Words"

Philippians 4:6–7

Do not be anxious about anything, but in every situation, by prayer and petition, with thanksgiving, present your request to God. And the peace of God, which transcends all understanding, will guard your hearts and your minds in Christ Jesus.

This week, I just couldn't catch up! I knew I had to prepare for a speaking engagement, but other work-related duties seemed to be overwhelming. I squeezed in time to prepare but was not comfortable with my presentation. The morning of the event, I had finished working on my delivery and headed for work, and then, it happened. My wife stopped me and asked me to come sit down. She asked for my hand, and then, she spoke some miraculous words: "I want to pray for you." My spirit calmed as she lifted me up to God and requested that he work through me and use me as his vessel to present his gospel. Her words flowed through my very soul and a "peace that transcends all understanding" was upon me.

2 Chronicles 30:27

And God heard them, for their prayer reached heaven, his holy dwelling place.

It was such a remarkable few minutes that several days later, I could still feel her hand on mine. I will never forget that moment and realize that through her, God was showing me another tremendous value of prayer. Husbands and wives need to be more perceptive of their spouses' anxious moments. All we have to do is say, "Sit down for a minute," then reach out our hand and say, "I want to pray for you."

1 Peter 3:12

For the eyes of the Lord are on the righteous and his ears are attentive to their prayer...

Prayer: Lord, help me to be more aware of the Holy Spirit's promptings. I don't want to just say that I will keep people in my prayers, but I want to reach out and hold their hands and pray for them.

FRIDAY
"God Is With Us"

My wife recently had to have her gallbladder removed. The surgery was much quicker than I expected, and she was in and out of the hospital in a few hours. Needless to say, I was concerned, and I prayed that God would keep her safe and reduce her apprehension. She said she felt calm and had an amazing peace (Philippians 4:7). I know there were angels in the operating room watching over the entire procedure, and she felt secure in their holy presence.

This event reminded me of Elisha in *2 Kings 6:8–23.*

The king of Aram was enraged with Elisha, and "he sent horses and chariots and a strong force to capture him. They went by night and surrounded the city." The next morning, Elisha's servant went outside and discovered the imposing army. Elisha said, "Don't be afraid. Those with us are more than those who are with them.

Elisha prayed, "O Lord, open his eyes so he may see." Then, the Lord opened the servant's eyes, and he looked and saw the hills full of horses and chariots of fire all around Elisha.

We have no idea of the angelic forces that encircle us every day. I know God is protecting me during all my daily activities. All the close calls or potential accidents were prevented by his supernatural force surrounding me. I know he was in that operating room watching over my wife as she had surgery. I know he directed the surgeon's hands and prompted the nurses to be quick and efficient.

The words of Elisha are imprinted in my mind:

"Those who are with us are more than those who are with them."

231

SATURDAY REFLECTIONS
Philippians 4:12–13

I know what it is to be in need,

And I know what it is to have plenty.

I have learned the secret of being content in any and every situation,

Whether well fed or hungry,

Whether living in plenty or in want.

I can do all things through Christ who strengthens me.

Lord, as I review the past week, I remember:

....

....

....

....

....

....

....

....

....

....

....

....

....

....

....

SUNDAY
Psalm 100:1–5

Shout for joy to the Lord, all the earth.
Worship the Lord with gladness;
Come before him with joyful songs.
Know that the Lord is God.
It is he who made us, and we are his;
We are his people, the sheep of His pasture.
Enter his gates with thanksgiving and his courts with praise;
Give thanks to him and praise his name.
For the Lord is good and his love endures forever;
His faithfulness continues through all generations.

For the Lord is good and his love endures forever;
His faithfulness continues through all generations.

Prepare to worship and count your blessings.

....

....

....

....

....

....

....

....

....

....

Week #30
Monday: TGIM

Psalm 115:15
May you be blessed by the Lord, the Maker of heaven and earth.

Kathy worked for the developer for several more years but then decided to change jobs to a real estate company. My business had recovered, and things were going well, so eventually, she wanted to concentrate on her volunteer job with CASA, otherwise known as a Court Appointed Special Advocate. CASA works with families that are struggling with parent/child relationships. Usually neglect or abuse is involved, and Kathy's job was to evaluate the case and determine who was at fault and how to rectify the situation. Her responsibility was to interview everyone involved in the children's home and school environments and report to the judge assigned to the case.

Many times, the kids are removed, and a search for foster or permanent parents begins. Each CASA volunteer is only involved in one case at a time, but they become totally immersed in the daily lives of these kids and try to help them recover from their undesirable lifestyles. Kathy fell in love with this work and had a major impact on each and every case she became involved.

Kathy and I moved several times and ultimately built our "final house" on an absolutely spectacular lot that backed up to creek and a forest. We had come such a long way from our modest little two-story house, and I was going to enjoy all the bells and whistles. Yes, a man cave was mandatory, and the video and sound system were remarkable—just ask the neighbors.

There were only two things I really wanted in a house. The first was a man cave, and second was tall ceilings in our great room so I could have my 16-foot Christmas tree. Number three (did I say two?) was a workout room with a sauna.

Yes, things were going well, and we enjoyed sharing our home with family and friends. We loved having the grandkids over to watch movies, and in the mornings when they woke up, we would sit by the window and discover all the animal life right in our backyard. We also enjoyed the porch overlooking the woods and opening the windows at night to listen to the cascading waters from the creek below.

MONDAY
"Too Late"

Romans 12:2

Do not conform to the pattern of this world...

Why am I so busy and forget about the people who really matter? Why am I repeatedly saying that I didn't get a chance to say goodbye? There have been so many times when I wished I had made a phone call or stopped to visit or sent a card or note, and then, it was too late.

Six months ago, I crossed paths with the son of one of my cousins. I had not seen his dad in a long time, and he gave me his new phone number. The next week, I called his dad and said, "Let's get together for lunch after I get back from my fishing trip." When I got back, there were so many things to do, and football practice was starting. I finally got around to calling him a month ago to see if we could go to lunch. He said he wasn't feeling good and had been sick with a cold for several weeks and couldn't shake it. He said he would call me the following week when he felt better.

This past weekend, I went to his funeral.

There is nothing to do now... absolutely nothing I can do! No words, no actions, no phone calls, nothing, except remember this feeling, remember this cramp in my stomach, and promise myself this will never happen again... never again!

Prayer: Lord, keep this memory on my heart. Impress upon me that not business, not pleasure, not anything is more significant than your most precious creation... people.

Isaiah 46:8

Do not forget this! Keep it in mind!

TUESDAY

"The Most Important Birthday"

There are several significant birthdays in our lives:

1. Your first birthday, your arrival on earth.
   Jeremiah 1:5
   Before I formed you in the womb, I knew you…

2. Your sixteenth birthday, your arrival behind the wheel. We all pray:
   Psalm 5:11
   Spread your protection over them…

3. Your eighteenth birthday, your arrival at the voting booth.
   2 Chronicles 1:10
   Give me wisdom and knowledge

4. Your twenty-first birthday, your arrival at the liquor store.
   Ephesians 5:18
   Don't be drunk with wine, because that will ruin your life

5. Your sixty-fifth birthday, your arrival at Medicare.
   Leviticus 19:32
   Stand up in the presence of the aged, show respect for the elderly…

6. Your second "birth" day, your arrival into eternal life. Jesus said:
   John 3:6
   Flesh given birth to flesh, but the Spirit gives birth to spirit.

   John 3:36
   Whoever believes in the Son has eternal life, but whoever rejects the Son will not see life.

All our earthly birthdays are insignificant in comparison to our birth into the kingdom of God. On January 30, 2018, I was one year closer to heaven.

Praise God.

WEDNESDAY
Two-Minute Drill

Isaiah 64:8
Yet, O Lord, you are our Father.
We are the clay, you are the potter.
We are all formed by your hand.

Have you ever watched a potter mold a piece of clay?
He starts with just a block of clay, but slowly,
Yes slowly,
The form takes shape.
Do you feel the potter's hands in your life?
Why do they seem so slow?

Psalm 66:10
For you, O God, tested us;
You refined us like silver.

As I look back on the trials in my life, it was not pleasant during the process, but I needed those experiences so I could learn to totally trust God.
I wouldn't change a thing.
God knew I needed to be refined.

PRAISE GOD!!!

THURSDAY
"Treasures In Heaven"

Psalm 33:6–9

By the word of the Lord the heavens were made, their starry host by the breath of His mouth…. For he spoke, and it came to be.

Do you believe God owns everything?

All your earthly possessions: your cars, your house, your golf clubs, your money… Are they yours? Did you earn them?

Or did God bless you with everything?

1 Corinthians 10:26

The earth is the Lord's, and everything in it.

Psalm 146:6

He made heaven and earth, the sea, and everything in them.

Is it your money or God's?

Why are we so possessive? If God truly gave us everything, is He asking too much for us to give back a small portion of His blessing?

Dr. David Jeremiah tells the story of a couple who worked hard and saved and retired to a beach house in Florida. Every day, they walked the beach and collected sea shells. They would sit on the porch and look at the miraculous ocean and then walk to find more shells.

One day, they were both killed in a car accident. They were transported to the throne of God, and as they stood before Him, they flashed back on all the money they saved and how they had neglected God. The Lord asked, "What have you done for me"? They both looked at each other and held out their tightly clenched hands, then slowly opened their fingers and revealed their shells.

Matthew 6:19–21

Do not store up for yourselves treasures on earth, where moths and vermin destroy, and where thieves break in and steal. But store up for yourselves treasures in heaven, where moth and vermin do not destroy, and where thieves do not break in and steal. For where your treasure is, there your heart will be also.

FRIDAY
"Prosperity"

Mark 8:36

What good is it for someone to gain the whole world, yet forfeit their soul?

A few years ago, during a very successful time of my life (in the world's eyes), I was approached with a very promising business proposal. I had several similar deals that were very profitable, so this was obviously another opportunity to seize the moment and continue my prosperity. God provided this real estate deal, so I should seize the moment... Wrong.

The one thing I forgot? Prayer.

I never thought twice about consulting God. Why? Because I didn't take the time, and I thought I was wise enough to evaluate the situation without His help. Why should God be involved in my life if I can't spend a little time with the Creator of the Universe? Realistically, I should be consulting the Lord for every business decision I make.

Sure, I go to church on Sunday, but is that supposed to be my filling station for the week? Absolutely not. We need to fill up every day by spending time with the Lord and prepare ourselves to really worship Him on Sunday.

James 4:8

Come near to God and He will come near to you.

If I am too busy for God, He is probably too busy for me!

SATURDAY REFLECTIONS
Philippians 4:12–13

I know what it is to be in need,

And I know what it is to have plenty.

I have learned the secret of being content in any and every situation,

Whether well fed or hungry,

Whether living in plenty or in want.

I can do all things through Christ who strengthens me.

Lord, as I review the past week, I remember:

....
....
....
....
....
....
....
....
....
....
....
....
....
....
....
....

SUNDAY

Psalm 145:1–4

I will exalt you, my God the King;
I will praise your name for ever and ever.
Every day I will praise you
And extol your name for ever and ever.
Great is the Lord and most worthy of praise;
His greatness no one can fathom.
One generation commends your works to another;
They tell of your mighty acts.

One generation commends your works to another;
They tell of your mighty acts.

Prepare to worship and count your blessings.

....

....

....

....

....

....

....

....

....

....

....

Jeremiah 29:11

"For I know the plans I have for you," declares the Lord, "plans to prosper you and not to harm you, plans to give you hope and a future."

Proverbs 3:6

In all your ways acknowledge him, and he will make straight your paths.

We were experiencing a super economic boom, and we were building and developing everywhere. The banks were begging to lend us some money, and I accommodated them by borrowing as much as I could because I knew my projects would be successful. We looked at an expensive acreage site and crunched the numbers and thought this was another opportunity to make money.

As we did our due diligence, there seemed to be a few roadblocks, but we bulldozed ahead and knew we could make it work. Please notice the plural pronoun "we." That means my partners and myself, because God was not included. The Lord had given us these opportunities, and "we" could make them successful.

The people we were buying the property from tried to take the contract away from us, but we gave them more money so we would have time to work out the bugs. Eventually, we closed the property and didn't even have our zoning complete, but fortunately, we were finally approved, and construction began. We had a magnificent piece of real estate, and developing soon began on our new model home. This was the fall of 1995, and the economy had slowed down, but everyone was expecting it to turn around in the spring of 1996.

Monday
"My Friend Steve" Part 1

Romans 8:6

The mind governed by the flesh is death...

Twenty years ago, Steve was a healthy young golf pro who dated my daughter. I liked Steve (free golf lessons!). But my daughter broke up with him, and his life seem to spiral downward. He lost his job, and I hired him, trying to help out. I caught him smoking marijuana on the job and fired him. His drug dependency escalated, and he collapsed in his shower and was rushed to the hospital where he almost died. He had a major stroke, was partially paralyzed, and his speech was slurred. I went to see him at rehab, and I struggled to understand him, but he explained that God had saved his life and he asked Jesus to be his Savior. He was so excited, and for 10 or 15 minutes, I couldn't figure out if he was laughing or crying.

Romans 8:6

But the mind governed by the Spirit is life and peace...

Steve got out of rehab and began his quest for a closer relationship with the living God. Three and a half years ago, I baptized him, and this past summer, I went to his four-year anniversary of being sober. He recently completed a two-year Bible study and is now counseling people with dependencies.

Steve's past life destroyed his kidneys and pancreas, and he currently undergoes dialysis three days a week. For the past year, he has been waiting on a transplant. Three months ago, his mom texted me on the way to the hospital to replace his damaged organs. Prior to the operation, they discovered that the donated organs were not acceptable. Last week, I received another text from his mom that he was on his way to the hospital to receive new organs. Again, those organs were damaged too. I spoke with Steve recently and kidded him about having all these false alarms. He nonchalantly replied that he wasn't worried about it because God has a plan. You see, Steve is not worried about a new organs because......He has a new heart.

Romans 10:10

For it is with your heart that you believe...

TUESDAY
"My Friend Steve" Part 2

Luke 18:1

Jesus told his disciples....always pray and never give up.

Many of you have family or friends who are addicted to drugs or alcohol. Recently, one of my friends had a brother who died from an overdose. Another friend has an addicted brother that has been in and out of jail and refuses to seek help. Steve's mom said his addiction seemed hopeless, but she continued to pray for his recovery and, most importantly, for his salvation. Steve asserts that we are all addicts who need a savior. Prior to my conversion, I know for a fact that I was addicted to myself and that my entire life revolved around me.

1 Timothy 4:7

Train yourself to be Godly.

Steve drowns out his cravings by immersing himself in God's word (Heb. 4:12). He is so excited just to get up and start his morning reading and talking to God. He knows God will speak to him if he makes himself available every day. I must discipline myself to do the same to prevent from being addicted to myself and the world.

John 3:18

Whoever believes in him is not condemned...

My dad was an alcoholic who could dry up for more than six months at a time and then return to the bottle. During those dry spells, he would go back to church and was an outstanding Sunday school teacher who everybody loved. Unfortunately, he always returned to the whiskey until it eventually killed him. My dad never could conquer the bottle, but most importantly, he did know Jesus as his Lord and Savior. He could not escape his addiction on earth, but I know he is at peace and resides in heaven with my Jesus.

John 3:36

Whoever believes in the son has eternal life...

Lord, my prayer is for those with addictions to recover, but more importantly, that they receive Jesus as their Lord and Savior.

WEDNESDAY
Two-Minute Drill

Psalm 106:7
When our ancestors were in Egypt,
They gave no thought to your miracles;
They did not remember your many kindnesses,
And they rebelled by the sea, the Red Sea.

The Israelites had witnessed all the miracles over and over, and yet, they still doubted the living God.
God continued to miraculously save them over and over and...

Psalm 106:13
But they soon forgot what he had done
And did not wait for his plan to unfold.

Why did God have so much patience?
Why did He allow them to treat Him this way?
I could not understand until
I finally realized that I am just like the Israelites.
God shows me miracles, and I believe for a while, but...
I soon forget.
And yet, He still loves me.

THURSDAY
"My Friend Steve" Part 3

Romans 3:23

For all have sinned and fall short of the glory of God...

Steve was an addict for more than 20 years and finally asked Jesus to be his Lord and Savior. During those years, he didn't think he was worthy to come before God and ask for forgiveness. Through my college life and my first year of playing pro ball, I knew my behavior was inappropriate, and whenever I thought about God, I was ashamed of all my transgressions. How could a Holy God associate with a sinner like me? If I was really interested in a relationship with the God of the universe, I needed to stop cussing, drinking, and doing bad things.

John 1:29

The Lamb of God, who takes away the sin of the world!

Steve and I both finally realized that God doesn't care if you are a drug addict, a criminal, or a person with sinful habits. God wants you just the way you are! You don't have to clean up your act to come before our all merciful God. The apostle Paul murdered Christians, and God forgave him. The adulterous woman was brought before Jesus for judgement, and our Lord responded, "Neither do I condemn you."

God wants you just the way you are!

So, if you are tired of who you are and have a desire to change, all you have to do is humbly ask for forgiveness and invite Jesus Christ to be your Lord and Savior.

Revelation 3:20

Here I am! I stand at the door and knock. If anyone hears my voice and opens the door, I will come in and eat with that person, and they with me.

All you have to do is open the door.

FRIDAY
"My Friend Steve" Part 4

Roman 12:12

Be joyful in hope, patient in affliction, faithful in prayer.

We have all prayed for loved ones and friends and even people we don't know. Many times, we see some miraculous answers, and other times, our requests are denied. Why does God heal some while others die? I always return to Scripture when I question our God.

Proverbs 3:5

Trust in the Lord with all your heart and lean not on your own understanding.

This scripture says it all: trust, and don't try to understand.

In yesterday's devotional, I reviewed Steve's life in drug addiction, recovery, salvation, being partially paralyzed, and currently going through dialysis three times a week. Steve needed a new kidney and a pancreas, and the prospects seemed dim, especially when two potential replacements failed because the donated organs were unacceptable. Steve's attitude was not diminished after two false alarms, and he totally trusted God regardless of his future. He continually said, "God has a plan. If my body fails, I will be with Jesus in heaven." Steve's demeanor reminded me of Paul and Silas after being stripped, severely flogged, and thrown into prison one afternoon. Then, around midnight...

Acts 16:25

Paul and Silas were praying and singing hymns to God, and the other prisoners were listening to them.

It's been almost a year since Steve got a healthy kidney and pancreas. He is no longer a diabetic and has been doing remarkably well. He is a great public speaker and continues his ministry and to deliver his salvation message to people with addictions........Praise God!

Proverbs 3:6

In all your ways acknowledge Him, and He shall direct your paths.

SATURDAY REFLECTIONS
Philippians 4:12–13

I know what it is to be in need,

And I know what it is to have plenty.

I have learned the secret of being content in any and every situation,

Whether well fed or hungry,

Whether living in plenty or in want.

I can do all things through Christ who strengthens me.

Lord, as I review the past week, I remember:

....

....

....

....

....

....

....

....

....

....

....

....

....

....

....

....

SUNDAY

Psalm 145:13–18

The Lord is trustworthy in all he promises
And faithful in all he does.
The Lord upholds all those who fall and
Lifts up all who are bowed down.
The eyes of all look to you,
And you give them their food at the proper time.
Your open your hand and satisfy
The desires of every living thing.
The Lord is righteous in all his ways
And faithful in all he does.
The Lord is near to all who call on hlm,
To all who call on him in truth.
The Lord is near to all who call on him,
To all who call on him in truth.

Prepare to worship and count your blessings.

....
....
....
....
....
....
....
....
....
....
....
....

Week #32
Monday: TGIM

Proverbs 3:5

Trust in the Lord with all your heart and lean not on your own understanding.

The building market was on the verge of collapse, nothing was selling, and the interest meters kept ticking. We kept digging deeper into our cash reserves. How could I have borrowed so much money? Who would have ever thought that with all the building going on that the market could possibly tank? I had not deserted the Lord during all the good times. In fact, I spent every morning reading devotionals and searching His word. However, I did not include him in my business decisions. I thought God was too busy to be bothered with me creating a successful business, and after all, I was providing for my son and his family as well as my other employees and many other subcontractors.

I struggled for many weeks, trying to hold things together, and many days, I would walk into our house and my wife would immediately know it had been another bad day. I brainstormed constantly and would come up with new possibilities and feel like there was hope, and at the end of the day, I would get shot down again and again and again.

After countless attempts to secure more funds, my wife and I finally decided to consult our God and let him control the future. What took so long? I was close to the Lord, and I spent time with him every day. Maybe since I got myself into this mess, I thought I needed to rescue the sinking ship. This was just like my experience in pro football almost 30 years prior. I finally had a flashback of that amazing day at training camp with my fellow team mate Norm Evans, and just like then, I decided to trust God. No matter what happened with our creditors, we were going to turn it over to the Lord.

My wife and I prayed, and I told the Lord that I had been too busy to approach Him and thought I could do it myself. I asked Him to please forgive me and told him that I was ready to accept whatever He had planned. I actually visualized living in a dilapidated trailer, and I said, "That's okay. We are going to be happy regardless of the circumstances." What a glorious relief—just like what happened 30 years ago. I was so stubborn and independent and forgot the source of my happiness. Our joy wasn't in the house or cars or the world but in the living God.

MONDAY
"How Quickly We Forget"

Mark 8:36

What good is it for someone to gain the whole world, yet forfeit their soul?

A few years ago, during a very successful time of my life (in the world's eyes), I was approached with a very promising business proposal. I had several similar deals that were very profitable, so this was obviously another opportunity to seize the moment and continue my prosperity. God provided this real estate deal, so I should seize the moment... Wrong.

The one thing I forgot? Prayer.

I never thought twice about consulting God. Why? Because I didn't take the time, and I thought I was wise enough to evaluate the situation without His help. Why should God be involved in my life if I can't spend a little time with the Creator of the Universe? Realistically, I should be consulting the Lord for every business decision I make.

Sure, I go to church on Sunday, but is that supposed to be my filling station for the week? Absolutely not. We need to fill up every day by spending time with the Lord and prepare ourselves to really worship Him on Sunday.

Proverbs 8:17

I love those who love me, and those who seek me find me.

James 4:8

Come near to God and He will come near to you.

TUESDAY
"Letter from a Fan"

I received a letter from a fan named Joe asking about my most memorable experience as a pro. Here is my response:

Dear Joe,

Some of the most memorable experiences were winning the NFC championships. Not many players get a chance to play in three super bowls. One season, I had a fumble recovery against the Green Bay Packers, and I ran it in for touchdown. This just happened to be the only game my sister ever got to see. She was from Madison, Wisconsin, and we were playing at the Packer's home field. When I scored, she went crazy yelling in the stands and almost started a riot.

However, my most memorable experience was prior to an exhibition game in Oakland, California. I went to chapel service the morning of the game, and a former player spoke about having a personal relationship with God. I did not have a very close walk with the God of the universe, and I had neglected Him for years. The speaker said, "All you have to do is ask the Lord to take control of your life." So, on that day, I asked Jesus Christ to be my Lord and Savior. That was not only my greatest football experience but the most important decision I ever made, and I am so very thankful that Jesus came into my heart on that very day.

Revelation 3:20
Look! I stand at the door and knock. If you hear my voice and open the door, I will come in, and we will share a meal together as friends.

Your Friend,
Amos Martin

WEDNESDAY
Two-Minute Drill

Psalm 107:1
Give thanks to the Lord, for He is good;
His love endures forever.

Romans 6:11–12
In the same way, count yourselves dead to sin
But alive to God in Christ Jesus.
Therefore do not let sin reign in your mortal body
So that you obey its evil desires.

Do you have any sin in your life?
I've had sin in my life, and it haunted me.

Psalms 32:3
When I kept silent,
My bones wasted away through my groaning all day long.
For day and night your hand was heavy on me;
My strength was sapped as in the heat of summer.

My sin had created a gap between God and myself.
We didn't talk like we used to.
I must rid myself of this separation.
I am so lonely for my God.

THURSDAY
"The Turmoil Within"

Proverbs 14:10

Each heart knows its own bitterness...

You know it's there, but you have ignored its destructive force. You were hurt—no, crushed—and you just can't forget. How could anyone treat you this way?

Matthew 6:14

For if you forgive other people when they sin against you, your heavenly Father will also forgive you.

Several years ago, a homeowner owed me a substantial amount of money and refused payment. He argued that many things were wrong with the house, and he wouldn't allow me to correct what I thought were insignificant repairs. Weeks went by, and my thoughts were always on retribution and justice. My resentful emotions gradually squeezed the joy from my life and inhibited my love for my friends and family.

I was driving to an early morning Bible study, and I was extremely angry about this frustrating experience. Suddenly, I realized I was becoming vindictive just like the man withholding my money. I asked the Lord to help me let this go. My prayers were answered when I asked for forgiveness and a solution to the problem. I wrote a letter to the homeowner expressing my desire to rectify the problems, but if not, I forgave him for his actions. I remember signing the letter, putting it in the envelope, attaching the stamp, and sliding it into the mailbox. As the letter descended, I told the Lord this episode in my life was over and that I was releasing all my anger and bitterness. The poison that had saturated my very soul instantaneously disappeared, and I could feel my joy and peace return.

Ephesians 4:31

Get rid of all bitterness, rage and anger... forgiving each other just as in Christ God forgave you.

Prayer: Lord, make me aware of any repressed anger and bitterness stored within my soul. You forgave me despite my selfishness and my many transgressions. Help me to do the same.

FRIDAY
"The Son Is Coming"

James 1:2–3

Consider it pure joy, my brothers, whenever you face trials of many kinds, because you know the testing of your faith develops perseverance.

"Life isn't about waiting for the storm to pass. It's about learning to dance in the rain."

–Vivian Greene

My wife and I discussed some of our own personal trials, and we certainly weren't dancing during the storm. Fortunately, we continued to seek God's will and accepted the fact that we were just not capable of comprehending what God had planned for us.

Proverbs 3:5

Trust in the Lord with all your heart and lean not on your own understanding.

During those trials, we realized that we really didn't trust God with our futures. We had lost a lot of money and material possessions and were worried and fearful about the days ahead. Those were very stressful days, but I wouldn't trade those moments for anything. We needed—I needed—those hard times to increase my dependence and faith in the living God.

Everybody reading this is going through, has been through, or will go through tough times. We will all stumble and lose our balance occasionally. We will all muddle in the darkness of partial depression. The good news is the there is an eternal glowing light of hope and a perpetual loving Father who wants the absolute best for us.

Proverbs 3:6

In all your ways acknowledge Him, and He shall direct your paths.

We are learning to dance in the rain…

The Son is coming!

SATURDAY REFLECTIONS
Philippians 4:12–13

I know what it is to be in need,

And I know what it is to have plenty.

I have learned the secret of being content in any and every situation,

Whether well fed or hungry,

Whether living in plenty or in want.

I can do all things through Christ who strengthens me.

Lord, as I review the past week, I remember:

....

....

....

....

....

....

....

....

....

....

....

....

....

....

....

SUNDAY

Proverbs 2:1–5

My son, if you accept my words

And store up my commands within you,

Turning your ear to wisdom and

Applying your heart to understanding—

Indeed, if you call out for insight and

Cry aloud for understanding, and

If you look for it as for silver and search for it as for hidden treasure,

Then you will understand the fear of the Lord and

Find the knowledge of God.

Then you will understand the fear of the Lord

And find the knowledge of God

Prepare to worship and count your blessings.

....

....

....

....

....

....

....

....

....

....

....

....

....

Week #33
Monday: TGIM

Hebrews 13:5

Keep your lives free from the love of money and be content with what you have…

We ultimately sold our dream house, and my wife and I split the proceeds. I put my share back into the company so we could hang on a little longer. When my money was almost depleted, I prayed, asking God what to do. There was only one thing to do, and no, it was not bankruptcy.

I decided to schedule a meeting with all the bankers individually, be upfront with them, and tell them I had no more money and could not pay my interest payments. On my first meeting with the bankers, I checked to make sure they didn't have any guns and after "shooting" the breeze, I finally told them, "I cannot pay you anymore." I expected them to get up and leave and say, "Our attorney will be in touch," but they remained very calm and asked specific questions about how to proceed. Amazing! I did not have to go to jail, and they left and said we will get back with you.

Unbelievable! Praise God!

I continued to meet with the various bankers, and most were very kind and never really got upset. They knew I was honest, and I seriously did not have anything left. Everyone remained patient, anticipating the economy turning around, but it never happened, and eventually, the lawsuits began. During this time, I was forced to let several of my dedicated employees go. This was heartbreaking, but I could not continue paying them even though Al and I had almost 20 years working together. We had run out of work, and shortly after letting Al go, I didn't have enough work for my son either. I thought it would be best for him to start his own company and run his own organization, and fortunately, he had several remodeling jobs to keep him busy.

Monday
"Trust God"

Philippians 4:6

Do not be anxious about anything, but in everything, by prayer and petition, with thanksgiving...

Several years ago, I was at a critical juncture in my life and had to make a tough decision regarding my future employment. There were several options. In fact, there were three different paths I could choose.

I met with a buddy of mine for advice and explained the problem and the choices. He responded, "Yes, Amos, those are all possibilities, but I think you left one out." I couldn't believe that after all my anxiety and apprehension I left out a potential answer to the problem. So, I asked for the mysterious answer. He said it so simply: *"Trust God."*

I couldn't believe what he just said. All my mental anguish and contemplation to find a solution, and there it was right in front of me. How could I have been so selfish and stubborn and neglected my most trusted ally, my Lord and my God?

I promised God that I would continue to work extremely hard, and I turned the problem over to him that day. We finished praying, and as I left his room, there was a remarkable confidence and an amazing peace that came over me... God was finally in control.

Philippians 4:6–7

...Present your requests to God. And the peace of God, which transcends all understanding, will guard your hearts and your minds in Christ Jesus.

TUESDAY
"Decisions"

John 8:16

But if I do judge, my decisions are true, because I am not alone. I stand with the Father, who sent me.

When the real estate market was booming, I was approached with a very profitable business deal. The land was expensive, and it would take a rather sizable loan to proceed. If the bank would lend the money, then it must be a good deal.

The bank approved the loan, but during the contractual time period for our due diligence, several issues surfaced. They were eventually resolved, but our time was expiring. The sellers refused to extend our contract, so we had to offer an additional deposit to keep the deal alive. Our zoning was delayed, but the bank still closed on the property despite several unknown circumstances.

Psalm 37:7

Be still before the Lord and wait patiently for him...

Sometimes, when things are going good, the first one we forget about is God. I figured he had presented this business opportunity, and of course, I steamrolled ahead and never once paused to ask his advice. During the process, there were many signs that told me not to go through with the deal, but of course, I was not paying attention.

God wants to be involved in every decision we make, and if we are diligent in our pursuit, he will gives us the answer. Sometimes, we continue on our path and deny his concern because we want our way and not his way. I have to ask myself if I really want His opinion. Everything is so easy and good, so how could this not be of God?

Obviously, there were many signs along the way that had I been attentive to God's plan, would have told me not to do the deal.

Psalm 27:14

Wait for the Lord; be strong and take heart and wait for the Lord.

WEDNESDAY
Two-Minute Drill

Psalm 32:5
Then I acknowledged my sin to you and did not cover up my iniquity.
I said, "I will confess my transgressions to the Lord."
And you forgave the guilt of my sin.
2 Chronicles 7:14
If my people, who are called by my name,
Will humble themselves and pray and seek my face
And turn from their wicked ways,
Then will I hear from heaven, and I will forgive their sin and heal their land.

We have sinned, and we will continue to sin.

Romans 3:23
For all have sinned and fall short of the glory of God.
The great news is God promises us forgiveness.
Forgiveness requires repentance.
A footnote in my Bible reads,
"Repentance is a change of mind and will arising from sorrow for sin and leading to transformation of life."
I must ask myself, "Do I really mean it?"

Jeremiah 15:19
If you repent, I will restore you…

THURSDAY
"Sanctify"

John 17:16–17
They are not of this world, even as I am not of it. Sanctify them by the truth; your word is truth.

I constantly run across the words "sanctify" and "sanctification."

Sanctify means "to set apart, declare holy, consecrate."

Webster's definition of sanctification is "the state of growing in divine grace as a result of Christian commitment after baptism or conversion."

Sanctification is "a state of separation unto God."

You are separated unto God by your rebirth into the world.

Jesus said, "I tell you the truth, no one can see the kingdom of God unless they are born again."

One of the best definitions of sanctification I found was by John Piper: "Progressively becoming like Jesus."

How do we become more like Jesus?
Jesus said, "Sanctify them by the truth; your word is truth."

Psalm 119:9
How can a young person stay on the path of purity? By living according to your word.

Psalm 119:11
I have hidden your word in my heart that I might not sin against you.

Psalm 119:105
Your word is a lamp to my feet and light to my path.

FRIDAY
"Appreciation"

1 Corinthians 13:8

Love never fails.

I wasn't the same this morning when I woke up. I remembered the words my wife told me last night. We were watching TV, and she grabbed the remote, turned off the sound, and said, "I really appreciate you, and I know I don't tell you enough. You are my number one priority."

I thought about those words all day today, and I can hear my wife's voice and feel her embrace as I write this post.

I need to tell her more often too. Not only speak the words but show her my heart.

There are others I need to encourage and appreciate too...

I haven't told my best friend lately how important he is to me.

My kids, grandkids, and other family members need to hear those words too. In fact, everyone I know needs to hear me say, "I appreciate you."

Thanks, dear, for those powerful words. I praise God for the gift of you!

1 Corinthians 13:13

And now these three remain: faith, hope and love. But the greatest of these is love.

To anyone reading this devotional... I appreciate you.

SATURDAY REFLECTIONS
Philippians 4:12–13

I know what it is to be in need,

And I know what it is to have plenty.

I have learned the secret of being content in any and every situation,

Whether well fed or hungry,

Whether living in plenty or in want.

I can do all things through Christ who strengthens me.

Lord, as I review the past week, I remember:

....

....

....

....

....

....

....

....

....

....

....

....

....

....

....

....

Proverbs 2:6–10

For the Lord gives wisdom;

From his mouth come knowledge and understanding.

He holds success in store for the upright,

He is a shield to those whose walk is blameless,

For he guards the course of the just

And protects the way of his faithful ones.

Then you will understand what is right and just

And fair—every good path.

For wisdom will enter your heart,

And knowledge will be pleasant to your soul

For wlsdom will enter your heart,

And knowledge will be pleasant to your soul.

Prepare to worship and count your blessings.

....

....

....

....

....

....

....

....

....

....

....

....

Week #34
Monday: TGIM

Proverbs 14:23
All hard work brings a profit, but mere talk leads only to poverty.

Our income had dropped substantially, and my wife was unsure if she should go back to work. She was at the CASA office one day, and they mentioned that they needed some help in the office. I didn't want her to go back to work, but she insisted and took over some office duties at CASA. It wasn't long until she became the administrative assistant to the Executive Director. This was quite a sacrifice for her to be out of the work force for almost 10 years and then jump into the grind of the daily work routine. She has always been a workout guru, so her day would start at 5:00 in the morning so she could get her exercise in before office duty.

After a year as second in command, she took over as Executive Director. I remember praying with her about accepting the job, and I knew she did not really want all the responsibility of dealing with all the people connected to a non-profit organization. I told her I would support her either way, but she knew we needed the money, and despite her hesitancy, she sacrificed for our future. She worked so hard, and the pressure was tremendous. There were so many different people and personalities to deal with—not only the financial supporters but a very diverse staff as well.

How blessed I am to have a wife who sacrificed for me…. Praise God!!!

"Anger Is One Letter Away from Danger"

Ephesians 4:31

Get rid of all bitterness, rage and anger...

Sin has a way of creeping into our lives. Recently, I dealt with a frustrating business deal that seemed extremely unfair. I did not have any options and was basically forced to accept the resolution. For several nights, I could not sleep because I was just thinking of sarcastic comments or some form of retribution.

Colossians 3:8

But now you must rid yourselves of all such things as these: anger, rage, malice, slander and filthy language from your lips.

When we have these feelings active in our mind, the Holy Spirit prompts us to rid ourselves of these destructive emotions. The devil's goal is to separate us from our relationship to the living God. I was consumed with thoughts of retaliation because anger and bitterness have a tendency to expand and grow if not removed. We have all witnessed friends or families that are torn apart by insignificant squabbles that morphed into total seclusion or separation.

James 1:20

For man's anger does not bring about the righteousness that God desires.

I still have random thoughts about the business deal, but I continually remind myself that it's is not worth sacrificing my communication with my Lord. I continually have to pray and ask the Lord to reveal any angry or bitter thoughts so I can confess and cleanse myself from all unrighteousness (1 John 1:9).

Romans 8:6

The mind governed by the flesh is death, but the mind governed by the Spirit is life and peace.

TUESDAY
"What if Jesus Had Not Come?"

If Jesus had not come, we would have no opportunity for salvation.

Acts 4:12

Salvation is found in no one else, for there is no other name under heaven given to mankind by which we must be saved.

Webster's definition of salvation is "deliverance from sin and its consequences, believed by Christians to be brought about by faith in Christ." Without Jesus, we cannot be delivered from sin. We are hopelessly separated from God, and the consequences of sin will eventually destroy us.

If Jesus had not come, then the Holy Spirit wouldn't have come either.

John 16:7

But I tell you the truth: it is for your benefit that I am going away. Unless I go away, the Advocate will not come to you; but if I go, I will send Him to you.

Without the Holy Spirit, we are not convicted of sin and made aware of our trespasses. We have no regard for righteousness or judgement (John 16:8). The "Advocate" makes us aware of our relationship to God and continually informs us of His all-encompassing love and compassion.

If Jesus had not come, we could not have eternal life.

1 John 5:11–12

And this is the testimony: God has given us eternal life, and this life is in his Son. Whoever has the Son has life; whoever does not have the Son does not have life.

But *Jesus did come*. All the Lord's precious gifts are ours if...

We receive Him (John 1:12).

WEDNESDAY
Two-Minute Drill

Psalm 23:1
The Lord is my shepherd,
Is He really your shepherd?
Sheep are virtually defenseless.
Sheep must be protected by the shepherd.
Are you dependent on the shepherd?
Sheep must be led by the shepherd.
Is God leading you?

The Lord Is my shepherd.

Psalm 23:1
I shall not want.
Are you satisfied with all you have?
Totally satisfied?
Or do you need a bigger house, a nicer car,
A better job, and new clothes?
Will you be happy if you don't get what you want?
Do you desire, or do you crave?

I shall not want.

THURSDAY
"Babysitting"

Matthew 18:5

And whoever welcomes one such child in my name welcomes me.

We have been praying for a year for one of the couples in our Bible study group who applied for a foster baby. They finally received a two-week old baby boy who was removed from an addicted mother. The only relative is an aunt, and she cannot take care of a young child, so hopefully, this leads to adoption. How could someone relinquish this gift from heaven? How could drugs be more desirable than a human life?

Isaiah 49:15

Can a mother forget the baby at her breast and have no compassion on the child she has borne?

This past weekend, the couple was tied up on a Saturday and asked our group if anyone could babysit. The phone exploded with volunteers, and we got the first shift. It has been a while since I have been around a two-week old baby, but this event was incredible. He was so small and had such little fingers and toes. You could feel the Spirit of God so alive in this baby boy. As I held this child in my arms, I could feel the presence of God. His handiwork, His design, and His breath inhaling and exhaling through His creation. I can feel His warmth radiating through my soul. We are blessed to experience this gift of life. Praise God! Thank you, Jesus.

1 John 5:1

Everyone who loves the Father loves his children...

I don't have any babies anymore, but I do have children and grandchildren. Next time I see any of them, I am giving them a serious bear hug. I want them to feel the amazing Spirit of God that flows through each and every one of us.

Romans 8:16

The Spirit himself testifies with our spirit that we are God's children.

FRIDAY

"Does God Speak?"

Psalm 50:7

"Hear, O my people, and I will speak."

Do you think God speaks to us? There is no question in my mind!

Here is an example, and I can't begin to tell you how many times this has happened. I've prayed, "Lord, I really need you to tell me how to help my friend. He is angry and struggling with some issues with his family, and I don't know how to advise him. Speak to me today through your mighty word as I read today's scriptures and devotionals."

The verses that day:

James 1:19

Everyone should be quick to listen, slow to speak and slow to become angry.

1 Corinthians 16:13–14

Be on your guard; stand firm in the faith; be courageous; be strong. Do everything in love.

1 Corinthians 13:8

Love never fails.

That's it! That's what he wanted me to tell my friend. Stand firm regarding the rules and consequences, but discipline can be administered without anger. The most important objective is doing everything in love. Sometimes, we get quick answers, and sometimes, we just have to be patient and keep searching and praying. One thing I am absolutely, unequivocally, 110% positive about is the fact that God speaks through his all-powerful and everlasting word.

Psalm 119:2

Blessed are those who keep his statutes and seek him with all their heart—

SATURDAY REFLECTIONS
Philippians 4:12–13

I know what it is to be in need,

And I know what it is to have plenty.

I have learned the secret of being content in any and every situation,

Whether well fed or hungry,

Whether living in plenty or in want.

I can do all things through Christ who strengthens me.

Lord, as I review the past week, I remember:

....

....

....

....

....

....

....

....

....

....

....

....

....

....

....

....

Proverbs 3:5–6

Trust in the Lord with all your heart,
And lean not on your own understanding.
In all your ways acknowledge Him,
And He shall direct your paths.

In all your ways acknowledge Him,
And He shall direct your paths.

Prepare to worship and count your blessings.

....
....
....
....
....
....
....
....
....
....
....
....
....
....
....
....

Week #35
Monday: TGIM

Job 8:21

He will yet fill your mouth with laughter and lips with shouts of joy.

During this period, I had several attorneys. One would handle the lawsuits, and one would advise us on filing bankruptcy. At this juncture in my life, I could file for bankruptcy and leave everybody hanging, including my subcontractors who I had worked with for years. I met with both attorneys, and we decided to hang on and see what happened. Needless to say, my wife and I were praying for guidance to make wise and Godly decisions.

During this time, we were unsure where we going to live, but I did have a speculative unit in one of my developments that had been sitting for a while. We talked to a mortgage person who thought my wife could pull off the mortgage, so we started making plans and designing our next home.

In the meantime, we needed to move into an apartment while I finished the unit. We moved into a 1000-square foot unit, and this was quite a shock since we had just moved out of a 4300-square foot house. We put all of our furniture in storage and rented everything for our new abode on the second floor. Moving clothes and all of our other belongings just about killed me.

Shortly after moving in, our mortgage lady called and said my wife's income would not support the amount of money we needed to borrow. We put our future house plans on hold and settled into our apartment. The kitchen adjoined the family room, and as Kathy was cooking one evening, I sat down to watch television, and a very important revelation hit me. I thought, "This place is not so bad. We could live here and be just as happy as we were in the big house. We are so blessed to have made it this far, and God is going to take care of us no matter what happens."

MONDAY

"Do You Really Trust Me?"

Proverbs 3:5

Trust in the Lord with all your heart...

I lost both of my parents very unexpectedly. My dad died suddenly of a heart attack, and my Mom had had a stroke and was recovering when she had a second one that took her life. The second stoke would have paralyzed her for life. She was only 74 years old and very active, and I was crushed when she left this earth. But she would not have been the same after the second stroke, and I know she would prefer to be with Jesus. My dad was a good man, and my mom was a saint. They were both Christians, and I am confident they are with the Lord.

Proverbs 3:5

...And lean not on your own understanding.

I do not know why God took them so early in their lives, but as the second part of this scripture says: "lean not on your own understanding." We are not capable of understanding God's plan, and the scripture does not read: "Trust in the Lord with all your heart once you understand." The definition of trust is a "*firm* belief in the reliability, truth, ability, or strength of someone." If I have anger or resentment after they have gone to heaven, then I am not really trusting God. And I still believe that my way would have been much better?

So, when you lose a loved one, do you really trust God?

Prayer: Lord, I miss my mom and dad, but I am so very thankful that they are with you. I would really like to have them back to tell them I love them one more time, but Lord, I am counting on you to take care of them. Forgive me for doubting you and being angry regarding your decision to take them. You know what's best, and I totally trust you!

Proverbs 3:6

In all your ways acknowledge him, and he will make straight your paths.

TUESDAY
"How Much Time?"

Psalm 119:105
Your word is a lamp for my feet, a light on my path.

Psalm 119:2
Blessed are those who keep his statutes and seek him with all their heart-

Years ago, I went to a seminar regarding the presence of the Holy Spirit in our lives. The speaker asked these questions regarding our daily routines.

How much time do you spend watching TV? Answer: *a lot.*

How much time do you spend reading the newspaper? *A lot.*

How much time do you spend reading magazines? *A lot.*

How much time do you spend on your phone/computer? *A lot.*

Then came the big question:

How much time do *you* spend with God? Answer: *Very little, if any.*

I was not prepared for this question, but I immediately felt ashamed.
I was so blessed, and all these worldly influences were controlling my everyday life. I have time for everything else but God.

Now the question is: What am I going to do about it?

WEDNESDAY
Two-Minute Drill

Psalm 23:2
He makes me lie down in green pastures...

Can you picture lying in a vast green meadow, gazing at the blue sky,
And just relaxing and feeling calm?
Praising God for the beauty of His world...
Praising Him for sending His Son...
Realizing how blessed you are.
And so very thankful for all His gifts!

Psalm 23:2
He leads me beside quiet waters...

Visualize walking beside a babbling brook
And being so engrossed in the sound of the cascading water
As it flows down the stream.
As you walk, you feel the calming presence of God.
You can feel His presence.
You can almost feel Him holding your hand.
Thanks for being here, Lord.

THURSDAY
"Apathy"

1 Samuel 23:21

"The Lord bless you for your concern for me."

The average age of the world's great civilizations is 200 years. These nations have progressed through the following sequence: From bondage to spiritual faith, from spiritual faith to courage, from courage to liberty, from liberty to abundance, from abundance to selfishness, from selfishness to complacency, from complacency to apathy, from apathy to dependency, from dependency back to bondage.

Merriam-Webster's definition of apathy is "indifference, lack of interest or concern, unresponsiveness."

Review a few of the events of the past 50 years:

1962: The justices ruled that official prayer had no place in public education.

1963: The court declared school-sponsored Bible reading and the recitation of the Lord's Prayer as unconstitutional.

1973: Roe vs. Wade. States were denied the authority to prohibit abortion.

A lack of interest in voting is directly related to the appointment of more liberal judges. Here are several things that we cannot afford to be apathetic about:

1. Prayer

2 Chronicles 7:14

If my people, who are called by name, will humble themselves and pray and seek my face and turn from their wicked ways, then I will hear from heaven, and I will forgive their sin and heal their land.

2. Voting

We must elect strong Christian leaders who are not ashamed of their faith and who are dedicated to God, not man (*Colossians 3:23*).

3. Expressing our opinions with a compassionate love for our neighbors.

Mark 12:31

"Love your neighbor as yourself."

FRIDAY
"Tear the Roof Off"

Luke 7:6

"Lord, don't trouble yourself, for I do not deserve to have you come under my roof."

How many times at indoor football games or basketball arenas have you heard the expression, "blow the roof off?" I have been at games where the entire building vibrates from the exuberant fans stomping, clapping, pounding, and yelling.

Jesus was preaching in a house overloaded with people, and some dedicated men were compelled to bring their friend to our Lord.

Mark 2:3–4

Some men came, bringing to him a paralyzed man, carried by four of them. Since they could not get him to Jesus because of the crowd, they made an opening in the roof above Jesus by digging through it and then lowered the mat the man was lying on.

Can you imagine Jesus standing there when, suddenly, a man is lowered from the roof and appears on a mat in front of Him? How long had these four men carried their friend? How did they lift him on top of the building? They must have been exhausted, but then, they tore a portion of the roof off, made an opening, and lowered him to Jesus.

Mark 2:5

When Jesus saw their faith, he said to the paralyzed man, "Son, your sins are forgiven."

Notice the first part of this scripture: *"When Jesus saw their faith."*

I have people in my life who don't know Jesus. The big question I ask myself is, "How badly do I want to bring them to the throne of grace?"

Am I willing to tear the roof off?

SATURDAY REFLECTIONS
Philippians 4:12–13

I know what it is to be in need,

And I know what it is to have plenty.

I have learned the secret of being content in any and every situation,

Whether well fed or hungry,

Whether living in plenty or in want.

I can do all things through Christ who strengthens me.

Lord, as I review the past week, I remember:

....

....

....

....

....

....

....

....

....

....

....

....

....

....

....

....

SUNDAY

Proverbs 3:13–18

Blessed are those who find wisdom,

Those who gain understanding,

For she is more profitable than silver

And yields better returns than gold.

She is more precious than rubies;

Nothing you desire can compare with her.

Long life is in her right hand;

In her left hand are riches and honor.

Her ways are pleasant ways,

And all her paths are peace.

She is a tree of life to those who take hold of her;

Those who hold her fast will be blessed

Those who hold her fast will be blessed.

Prepare to worship and count your blessings.

....

....

....

....

....

....

....

....

....

....

....

....

Matthew 10:12–13

As you enter the home, give it your greeting. If the home is deserving, let your peace rest on it; if it is not, let your peace return to you.

Within a few months, we finally decided on a new three-bedroom condo with about 1,400 square feet. We caught it early in the construction phase, and we enjoyed the decorating process again. This was probably our seventh house, and we loved watching our unit come to life.

In the meantime, all of my properties had been either taken back by the bank or were given back with no recourse. There was one property that the bank kept alive and allowed me to manage. They even paid me for completing and selling any units. The economy finally turned around, we started moving some of the condos, and the momentum was unbelievable. Eventually, the bank called me one day and asked for a meeting regarding selling the property to some investors.

Going into the meeting, I expected them to tell me they would sell the property if I agreed to pay them hundreds of thousands of dollars, but to my surprise, they said if I sold it that they would release me from any debt. God was in control, and it was absolutely amazing.

There were so many unbelievable occurrences with our finances, attorneys, and banks. Kathy continued to work hard, and we finally reached an agreement with the investors and sold out. The bank released me from all my debt on the property. I assumed this investment group would get rid of me and hire their own manager, but they asked me to continue and offered me a job. With this income, Kathy could retire from her job, especially since she was becoming extremely stressed.

MONDAY

"Our Government"

2 Chronicles 7:14

If my people, who are called by my name, will humble themselves and pray and seek my face and turn from their wicked ways, then I will hear from heaven and will forgive their sin and will heal their land.

Everyone would agree that all of our government officials have been elected by the people. Of course, there are exceptions when someone does not finish their term, but the American people are responsible to vote and make the initial selections. Personally, I do not agree with some of our officials, both past and present, but I still have a direct responsibility assigned to me by God... PRAYER!

1 Timothy 2:1

I urge, then, first of all, that petitions, prayers, intercessions, and thanksgiving be made for all people—for kings and all those in authority, that we may live peaceful and quiet lives in Godliness and holiness.

Jesus never responded negatively about the Roman dictatorship. He focused on people. The Pharisees attempted to trap Jesus by asking questions regarding paying taxes to Caesar. Our Lord responded:

Mark 12:17

"Give to Caesar what is Caesar's and to God what is God's."

We can voice our opinions, but our president needs our prayers for wisdom and power (Job 12:13). You may choose to ridicule and make derogatory comments about the administration, but keep in mind:

Romans 13:1

Everyone must submit himself to the governing authorities, for there is no authority except that which God has established. The authorities that exist have been established by God. Consequently those who rebel against what God has instituted, and those who do so will bring judgment on themselves.

THE AUTHORITIES THAT EXIST HAVE BEEN ESTABLISHED BY GOD.

"Stepping Out"

Matthew 14:26–31

When the disciples saw him walking on the lake, they were terrified. "It's a ghost," they said, and cried out in fear. But Jesus immediately said to them: "Take courage! It is I. Don't be afraid." "Lord, if it's you," Peter replied, "tell me to come to you on the water." "Come," he said. Then Peter got down out of the boat, walked on the water and came toward Jesus. But when he saw the wind, he was afraid and, beginning to sink, cried out, "Lord, save me!" Immediately Jesus reached out his hand and caught him. "You of little faith," he said, "why did you doubt?"

The story of Jesus walking on the water is truly amazing and inexplicable. Jesus performed countless miracles, and yet many, including his disciples, did not believe. But Peter did. Jesus said, "Come," and Peter did. Jesus is calling all of us and He reaches out His nail scarred hand and says come.

What is God calling you to do today that you just haven't had the courage to do? Compassionately stand up to your coworkers regarding your faith? Revealing your belief in Jesus Christ to neighbors, friends, or family? Maybe the Holy Spirit has been prompting you to change the direction of your life. Maybe God is just saying, "Trust Me!"

So, the question is… Are you willing to get out of the boat?

The unbeliever must make a huge decision about getting out of the boat. Are you willing to commit your life to Jesus? This takes a truly humble heart that says *I* can't continue my life like this, *I* am not capable of living the way *I* should, and *I* need someone to help and guide me.

Maybe today is your decision day, recommitment day, or action day that proclaims, "I am yours, Lord, heart and soul and mind. I realize I can't do it without you. Today, *this day*, I commit my life and actions to you. Please come and take my life and mold me into the person *you* want me to be."

John 10:10

I have come that they may have life, and have it to the full.

John 14:6

Jesus answered, "I am the way the truth and the life. No one comes to the Father except through me."

WEDNESDAY
Two-Minute Drill;

Psalm 23:3
He restores my soul.

I remember being so depressed over my finances.

There seemed to be no hope.

We finally gave it to the Lord.

My wife and I prayed and opened our hearts and told God we didn't care about the outcome.

We have each other, and whatever happens, we are in your mighty hands.

What an awesome relief.

We could feel the stress leave our bodies.

Why did this take so long?

Because I had tried everything on my own.

God was not involved!

It was all me!

I thought I could do it on my own!

Since then, I have declared my independence several other times.

I can do it on my own!

Fortunately, those times are becoming fewer and fewer.

These have been tough lessons, but I am pretty hard-headed until I finally remember who God is and I can trust Him because....

HE RESTORES MY SOUL.

THURSDAY

"Temptation" Part 1

1 Corinthians 10:13
No temptation has seized you.
After fasting and praying in the desert for 40 days, Jesus was prepared for the devil's attack. He responded quickly with scripture, and the devil ultimately left. Unfortunately, sometimes, we are not ready for the temptation, and this is clearly exhibited in the life of Joseph. He was prepared for Potiphar's wife:

Genesis 39:7
After a while his master's wife took notice of Joseph and said, "Come to bed with me!"
But he refused and responded:

Genesis 39:9
"How then could I do such a wicked thing and sin against God?"
Potiphar's wife continued stalking Joseph, and I am sure he had noticed her flirtatious comments. He was prepared to express his feelings about violating one of God's commandments, but she was not going to give up.

Genesis 39:11–12
One day he went into the house to attend to his duties, and none of the household servants was inside. She caught him by his cloak and said, "Come to bed with me!"
Nobody around when you are sexually approached by a beautiful woman? What scripture can you come up with now? So, what did Joseph do?

Genesis 39:12
But he left his cloak in her hand and ran out of the house.
Sometimes, our only option is to run. Don't pause, don't hesitate, just get away from the temptation. The best thing to do is avoid a compromising situation. The cardinal rule for married men and woman is to never be alone with the opposite sex in a car, coffee shop, office with a closed door, or anywhere else. Many have violated this rule and have suffered serious consequences.

1 Corinthians 10:13
And God is faithful; He will not let you be tempted beyond what you can bear. But when you are tempted, He will also provide an escape, so that you can stand up under it.

FRIDAY

"Temptation" Part 2

On Thursday, I wrote that Joseph was grabbed by a seductive married woman, and she asked him to come to bed with her.

Genesis 39:12

But he left his cloak in her hand and ran out of the house.

Many times, our only option is to run or remove ourselves from the temptation entirely. Some say that will never happen to them, but there are similar temptations we face every day. I asked a friend of mine if he read any of my devotionals on Facebook. He responded that he refused to open an account because he had four different friends who had gotten divorced after finding someone else on Facebook. When the web, TV, and movies involve our eyes in sexually suggestive material, we must remember to *run!* The devil will do anything to pull us away from our relationship with the Lord. Many a person started unsuspectedly looking at suggestive pictures and ultimately became addicted.

Another option when confronted with temptation is waiting. My wife and I very rarely argue, but the other day, she said something that irritated me. My immediate response was to attack, but I decided to hold my tongue. A little later after some soul-searching and prayer, I made her apologize (just kidding). Seriously, we discussed the situation, I explained my concern, and we amicably resolved the situation.

Psalm 40:1

I waited patiently for the Lord; he turned to me and heard my cry.

Psalm 103:8

The Lord is compassionate and gracious, slow to anger...

We erupt too quickly with our kids, friends, and business associates. Something they say or do that hits a nerve, and "open mouth... insert foot!" Why are we so quick to lash out instead of analyzing the comments, diffusing the volcanic explosion, and calmly responding?

Matthew 26:63

But Jesus kept silent

SATURDAY REFLECTIONS
Philippians 4:12–13

I know what it is to be in need,

And I know what it is to have plenty.

I have learned the secret of being content in any and every situation,

Whether well fed or hungry,

Whether living in plenty or in want.

I can do all things through Christ who strengthens me.

Lord, as I review the past week, I remember:

....

....

....

....

....

....

....

....

....

....

....

....

....

....

....

Proverbs 3:21–24

My son, preserve sound judgement and discernment.
They will be life to your soul and adornment for your neck.
Then you will go on your way in safety,
And your foot will not stumble.
When you lie down, you will not be afraid;
When you lie down, your sleep will be sweet.

When you lie down, you will not be afraid;
When you lie down, your sleep will be sweet.

Prepare to worship and count your blessings.

....
....
....
....
....
....
....
....
....
....
....
....
....
....

Week #37
Monday: TGIM

Ephesians 2:10

We are God's workmanship created in Christ Jesus to do good works, which God prepared in advance as our way of life.

As my son was growing up, I coached him in football from the fifth grade until he went to high school. I retired so I could watch him play high school ball, and when he went to college, I was asked to coach seventh and eighth graders. I accepted despite the fact that the program had been decimated over the years. Our team was short on talent and big on heart. I stayed with this arrangement for a couple of years, but after three years of getting our butts kicked, I was ready for a new adventure. We had a great banquet in November, and I had been praying for guidance. I held back on announcing my retirement.

I was sitting in my office around Christmas and through my window, I saw my previous season's quarterback and his mom walking into my office. I greeted them, and this young man gave me an NFL highlight book that was not only expensive but heavy. He thanked me, and so did his mom. After they left, I opened the front cover, and he had written, "Thanks, coach, for the greatest year of my life." There was no question what God wanted me to do, and I continued coaching for another 15 years. And guess what?

We won the championship the next year!

Praise God!

MONDAY

"Obedience" Part 1

2 Chronicles 1:1

Solomon son of David established himself firmly over his kingdom, for the Lord his God was with him and made him exceedingly great.

Solomon, David's son, was extremely devoted and one of the great kings of the Old Testament. One night, the Lord appeared to Solomon and said to him:

2 Chronicles 1:7

"Ask for whatever you want me to give you."

Solomon requested:

2 Chronicles 1:10

Give me wisdom and knowledge, that I may lead this people, for who is able to govern this great people of yours?

Solomon was considered the wisest man of his time, and his fame spread throughout the surrounding nations. He built a magnificent temple for the Lord, and after the dedication, the Lord was so impressed with his devotion that He appeared to him at night after hearing his prayers and said:

2 Chronicles 7:14

If my people, who are called by my name, will humble themselves and pray and seek my face and turn from their wicked ways, then I will hear from heaven, and I will forgive their sin and heal their land.

Solomon was extremely faithful and was tremendously blessed by the Lord.

2 Chronicles 9:13–14

The weight of the gold that Solomon received yearly was 666 talents, not including the revenues brought in by merchants and traders. Also the kings of Arabia and the governors of the territories brought gold and silver to Solomon.

Solomon's wealth was almost immeasurable. He was gifted 666 talents of gold, which was 50,000 pounds, and this did not include his other revenues. He had wisdom and wealth beyond our imagination, so what could possibly go wrong?

TUESDAY

"Obedience" Part 2

2 Chronicles 9:22–24

King Solomon was greater in riches and wisdom than all the other kings of the earth. All the kings of the earth sought audience with Solomon to hear the wisdom God had put in his heart. Year after year, everyone who came brought a gift—articles of silver and gold, and robes, weapons and spices, and horses and mules.

Unfortunately, Solomon's glory would fade because of his love for foreign women, and this lead to disobedience of a direct command the Lord had told the Israelites:

1 Kings 11:2

"You must not intermarry with them, because they will surely turn your hearts after their Gods."

God's laws have been established in the Bible, and everyone thinks they can rationalize (rational lies) their obedience to His sacred rules.

1 Kings 11:4

As Solomon grew old, his wives turned his heart after other Gods, and his heart was not fully devoted to the Lord his God, as the heart of David his father had been.

When we are not obedient, there are always consequences, and there are no exclusions—even if you are one of the wisest and wealthiest men in the world.

1 Kings 11:11

So the Lord said to Solomon, "Since this is your attitude and you have not kept my covenant and my decrees, which I commanded you, I will most certainly tear the kingdom away from you and give it to one of your subordinates."

OBEDIENCE = WELLNESS   DISOBEDIENCE = CONSEQUENCES

Jeremiah 7:23

But I gave them this command: Obey me, and I will be your God and you will be my people. Walk in obedience to all I command you, that it may go well with you.

Praise God that Jesus died for the forgiveness of our sins!

WEDNESDAY
Two-Minute Drill

Psalm 23:3
He guides me in the paths of righteousness for the sake of His name.

Does He guide you?

How?

Do you know subconsciously what is righteous?

Sometimes, we are just not sure, so where do you go to find out?

Go to the instruction book...

The Bible!

All of God's rules are displayed in living color.

2 Timothy 3:16
All scripture is inspired by God.

God loves when we are obedient.

Why?

Because we were righteous for...

HIS NAME'S SAKE.

THURSDAY
"Obedience" Part 3

Romans 3:23

For all have sinned and fall short of the glory of God...

David was one of the greatest kings appointed by God.

2 Samuel 7:9

"I have been with you wherever you have gone, and I have cut off all your enemies from before you. Now I will make your name great, like the names of the greatest men of the earth."

David's passion for the Lord is revealed in the Book of Psalms. He wrote more than half of the 150 chapters in the longest book in the Bible. Review several of his psalms, and feel his dedication and his devotion to the Lord.

Psalm 8:9

Lord, our Lord, how majestic is your name in all the earth!

Psalm 19:14

May the words of my mouth and the meditation of my heart be pleasing in your sight, O Lord, my Rock and my Redeemer.

Psalm 103:1

Praise the Lord, my soul; all my inmost being, praise his holy name.

In Tuesday's devotional, we read about the spiritual demise of King Solomon, David's son, who took over the throne upon his father's death. While David was king, he was also confronted with temptation from a beautiful woman. Despite his closeness to the Lord, he was entrapped in sin.

2 Samuel 11:4

Then David sent messengers to get her [Bathsheba]. She came to him, and he slept with her.

The plot thickens as Bathsheba becomes pregnant. Her husband is off to war, and eventually, David sends him to the front line to be killed in battle. One sin leads to another, and the mighty king was guilty of adultery and murder.

Not only did David violate God's laws, but Israeli law demanded death for the adulterers.

"Obedience" Part 4

2 Samuel 12:4

"Now a traveler came to the rich man, but the rich man refrained from taking one of his own sheep or cattle to prepare a meal for the traveler who had come to him. Instead, he took the ewe lamb that belonged to the poor man and prepared it for the one who had come to him."

The prophet Nathan had been with David for several years. He guided, advised, and consulted with the Lord on David's behalf. He came to the king with a parable that compared David's behavior with Bathsheba to the man in the story. David erupted with anger and threatened to kill the man, and Nathan responded:

2 Samuel 12:7

Then Nathan said to David, "You are the man!"

It took David a moment to realize that his sin had betrayed him, and Nathan, a prophet from God, called him out. After Nathan announced the punishment, King David realized his grievous actions and his guilt before God.

2 Samuel 12:13

David said to Nathan, "I have sinned against the Lord."

We all have sinned before our God, and many times, we rationalize our actions. We make excuses for our behavior, but hopefully, we realize that our sin has damaged our relationship to our God.

Acts 3:19

Repent, then, and turn to God, so that your sins may be wiped out, that times of refreshing may come from the Lord...

A footnote in my Bible reads: "Repentance is a change of mind and will arising from sorrow for sin and leading to transformation of life." We have such a great God that no matter what we have done, if we truly repent, He will always take us back and restore us to His glorious fellowship.

1 John 1:9

If we confess our sins, he is faithful and just and will forgive us our sins and purify us from all unrighteousness.

Jeremiah 15:19

"If you repent, I will restore you..."

SATURDAY REFLECTIONS
Philippians 4:12–13

I know what it is to be in need,

And I know what it is to have plenty.

I have learned the secret of being content in any and every situation,

Whether well fed or hungry,

Whether living in plenty or in want.

I can do all things through Christ who strengthens me.

Lord, as I review the past week, I remember:

....

....

....

....

....

....

....

....

....

....

....

....

....

....

....

....

SUNDAY

Psalm 40:1–4

I waited patiently for the Lord;

He turned to me and heard my cry.

He lifted me out of the slimy pit,

Out of the mud and mire;

He set my feet on a rock

And gave me a firm place to stand.

He put a new song in my mouth,

A hymn of praise to our God.

Many will see and fear the Lord

And put their trust In hIm.

Blessed is the one

Who trusts in the Lord.

Blessed is the one

Who trusts in the Lord.

Prepare to worship and count your blessings.

....

....

....

....

....

....

....

....

....

....

Week #38

Monday: TGIM

2 Timothy 3:16

All Scripture is inspired by God and is useful to teach us what is true and to make us realize what is wrong in our lives. It corrects us when we are wrong and teaches us to do what is right.

After 15 years of coaching, it was time to retire. Practices were three nights during the week, we had games on Saturday, and I was tired. I missed coaching, but after taking it easy for a couple of years, I knew God had other plans for me. I signed up for a two-year Bible study called "DC," short for discipleship curriculum. We met once a week for two years, and yes, we had some weeks off for spring break, Christmas, etc., so it wasn't a mind-boggling sacrifice.

I never had been an Old Testament fan and even questioned God why He even inspired this section of the Bible. Why didn't He just give up on these Israelites? He would continually save them from their oppressors, and then they would do evil again and again. However, after several months of classes, I realized that I am no different than they were. How many times has God rescued me? I have promised to do better, and then, I desert Him again. I can't begin to tell you how eye-opening this class was, and my perspective completely changed. By neglecting the Old Testament, I had missed out on some of the most amazing stories of God's power and love for mankind and for me.

MONDAY

"What Fragrance Are You?"

2 Corinthians 2:14

But thanks be to God, who always leads us as captives in Christ's triumphal procession and uses us to spread the aroma of the knowledge of him everywhere.

If Jesus is your Lord and Savior, you are the fragrance of life.

2 Corinthians 2:15

For we are the aroma of Christ...

Imagine God sitting on his majestic throne, and as He looks down on earth, He feels your heart for Him, and He knows your passion for Jesus and His gospel. He takes a deep breath and inhales the aroma of His Son in you. His radiant face illuminates even more, and all of the angels rejoice as His joy fills the heavenly realms.

2 Corinthians 2:16

But to those who are being saved, we are a life-giving perfume.

If you do not know Jesus as your Lord and Savior...

2 Corinthians 2:15–16

But this fragrance is perceived differently... by those who are perishing. To those who are perishing, we are a dreadful smell of death and doom.

Prayer: Lord, I need you in my life, and I am asking you to come into my life and take control. I want to commit my life to you, and I accept you as my Lord and Savior.

TUESDAY

"It's Mine!"

Psalm 89:11

The heavens are yours, and yours also the earth; you founded the world and all that is in it.

Why are we so possessive? This is mine... I earned it... my talent... my money... my accomplishment... mine... mine... mine.

Acts 17:24

The God who made the world and everything in it is the Lord of heaven and earth...

Hebrews 3:4

For every house is built by someone, but God is the builder of everything.

Psalms 24:1–2

The earth is the Lord's, and everything in it, the world, and all who live it; for he founded it upon the seas and established it upon the waters.

After reading these verses, I was reminded of something Dave Ramsey said at Southeast Christian Church several months ago. The topic of his talk was on teaching our kids how to handle money and finances.

He said something so simple and yet so profound. The number one rule:

"God owns everything."

Acts 17:25

He is not served by human hands, as if he needed anything. Rather, he himself gives everyone life and breath and everything else.

How easily we forget!

WEDNESDAY
Two-Minute Drill

Psalm 23:4
Even though I walk through the valley of the shadow of death,
I will fear no evil, for you are with me;
Your rod and your staff, they comfort me.

I remember the valley of the shadow of death.
I was broke!
I owed the banks a phenomenal amount of money.
Do I just file bankruptcy and leave town?
Do I avold the phone calls?
My wife and I talked about it, and we decided to pray.
Not just overnight, but as long as it took to get an answer.
The answer came.
I didn't like the answer, but I knew it had to be done.
I had to call each banker, meet with them, and tell them the truth.
I did… I assumed they would get mad and leave.
They didn't. They listened.
God was with me in the valley.
I can't say I was not fearful, but…
I was doing what He wanted me to do.

Thank you, Lord, for walking with me!

THURSDAY

"The New President"

Jeremiah 29:12

Then you will call upon me and come and pray to me, and I will listen to you.

My wife and I prayed continuously before the election. Our overwhelming concern was maintaining a conservative Supreme Court. Most every night before we went to sleep, we would pray for God's hand to be on the hearts of the American voters. For several days following the election, we continually thanked our God for His mighty showing and a miraculous victory. We also prayed for the unification of our country and the revitalization of American patriotism. Unfortunately, I noticed lately that my prayers for the President elect have not been as consistent as before the election, and have been, in fact, quite negligent.

1 Thessalonians 5:17

Pray continually...

This election was decided by people who pounded on the gates of heaven, and it is even more critical now to be persistent in our prayers for our country. Our President needs supernatural wisdom and God's divine intervention to lead this country. We must be even more diligent in prayer so we can restore our allegiance to our Creator and truly make this "one nation under God."

2 Chronicles 7:14

If my people, who are called by my name, will humble themselves and pray and seek my face and turn from their wicked ways, then I will hear from heaven, and I will forgive their sins and will heal their land.

FRIDAY
"Priorities"

1 Thessalonians 5:17

Pray continually...

During our Thursday morning men's group, there was an interesting question: Do you have a problem praying with your wife?

There was silence. One guy spoke up and said, "My wife enjoys her quiet time and really does not want to be disturbed." Someone asked, "Do you pray afterward?" His answer? Sometimes.

One man said, "We used to."

Almost everyone said they didn't have a problem praying with their wives but were very inconsistent and basically neglectful.

Why weren't we praying more with our most important earthly companion?

The simple answer? It is not a priority!

The question now is: What are you going to do about it? Each man felt somewhat ashamed at their selfishness, and we decided that we would improve our prayer time with our spouses. We would report back in a month to review our success or failure.

Romans 12:12

Be... faithful in prayer.

Prayer: Lord, forgive me for not sharing more often with my bride in prayer. She is such an unbelievable gift that you have bestowed and entrusted to me. Keep me faithful in prayer with her.

Last night, just before turning the lights out, I held my wife and prayed. We thanked the Lord for so many blessings.

Praise God!

SATURDAY REFLECTIONS
Philippians 4:12–13

I know what it is to be in need,
And I know what it is to have plenty.
I have learned the secret of being content in any and every situation,
Whether well fed or hungry,
Whether living in plenty or in want.
I can do all things through Christ who strengthens me.

Lord, as I review the past week, I remember:

....
....
....
....
....
....
....
....
....
....
....
....
....
....
....
....

SUNDAY
Proverbs 4:20–23

My son, pay attention to what I say;
Turn your ear to my words.
Do not let them out of your sight,
Keep them within your heart;
For they are life to those who find them
And health to one's whole body.
Above all else guard your heart,
For everything you do flows from it.
Above all else guard your heart,
For everything you do flows from it.

Prepare to worship and count your blessings.

....

....

....

....

....

....

....

....

....

....

....

....

Week #39
Monday: TGIM

Psalm 17:6
I call on you, my God, for you will answer me; turn your ear to me and hear my prayer.

Each week, we had to memorize specific verses in the Bible, and at the beginning of each class, we had to recite them to our fellow classmates. At first, this sounded difficult, but eventually, I enjoyed the challenge and looked forward to the new verse each week. There were so many learning experiences during this two-year program. I was still involved with the attorneys and lenders, and my study patterns helped me feel God's presence in His word every day. Each day, I was anxious to open my study books and fill in the blanks or read the appropriate material and answer questions.

After several months, I knew something was missing but I couldn't figure it out. I would never miss a lesson and would spend time finishing the day's homework, but I seemed to be losing my enthusiasm and my joy. I told God that I was working hard for him, so I asked him what I could possibly be neglectful about. The answer finally came... prayer. Because of my time commitment to the book work, I had totally skipped my prayer time. I was so busy that I wasn't taking any time to talk to God or allow him to talk to me.

Thank you Holy Spirit for making me aware of the void in my prayer life.

I missed you and I know you missed me.

MONDAY
"David and Bathsheba"

2 Samuel 11:1–2

In the spring, at the time when kings go off to war... David remained in Jerusalem. One evening David got up from his bed and walked on the roof of the palace.

Why did David stay home? He had been fighting every spring for years and was still a young man. Did he stay because he had been on the roof many times before and observed a beautiful young woman bathing? Was he waiting for her husband to go off to war? Everyone knows what happens next... the illicit affair and his mistress falling pregnant. The lies began, and eventually, they lead to the death of Bathsheba's husband.

We have all journeyed into the pit of sin. We have felt its grasp and struggled to remove ourselves from its grip. We make excuses, and our continued sin leads to more lies and deceit. No, maybe it wasn't an affair, but sin has a tendency to make us its slave (John 8:34). I have felt an immense anger and bitterness that conceived plans for retribution. I have felt greed and watched my selfishness expand. I have slandered my neighbor and gained an unholy righteousness. I have had an unforgiving spirit that tainted other relationships. I have felt distant from my Lord and seemed to drift further away because sin pulls us away from the living God.

King David finally recognized his sin and pleaded for mercy and restoration (Psalm 51). Amazingly, we have a God who will forgive our sins no matter what we have done. King David had committed adultery and murder, but our great God forgave him and renewed his steadfast spirit (Psalm 51:10).

1 John 1:8–9

If we claim to be without sin, we deceive ourselves and the truth is not in us. If we confess our sins, he is faithful and just and will forgive us our sins and purify us from all unrighteousness.

TUESDAY

"The Good Samaritan"

Luke 10:30

"A man was going down from Jerusalem to Jericho, when he was attacked by robbers. They stripped him of his clothes, beat him and went away, leaving him half dead."

Jesus told the story of the Good Samaritan after an expert in the law asked him, "And who is my neighbor?" Our Lord then presented the situation with a half-dead man lying on the side of the road. A priest and a temple assistant both passed by and ignored the dying man. Finally, a Samaritan stopped and rescued the man and delivered him to safety. The footnote in my Bible says, "Samaritans were viewed as half-breeds, both physically and spiritually, and people practiced open hostility toward them."

Our society today is so conscious of suspicious people and events. Even today, I am very wary of picking up a hitchhiker or responding to a needy person on the street corner. I know I have been too busy to recognize people in need, and sometimes, I avoid looking because I don't have time.

As I reviewed this parable, I questioned myself. Would I have stopped and saved this man from imminent death?

What would you do?

Prayer: Lord, help me to slow down and become more aware of other people's needs. Help me to pause and ask the Holy Spirit to guide me and advise me in these situations. Your will, Father, not mine.

Matthew 25:45

Truly I tell you, whatever you did not do for one of the least of these, you did not do for me.

WEDNESDAY
Two-Minute Drill

Psalm 23:5
You prepare a table before me
In the presence of my enemies.
You anoint my head with oil;
My cup overflows.

God loves us so.

Even when we are fighting a battle that seems hopeless, he prepares a Thanksgiving dinner for us.

They seem to be winning, but we are the honored guest!

As the meal continues, the King comes to me and anoints my head with oil!

His servants fill my cup till it overflows.

MY CUP OVERFLOWS.

Psalm 23:6
'Surely goodness and mercy shall follow me all the days of my life,
And I shall dwell in the house of the Lord forever.'

I can feel His presence, and I know He will never leave me.

How could I possibly leave His sanctuary where He protects me?

I shall dwell in the house of the Lord forever.

THURSDAY
"Prayer"

Psalm 119:105
Your word is a lamp to my feet and a light to my path.
My mom was a young woman and had a stroke that left her partially paralyzed. She was recovering and moving to rehab and had a second stroke and died.

My wife's mom had mesothelioma and had to have a lung removed. The operation was a great success and recovery was going well, but suddenly, she contracted pneumonia. I had just returned home and was totally shocked when I received the news from my tearful wife. I left for Cleveland immediately, and as I drove, I continually prayed and asked God to eliminate the virus and touch her with his healing hand. When I got there, the family decided it was time to let her go.

Did I pray hard enough? Did God hear our prayers? Why didn't He rescue them? I know my mom would not have been happy if she did not recover from her stroke, but why did He take these two young Christian women? So many questions, so many doubts, but God answered me in His word.

Isaiah 33:8–9
"For my thoughts are not your thoughts, neither are your ways my ways," declares the Lord. "As the heavens are higher than the earth, so are my ways higher than your ways and my thoughts than your thoughts."
God speaks through His word! When in doubt, God wants me to seek Him for answers. Why do I turn to the world and look for solutions? He is the only source, and as I continued my search, I found another scripture:

Proverbs 3:5
Trust in the Lord with all your heart and lean not on your own understanding.
We cannot comprehend or understand the Lord's will. We must accept His decisions and trust Him—TOTALLY TRUST HIM!

I recently lost two of my best friends. I don't understand, and I miss them both, but I can hear God whispering to me... TRUST ME!

FRIDAY

"God's Word"

Hebrews 4:12

For the word of God is alive and active. Sharper than any double-edged sword, it penetrates even to dividing soul and spirit, joints and marrow; it judges the thoughts and attitudes of the heart.

We talked about reading the Bible, and I know some of you really struggle with how to begin or how to maintain any consistency. After I found the translation I could understand, I would randomly open the Bible and feel like wherever I opened it, God was watching and directing my fingers. I am not saying he can't do that, but I was becoming distracted and started to lose my focus. Personally, I needed a guidebook or lesson plan to keep me on track. I found what I needed in several devotional books written by different authors. This gave me a daily calendar to follow and a coordinating scripture to relate to the author's analyses. Some of those verses came from books in the Old Testament I had never heard of (like Habakkuk), but it sparked my interest to research what they were and what they had to do with biblical history.

The original author I selected was Max Lucado, and I chose him because he was brief and simplistic in his writings. However, his interpretation and application of the scripture was quite thought-provoking. I was hooked, and to this day, I still have Max's dilapidated devotional book from several years ago that I still read every day. The pages are bent back and torn, but even after years of rereading each one, they always have a new message.

God's word is living.

God's word is active.

God's word penetrates.

God's word judges.

SATURDAY REFLECTIONS
Philippians 4:12–13

I know what it is to be in need,
And I know what it is to have plenty.
I have learned the secret of being content in any and every situation,
Whether well fed or hungry,
Whether living in plenty or in want.
I can do all things through Christ who strengthens me.

Lord, as I review the past week, I remember:

....

....

....

....

....

....

....

....

....

....

....

....

....

....

....

SUNDAY

Proverbs 8:11–17

For wisdom is more precious than rubies,

And nothing you desire can compare with her.

I, wisdom, dwell together with prudence; I possess knowledge and discretion.

To fear the Lord is to hate evil; I hate pride and arrogance,

Evil behavior and perverse speech.

Counsel and sound judgement are mine;

I have insight, I have power.

By me kings reign and rulers issue decrees that are just;

By me princes govern, and nobles—all who rule the earth.

I love those who love me,

And those who seek me find me.

Prepare to worship and count your blessings.

....

....

....

....

....

....

....

....

....

....

....

....

Week #40
Monday: TGIM

Psalm 66:19
But God has surely listened and heard my prayer.
Since I had retired from coaching, I knew God wanted to use me someplace, and I was anxious to find out where. The scripture in Ephesians continually drove my prayer life in my search to serve the living God.

Ephesians 2:10
We are God's workmanship, created in Christ Jesus to do good works, which God prepared in advance as our way of life.
Something was out there, and I prayed and told God I was ready and available to serve Him. My wife asked me if I wanted to help her with her third, fourth, and fifth graders and thought this might be the answer. I helped her for one week, and the following week, she asked me if I was coming back. My response was, "Honey, if I go back, somebody is going to die. Either they are going to kill me, or I am going to kill somebody." Obviously, this was not my calling from God, so I continued my vigil, and after two years away from football, I received a call from a middle school athletic director asking if I was interested in starting a program at one of the traditional schools. I said doubtful, but let's talk.

At my interview, I was informed that the practices were after school and the games were during the week, so I was immediately interested. I prayed and discussed everything with my wife, and all the pieces seem to fall together. I am now going into my sixth year. I know this is where God wants to use me, and working with these young men has provided an unbelievable amount of joy in my life.

God has a plan for each and every one of us, and it is up to us to search and find out exactly what He wants us to do. I picture God in heaven with a big book of assignments he would like people on earth to accomplish. The items listed will provide the most joy, not only for God, but for all the people involved. If we don't find our designated place to serve Him, then it might not get done. If you are serving God but not enjoying it, then you need to find something else. God promised us the abundant life, and by finding our specific placed to serve Him, everyone will be blessed.

MONDAY
"Listen to the Spirit"

Jonah 1:1–2

The word of the Lord came to Jonah son of Amittai: "Go to the great city of Ninevah and preach against it, because its wickedness has come up before me."

Jonah refused to go and, ultimately, ended up in the belly of the whale. Throughout our lives, we will be prompted by the Holy Spirit to do things, but sometimes, we ignore His calling.

It was the day before I left for Canada, and I had a zillion things to do. An older friend of mine was in rehab recovering from a broken hip, and I needed to see him before I left, but I was so busy. The Holy Spirit kept prodding me to visit and, reluctantly, I went. We had an amazing conversation about our faith in God and trusting Jesus with our lives.

I left for Canada the next day, and a week later when we came out of the wilderness, I had a message to call my wife. I called immediately, and she told me that my friend in rehab had had complications and died. I couldn't believe it! I paused and reflected on my reluctant visit prior to leaving for Canada. What if I had drowned out the Spirit's urging and listened to my busy world?

What is the Lord asking you to do today? Don't wait! We all have someone that needs a phone call, a visit, a card, or just a prayer. Take time to listen to the Holy Spirit's prompting. Don't ignore His call.

Proverbs 8:34

Blessed are those who listen to me, watching daily at my doors, waiting at my doorway.

TUESDAY
"The Train"

Matthew 22:29

Jesus replied, "You are in error because you do not know the Scriptures or the power of God."

I remember seeing an illustration that compared our spiritual life to a three-car train. There is a locomotive, a car for fuel, and a caboose. The engine is called faith, the fuel car is labeled fact, and the caboose is feeling. At some point in everyone's lives, our trains were sitting in the railroad yard rusting due to inactivity. The locomotive was virtually dead, but all of a sudden, something sparked the engine, and it came to life. That ignition was supplied by Jesus Christ.

1 Corinthians 15:22

So in Christ all will be made alive...

The powerful locomotive had come to life in the train yard but remained stationary. There seem to be plenty of fuel in the adjoining car, but nothing was being supplied to the locomotive engine. This is the same situation that happens in the early Christian experience. We accept Jesus Christ as Lord and Savior, but our power is limited because the Word of God has not come alive within us.

Hebrews 4:12

The Word of God is alive and active...

For many years, I went to church, and on Sunday, the preacher filled me up. I felt the increase in power, and as I left the building, I could *feel* God's presence. The next day I went back to work, and I soon forgot the message delivered the day before. I would quickly become immersed in the world. I had enough fuel to keep my engine starting, but the *feeling* I possessed had evaporated. I soon realized that without God's word, without *facts*, there would be no *feeling*.

Hebrews 11:6

Without faith it is impossible to please God...

If my *faith* is not producing *feelings*, then something is wrong with my fuel car (*facts*), so I need to absorb more of God's Holy Word. The Holy Spirit within our souls will provide plenty of *feelings* if we supply the fuel.

WEDNESDAY
Two-Minute Drill

Luke 10:38–42

As Jesus and his disciples were on their way, he came to a village where a woman named Martha opened her home to him. She had a sister called Mary, who sat at the Lord's feet listening to what he said.

But Martha was distracted by all the preparations that had to be made.

She came to him and asked, "Lord, don't you care that my sister has left me to do the work by myself? Tell her to help me!"

"Martha, Martha," the Lord answered, "You are worried and upset about many things, but only few things are needed. Mary has chosen what is better, and it will not be taken away from her."

Notice the highlighted verse.

Mary was distracted by the world.

Are you?

What are the priorities in your life?

Is church a priority?

God asks for only one day a week to gather in His name.

Can you spare an hour or two for God?

Do your kids know you will absolutely not miss church?

Is time with God on a daily basis a priority?

Are you spending any time with the Lord besides on Sundays?

Are you too busy for God?

If you start your day without God,

You are basically saying, "I don't need you today."

DON'T BE DISTRACTED BY THE WORLD!

THURSDAY
"Always Hopeful"

Isaiah 40:31

But those who trust in the Lord will find new strength.

We all have family, friends, and other loved ones who don't know Jesus Christ as their personal Lord and Savior. Many are not aware of God's grace, and some have strayed from the faith. Our hearts break every time we discuss our Christian beliefs, and they look at us with glossy eyes and ignore the gospel message. It is so frustrating because we only want them to experience an abundant life of joy, peace, and eternity with God.

Lee Strobel was a devout atheist who set out to disprove the Bible and God's plan for salvation. He documents his search in his book *The Case for Christ: A Journalist's Personal Investigation of the Evidence for Jesus*. The indisputable facts he discovered were too overwhelming, and ultimately, he accepted Jesus as his Lord and Savior. His wife, a Christian for many years, was aware of his atheism but did not know about his exploration for the truth. After he completed his comprehensive examination and accepted Jesus into his life, he went to his wife and told her about his confession of faith. She immediately jumped in his arms and sobbed for joy. After a long celebration of hugs and kisses, she said, "I prayed for you every day, and some days, I almost gave up."

1 Corinthians 13:7

Love never gives up, never loses faith...

As Christians, we need to live the gospel, present the truth, and keep the faith. God will do the rest, and only He can save!

2 Chronicles 30:27

And God heard them, for their prayer reached heaven, his holy dwelling place.

"Depressed?"

James 1:2

Consider it pure joy, my brothers and sisters, whenever you face trials of many kinds...

The day after a light workout and some pushups, my wrist swelled, and I could barely pick up a glass of water. The doctor informed me that I had gout and prescribed the proper medication. As I became frustrated and started feeling sorry for myself, I remembered one of my friends is in the hospital with an unknown bacterial infection and another is undergoing treatment for prostate cancer. I was also reminded of Paul and Silas as they were preaching in Philippi and were seized by the authorities for removing an evil spirit from a fortune teller. They were dragged before the magistrates and ordered to be stripped and flogged and then put in prison with their feet fastened in stocks. If I was beaten and imprisoned after sharing the gospel, I would have some serious questions for God. So, what did Paul and Silas do later that day?

Acts 16:25–26

About midnight Paul and Silas were praying and singing hymns to God, and the other prisoners were listening to them. Suddenly there was such a violent earthquake that the foundations of the prison were shaken.

They had been chained to the wall, bruised and bleeding from the harsh punishment, and later that evening were praying and singing praise music to God. My gout problem doesn't seem nearly as bad after reading about these two devoted men. Paul and Silas were just warming up because shortly after the earthquake, they witnessed to all the prisoners and shared Jesus with the jailer. He and his family members were all baptized.

As I review the previous trials I have experienced, many of those times were not pleasant. However, there is no question in my mind that those lessons were necessary to increase my faith and trust in my God.

James 1:3

Because you know that the testing of your faith produces perseverance. Let perseverance finish its work so that you may be mature and complete, not lacking anything.

SATURDAY REFLECTIONS
Philippians 4:12–13

I know what it is to be in need,

And I know what it is to have plenty.

I have learned the secret of being content in any and every situation,

Whether well fed or hungry,

Whether living in plenty or in want.

I can do all things through Christ who strengthens me.

Lord, as I review the past week, I remember:

....

....

....

....

....

....

....

....

....

....

....

....

....

....

....

....

Proverbs 8:32–35

Now then, my children, listen to me;
Blessed are those who keep my ways.
Listen to my instruction and be wise;
Do not disregard it.
Blessed are those who listen to me,
Watching daily at my doors,
Waiting at my doorway.
For those who find me find life
And receive favor from the Lord.
For those who find me find life
And receive favor from the Lord.

Prepare to worship and count your blessings.

....
....
....
....
....
....
....
....
....
....
....

Week #41
Monday: TGIM

Proverbs 17:6

Children's children are a crown to the aged, and parents are the pride of their children.

I dated Kathy for five years, and during that time, I really got to know her parents. Her mom and dad were very special people, and after we were married, they came to visit us and spent the night. I am usually an early riser, and not long after I got up and started my devotional time, here came Kathy's mom with her Bible. She asked if it would bother me if she sat in the adjoining room and read, and I said that it wouldn't at all. She mentioned that this was her daily routine, and the whole time they stayed with us, she was right behind me every morning. She had such a remarkable spirit, and I know it was due to her commitment to spend time with the Lord. Every morning, she looked forward to talking with Jesus.

We had been married for 10 years when Sharon (Kathy's mom) found out she had mesothelioma. The disease had infected one lung, and chemotherapy started immediately to halt the progress. She did remarkably well during the treatments, and after several weeks, it looked like the spreading had stopped. The question now was to continue with the treatments or have the entire lung removed. There were no doctors in Louisville capable of doing the surgery, so she went to the Cleveland Clinic, and after consultation and much prayer, the operation was scheduled.

MONDAY

"Imagine You Were There Almost 2000 Years Ago"

It was 33 AD and my friend Nicodemus, who was a member of the Jewish ruling council, asked me to come to Jerusalem to visit during Passover. As I arrived, people were everywhere waving their palms and talking about the arrival of a miracle worker named Jesus. Suddenly, the crowd erupted with jubilation as this man called Jesus rode in on a donkey. Everyone rejoiced and shouted:

John 12:13

"Hosanna!" "Blessed is he who comes in the name of the Lord!" "Blessed is the king of Israel!"

Rumors had spread that a man named Lazarus had been in a tomb for four days, and this Jesus had raised him from the dead. He was coming right past me, I looked into his eyes, and I could feel an overwhelming sensation of peace and joy. I reached to touch his robe, and a remarkable force moved through my body. I felt a calm like never before. Who was this man that penetrated my very soul?

I continued to follow Him and overheard the religious leaders say this Jesus was a criminal. How could this be? Then, I overheard Jesus say:

John 12:25

Anyone who loves their life will lose it, while anyone who hates their life in this world will keep it for eternal life.

What could this mean? I paused and thought about my life, and I didn't like who I was. I drank too much, had a bad mouth, and mistreated my family. Like Jesus said, I hated my life and regretted who I had become. So, what is this eternal life? What did Jesus mean? I asked Nicodemus, and he told me what Jesus had told him,

John 3:3

"Very truly I tell you, no one can see the kingdom of God unless they are born again."

Prayer: Lord, I know I am not worthy, but by your miraculous grace, you came and died for me. Please forgive my sins and accept me into your kingdom. I want you to be my Lord and Savior.

TUESDAY
"The Battle"

Psalm 23:4

Even though I walk through the valley of the shadow of death I will fear no evil, for you are with me.

As David entered the valley to face Goliath, he was not afraid because he felt the overwhelming presence of the living God. His opponent laughed, spit, and cursed him and his God. Then David, filled with the power of the Holy Spirit, boldly spoke:

1 Samuel 17:45–46

"You come against me with sword and spear and javelin, but I come against you in the name of the Lord Almighty, the God of the armies of Israel, whom you have defied. This day the Lord will deliver you into my hands, and I'll strike you down and cut off your head. This very day I will give the carcasses of the Philistine army to the birds and the wild animals, and the whole world will know that there is a God in Israel."

Notice his statement, "The Lord will deliver you into my hands." David didn't mention what "he" was going to do because he knew his supernatural strength came from the Lord. David recognized his power source, and he was just a servant being obedient to his master.

Many times, I have accomplished something, and I have immediately thought, "What a great job I did!" I think about all the praise I deserve. Why do I take credit for something that God made possible through the power of His mighty Holy Spirit? Why do I so quickly lose sight of where the goodness within my soul originates? When will I realize that it's not about me—it's about Him!

1 Corinthians 10:31

Whatever you do, do it all for the glory of God.

Prayer: Lord, forgive my lack of awareness of your presence and your power. Use me as your vessel, and may all the glory be yours, not mine.

324

WEDNESDAY
Two-Minute Drill

Ephesians 2:4
But because of His great love for us,
God, who is rich mercy...

God loves me so much. Why?

What have I done to be worthy?

Have I done good deeds, been nice to my wife and kids, treated people fairly?

Have I done enough?

Ephesians 2:5
Made us alive with Christ
Even when we were dead in our transgressions—
It is by grace you have been saved.

God loves me, not because of anything I have done or will do.

Ephesians 2:9
For it is by grace you have been saved,
Through faith—and this not from yourselves,
It is the gift of God—not by works,
So that no one can boast

THURSDAY
"Lazy Christians"

2 Timothy 3:17

So that the servant of God may be thoroughly equipped...

An interesting comment on the Christian radio station caught my attention. The host said, "Most Christians are lazy!" At first, I found this offensive because I work hard and am very committed to my various jobs. His remarks continued, "Many times after someone receives the helmet of salvation (1 Thessalonians 5:8), they relax or get sidetracked in their faith journey." The commentator was emphasizing that we must continue to strengthen our weapons and our armor.

Ephesians 6:13

Therefore put on the full armor of God...

In Ephesians, Paul also mentions in the belt of truth, breastplate of righteousness, and the shield of faith. These items are necessary to protect and prevent our enemy the devil from penetrating our defenses and damaging our spirit. But in order to fight, to really be aggressive, we need the sword of the Spirit and the word of God. Does this mean you have to memorize the Bible? No, but we must familiarize our minds with His powerful word. I can't count the number of times I have struggled with something and I turned on the Christian radio station or read a devotional and received an answer. The options for expanding our familiarity with God's word are overwhelming. Christian radio, church, TV, CDs, books, magazines, and devotionals (such as Charles Stanley, Tony Dungy, and Max Lucado).

Luke 11:28

"Blessed are those who hear the word of God and obey it."

After fasting for 40 days in the desert, Our Lord was tempted by the devil. Jesus' first response was a scripture from Deuteronomy. After the third satanic attack, Jesus answered, "Worship the Lord your God, and serve Him only." The devil then left Him. We must be prepared because we are all weak, and without the sword of the Spirit, our defenses are penetrable.

1 Timothy 4:7

Train yourself to be Godly.

I need to continually ask myself…. Am I a lazy Christian?

"What if It Never Happened?"

The resurrection is an essential fundamental tenant of the Christian faith, and even Jesus spoke about his own return from death and the grave:

John 2:19

Destroy this temple, and I will raise it again in three days.

Matthew 12:40

For just as Jonah was three days and three nights in the belly of the great fish, so the Son of Man will be three nights in the heart of the earth."

So, what if there was no resurrection?

Charles Stanley wrote, "Let's consider what the outcome of life and death would be without the resurrection. First of all, Jesus would still be dead. That means our faith in him would be worthless, and our message to the world would be a lie. What's more, Jesus himself would be proved to be liar since he claimed that he would rise from the dead. There would be no forgiveness of our sins, no possibility of reconciliation with God, and no hope of heaven. All deceased believers throughout history would have perished. Without the resurrection, there would be nothing positive for anyone to look forward to. Everybody's destiny after death would be hell.

Thank God, none of these scenarios are true. Our savior lives, our sins are forgiven, death has been defeated, and believers in Christ have assurance of eternity in heaven with him. After considering how hopeless we would be without a resurrection, let's rejoice all the more in the greatness of our salvation."

1 Peter 1:3–4

Praise be to the God and the Father of our Lord Jesus Christ! In his great mercy he has given us new birth into a living hope though the resurrection of Jesus Christ from the dead, and into an inheritance that can never perish, spoil or fade.

Praise God... He's alive.

SATURDAY REFLECTIONS
Philippians 4:12–13

I know what it is to be in need,

And I know what it is to have plenty.

I have learned the secret of being content in any and every situation,

Whether well fed or hungry,

Whether living in plenty or in want.

I can do all things through Christ who strengthens me.

Lord, as I review the past week, I remember:

....

....

....

....

....

....

....

....

....

....

....

....

....

....

....

SUNDAY

Proverbs 11:23–28

The desire of the righteous ends only in good,

But the hope of the wicked only in wrath.

One person gives freely,

Yet gains even more;

Another withholds unduly,

But comes to poverty.

A generous man will prosper;

Whoever refreshes others will be refreshed.

People curse the one who hoards grain,

But they pray God's blessing on the one who is willing to sell.

Those who trust in their riches will fall,

But the righteous will thrive like a green leaf

Those who trust in their riches will fall,

But the righteous will thrive like a green leaf.

Prepare to worship and count your blessings.

....

....

....

....

....

....

....

....

....

....

Week #42
Monday: TGIM

Psalm 68:20

Our God is a God who saves; from the Sovereign Lord comes escape from death.

All the immediate family was there the day of the surgery, and everyone would occasionally leave the waiting room to go to the chapel. After several hours, the doctor came and told us the operation was a success and that Sharon was doing fine. What a relief! We all praised God for this miraculous removal and the end of this cancer. The next day, I needed to get back home, but Kathy was going to stay the rest of the week until her sister got there. Kathy came home for a few days and went back the next Monday.

A few days later on Kathy's birthday, Sharon contracted an infection and was moved to Intensive Care. I was at home and got word from the hospital that the infection had set in overnight and that the antibiotics weren't working. How could there be such a turnaround in less than 24 hours? I left immediately, and by the time I got there, Kathy's mom had gone into a coma. I remember driving to Cleveland and praying continually that she would recover or at least wake up so everyone could say goodbye. I would never get to talk to her again. Everyone was in shock when I arrived, and it was time to let her go. It was so unexpected, and the cries of anguish were painful to listen to.

Sharon was the matriarch of the family and so dedicated to the Lord. Why did God choose to take her with so many years left to live? She would touch so many people, and everyone she met knew there was something special about her. Although we knew she was with Jesus and free from any suffering, it was so hard to let go. Though I had been part of the family for only a brief period, I could feel the pain of my wife and the rest of her family.

It was a long drive back from Cleveland.

MONDAY
"That Was Me"

John 12:12

The next day the great crowd that had come for the festival heard that Jesus was on his way to Jerusalem.

It started as Jesus entered Jerusalem (John 12:13)—*that was me* waving my palms and shouting, "Hosanna, blessed is the King of Israel."

It continued at Gethsemane when Jesus asked us to pray that you will not fall into temptation (Luke 22:40). *That was me* who fell asleep.

It continued when they arrested my Jesus and took him away. I followed, and several people accused me of being one of his followers (Luke 22:60). *That was me* who denied him.

It continued when they placed my Jesus in front of Herod, and his soldiers ridiculed him (Luke 23:11). *That was me* hurling insults.

It continued when Pilate offered us a choice between a murderer and my Jesus (Luke 23:18). *That was me* who shouted, "Give us Barabbas!"

It continued when Pilate was debating what to do with Jesus (Luke 23:20). *That was me* who yelled, "Crucify him, Crucify him!"

It continued after He was nailed to the cross and my Jesus said, "Father, forgive them, for they do not know what they are doing" (Luke 23:34). *That was me* casting lots for his clothing.

That was me who fell asleep, denied him, mocked him, and yelled for his crucifixion. And yet, despite all my transgressions against him...

He still died for me!

He still died for everybody!

Praise God!

Romans 5:8

But God demonstrates his own love for us in this: While we were still sinners, Christ died for us.

331

"How Do We Maintain Our Relationships to God?"

Joshua 6:18

But keep away from the devoted things, so that you will not bring about your own destruction by taking them.

The Book of Joshua reviews how the Israelites had violated the Lord's specific command and how someone had removed some of the devoted things. Achan responded to Joshua's questioning:

Joshua 7:20

"It is true! I have sinned against the Lord, the God of Israel. This is what I have done: When I saw in the plunder a beautiful robe from Babylonia, two hundred shekels of silver and a wedge of gold weighing fifty shekels, I coveted them and took them."

I asked myself, "Have I violated God's laws?" So, I reviewed the 10 Commandments: You shall have no other Gods before me (money, houses, beauty, cars, and possessions). You shall not misuse the name of the Lord your God (movies, video games, music). Remember the Sabbath and keep it holy (church, working on Sunday). Honor your mother and father (disrespectful adults and children, helping aging parents). You shall not covet (keep up with the Jones's). Other sinful actions include emotional and physical abuse, laziness, selfishness, price, arrogance, anger, and bitterness. How do we fight these temptations?

Joshua 1:8

Do not let the Book of Law depart from your mouth; meditate on it day and night, so that you may be careful to do everything written in it.

When we don't focus on God's word, the world sneaks in, and we rationalize our behavior just like Achan. However, if we succeed in meditating on it day and night and stay obedient, God has a promise for us:

Joshua 1:8

Then you will be prosperous and successful.

WEDNESDAY
Two-Minute Drill

Psalm 119

This is the longest chapter in the Bible and emphasizes how dependent we should be on the word of our Lord as spoken through the writer. Take time and digest some of the inspirational verses in this psalm, and feel the heart of the writer. The footnote in my Bible says:

"The author was an Israelite who was passionately devoted to the word of God as the word of life."

Psalm 119:11
I have hidden your word in my heart that I might not sin against you.
Psalm 119:24
Your statutes are my delight; they are my counselors.
Psalm 119:28
My soul is weary with sorrow; strengthen me according to your word.
Psalm 119:74, 81
For I have put my hope in your word.
Psalm 119:89
Your word, Lord, is eternal; it stands firm in the heavens.
Psalm 119:105
Your word is a lamp for my feet, a light on my path.
Psalm 119:147
I rise before dawn and cry for help; I have put my hope in your word.

THE WORD OF LIFE

THURSDAY

"What Are You Doing This Weekend?"

Genesis 2:2–3

By the seventh day God had finished the work he had been doing; so on the seventh day he rested from all his work. Then God blessed the seventh day and made it holy, because on it he rested from all the work of creating that he had done.

My wife and I were preparing for our vacation, and as usual, things were pretty hectic. We were leaving on Sunday morning and had planned on attending our normal church service on Saturday night.

On Saturday morning, a client called and wanted to meet at 4:30 to 5:00 p.m. to finalize his contract to build before I left town. This meant no church! I paused because I had been busy most of the day, and this would give me a little more time to finish up other things. Plus, I could then go to the gym, so I agreed to meet at 5:00 p.m.

I called my wife and told her and assumed she would be glad because she had been busy too. She sounded disappointed and said she wasn't sure if she would go by herself. I completed the contract signing and finished the meeting at 6:45 p.m. When I got home, I was surprised to find out that my wife went to church alone.

I asked her about the service, and she told me that the sermon was great and the music was awesome. The choir and soloist did one my absolute favorite songs that I had waited more than a year for them to repeat.

I wasn't there. I should have been there. My client would have waited until 6:15 to meet had my time with my God been a priority. Who suffered? I did, and I do every time I neglect the living God. I love that song, and it brings joy to my very soul. I missed it because of my selfishness.

Prayer: Thank you, Lord, for speaking to me. I can sign all the contracts in the world, but they mean nothing if I don't glorify the One who made it possible.

Help me remember this message, not only regarding church service, but also my daily devotional time with you. Without you, it is all about me.

FRIDAY
"Only One Thing"

Joshua 1:7

Be strong and very courageous. Be careful to obey all the laws my servant Moses gave you.

After wandering in the desert for 40 years, the Israelites crossed over the Jordan into the Promised Land. This would be the most successful time in the history of their nation, and their first challenge was Jericho. The walls of Jericho were 35 to 40 feet in height and 5 to 10 feet in depth and seemed virtually impenetrable. After circling the city for seven days, Joshua gave the command for the trumpet blowers to blow the horns and the people to shout:

Joshua 6:20

When the trumpets sounded, the people shouted, and at the sound of the trumpet, when the people gave a loud shout, the wall collapsed; so every man charged straight in, and they took the city.

The Israelite warriors were undefeatable and conquered 31 Kings and possessed their land. Eventually, all the kingdoms were divided among the 12 tribes, and Joshua announced his dedication to God. He then asked the people who they would serve, and all the people responded, "We too will serve the Lord, because He is our God."

Why were the Israelites so successful during this period? Prior to crossing the Jordan, God told them to do one thing, and they obeyed.

Joshua 1:8

Do not let the Book of Law depart from your mouth; meditate on it day and night so that you are careful to do everything written in it. Then you will be prosperous and successful.

Our only source should be God's word. If we are obedient, the Lord will provide all our needs.

2 Timothy 3:16

All scripture is God-breathed.

SATURDAY REFLECTIONS
Philippians 4:12–13

I know what it is to be in need,

And I know what it is to have plenty.

I have learned the secret of being content in any and every situation,

Whether well fed or hungry,

Whether living in plenty or in want.

I can do all things through Christ who strengthens me.

Lord, as I review the past week, I remember:

....

....

....

....

....

....

....

....

....

....

....

....

....

....

....

SUNDAY

Proverbs 12:14–20

From the fruit of their lips people are filled with good things,

And the work of their hands brings reward.

The way of the fool seems right to them,

But the wise listen to advice.

Fools show their annoyance at once,

But the prudent overlook an insult.

An honest witness tells the truth,

But a false witness tells lies.

The words of the reckless pierce like swords,

But the tongue of the wise brings healing.

Truthful lips endure forever,

But a lying tongue lasts only a moment.

Deceit is in the hearts of those who plot evil,

But those who promote peace have joy.

But those who promote peace have joy.

Prepare to worship and count your blessings.

....

....

....

....

....

....

....

....

....

....

Week #43
Monday: TGIM

Psalm 53:2

God looks down from heaven on all mankind to see if there are any who understand, any who seek God.

Matthew 25:23

"His master replied, 'Well done, good and faithful servant! You have been faithful with a few things; I will put you in charge of many things. Come and share your master's happiness!'

The funeral arrangements were made, and as we prepared, I asked Kathy if I could say a few words at the funeral. For some reason, I felt God was telling me to speak. My message was short, and I described my drive back to Cleveland when things turned for the worse. On the way, I listened to Christian music and prayed the entire way for a miracle and quoted one of my favorite scriptures:

Proverbs 3:5

Trust in the Lord with all your heart and lean not on your understanding.

We were not capable of comprehending God's plan. Maybe the cancer wasn't gone and she would have suffered from the after-effects. Maybe someone she had spoken to finally realized they needed Jesus Christ in their life. We just can't understand, but we know He had a plan for Sharon Compton, and His plan was best.

Proverbs 3:6

In all your ways acknowledge Him, and He will make your paths straight.

It is hard to accept, but I know Sharon was welcomed into heaven and that the angels were singing. I can picture Jesus reaching out his hand and saying, "Well done, good and faithful servant."

MONDAY
"Memories"

Psalm 9:10

Those who know your name will put their trust in you.

There are always events and festivities that bring back memories of the loved ones who are no longer with us. Many of the people we have lost over the years had influenced so many yet seemed to die prematurely. I questioned why the Lord would take such significant people. They were obviously devoted followers and dedicated to spreading His gospel, so why were they not spared? God's word always provides answers:

Ecclesiastes 11:5

As you do not know the path of the wind, or how the body is formed in a mother's womb, so you cannot understand *the work of God, the maker of all things*.

Proverbs 3:5

Trust in the Lord with all your heart and lean not unto your own **understanding.**

We are not capable of understanding God's will. This does not make it any easier, but we just have to trust our great God and realize that despite our pain, His way and His plans are the best. We were so blessed to know these humble, committed, and loyal servants in our lives, and the way to honor them is to be more like Jesus. I know they would sacrifice their lives just to know their deaths had an impact on me. We must also be aware that their reward for all their earthly work was realized at the gates of heaven when they saw Jesus extending his nail-scarred hand and saying, "Well done, good and faithful servant".

1 Corinthians 2:9

However, as it is written: "What no eye has seen, what no ear has heard, and what no human mind has conceived"—the things God has prepared for those who love him—

Prayer for all our loved ones who have gone to be with the Lord:

We miss you, but we know you are enjoying your time with the Lord!

"Good Works" Part 1

Matthew 5:16

In the same way, let your light shine before others, that they may see your good deeds and glorify your Father in heaven.

What are your good deeds?

Do you do volunteer work at the church, visit nursing homes, donate to the Salvation Army, sing in the choir, or participate as an elder or deacon in the church? Do you lead a Bible study? I am sure I have left out many other contributions that people are making for the ministry of Jesus Christ. So, are we saved by all our good works? Absolutely not. It is only through God's amazing grace and our faith in Jesus Christ that we are saved.

Ephesians 2:8–9

For it is by grace you have been saved, through faith—and this is not from yourselves, it is the gift of God—not by works, so that no one can boast.

Does religion offer us salvation?

The Pharisees and Sadducees were the most "religious" men during our Savior's life, and Jesus told them they were hypocrites because their hearts were far from him (Matthew 15:7–9). These same men *rejected* our Lord and ultimately sent him to the cross.

John 3:36

Whoever believes in the Son has eternal life, but whoever <u>rejects</u> the Son will not see life, for God's wrath remains on them.

Salvation is not something you can earn through works or religion. Only by the grace of God through faith in Jesus Christ can we obtain eternal life. God speaks about a judgement day when he will evaluate our relationship with him. He will open the Book of Life to see if our names have been recorded. If we have accepted Jesus Christ as our Lord and Savior, our name will be revealed. If not…

Revelation 20:15

Anyone whose name was not found written in the Book of Life was thrown into the lake of fire.

Two-Minute Drill

Proverbs 3:5–6
Trust in the Lord with all your heart
And lean not on your own understanding;
In all your ways submit to him,
And he will make your paths straight.

Trust in the Lord with all your heart.
Do you trust Him?
Do you totally trust Him?

Lean not on your own understanding.
Do you try to figure it out?
Do you ask why?

In all your ways submit to him.
Do you do things your way or His?

And he will make your paths straight.
Do you accept His decision?
Do you praise Him for His guidance?

TRUST HIM!

THURSDAY
"Good Works" Part 2

Acts 26:20

I preached that they should repent and turn to God and demonstrate their repentance by their deeds.

How do I prove my repentance by my deeds?

Several years ago, I had retired from coaching middle school football and was looking for a different way to serve the Lord. I prayed for months, imploring God to show me where He wanted to use me. As I searched and studied God's word, I found an amazing scripture:

Ephesians 2:10

For we are God's handiwork, created in Christ Jesus to do good works, which God prepared in advance for us to do.

God has something specifically planned just for me? I continued to pray, and I received a call from a friend asking if I was interested in coaching middle school football again, and I said if the conditions were right, maybe. Everything worked out, and after much prayer, I accepted the job. This was one of the most rewarding experiences in my life, and God had been planning it the whole time.

According to Ephesians 2:10, the work God prepared in advance is waiting for me to find it. Once I discover my calling, this is where I will receive the most joy because He planned it. When you find where God wants to use you, you will feel a peace and a joy that transcends all understanding (Philippians 4:7).

If you are driving a bus, going to nursing homes, etc. and loathe every minute of it, then you are not where God wants you. God promised us the abundant life, and only He knows where we can accomplish what He wants. We must find what *"God prepared in advance for us to do."*

FRIDAY
"Good Works" Part 3

2 Corinthians 5:10

For we must all appear before the judgment seat of Christ, so that each of us may receive what is due us for the things done while in the body, whether good or bad.

When we die, everyone will appear before the living God at the judgement seat of Christ. He will open the Book of Life to see if our name is recorded. If we have accepted Jesus Christ as our Lord and Savior, our name will be revealed. Once our name is found in the Book of Life, we are assured of eternal life, but there will be an evaluation of our works...

1 Corinthians 3:13–15

Their work will be shown for what it is, because the Day will bring it to light. It will be revealed with fire, and the fire will test the quality of each person's work. If what has been built survives, the builder will receive a reward. If it is burned up, the builder will suffer loss but yet will be saved--even though only as one escaping through the flames.

Our great God will review a specific list of what we have done for Him. As I mentioned in Part 2, we need to continually search for the works God prepared in advance for us to do (Ephesians 2:10). While we are on earth, we will receive the most joy once we find the predetermined good deeds God planned long ago, and those works will be revealed on Judgement Day. If we don't find and complete those works, they may not get done, and we will not receive the rewards.

Once we accept Jesus as Lord, we receive the remarkable gift of the Holy Spirit. That Spirit that dwells within our souls and desires for us to grow closer to God. As our Spirit matures, we realize God has work here on earth that He wants us to accomplish for His glory.

Revelation 22:12

Look, I am coming soon! My reward is with me, and I will give to each person according to what they have done.

SATURDAY REFLECTIONS
Philippians 4:12–13

I know what it is to be in need,

And I know what it is to have plenty.

I have learned the secret of being content in any and every situation,

Whether well fed or hungry,

Whether living in plenty or in want.

I can do all things through Christ who strengthens me.

Lord, as I review the past week, I remember:

....

....

....

....

....

....

....

....

....

....

....

....

....

....

....

....

Proverbs 15:1–5

A gentle answer turns away wrath,

But a harsh word stirs up anger.

The tongue of the wise adorns knowledge,

But the mouth of the fool gushes folly.

The eyes of the Lord are everywhere,

Keeping watch on the wicked and the good.

The soothing tongue is a tree of life,

But a perverse tongue crushes the spirit.

A fool spurns a parent's discipline,

But whoever heeds correction shows prudence.

A fool spurns a parent's discipline,

But whoever heeds correction shows prudence.

Prepare to worship and count your blessings.

....

....

....

....

....

....

....

....

....

....

....

....

Week #44
Monday: TGIM

Jeremiah 29:13
You will seek me and find me when you seek me with all your heart.

In August of 2007, my wife and I won a trip to Lake Tahoe. While we there, we decided to extend our stay in the small town of Arnold, California. Prior to leaving for the trip, we went to the Christian bookstore to look for something we could study together. My wife and I decided on a book called *Fireproof Your Life: Building a Faith That Survives the Flames* by Michael Catt. This was not the same as the movie, which was about a troubled marriage, but this book described the life of the sequoia tree and how it related to our lives. This was a remarkable book, and even more surprising while visiting in Arnold, we were only an hour away from the Sequoia National Forest. Each day, we would read a chapter, then discuss it while we drove to our various destinations in California.

The timing was certainly God-ordained as we were going through the real estate recession and our future was definitely in question. This just happened to be 30 years to the month of my last major employment conflict with the Seattle Seahawks. At that time, my job future was hanging by a slim thread, and now, with the economy crashing and tremendous debt, the *Fireproof* book was extremely helpful.

In a previous devotional, I discussed my visit with my teammate and my decision to trust God. This was the identical situation, and after our daily readings, my wife and I were convinced that God had a plan. We promised the Lord we would continue our daily devotions and search for His direction.

"Worship"

Genesis 2:3
God blessed the seventh day and made it holy.

How blessed we are to have the opportunity to attend church and truly praise and worship the creator of the universe. I used to think Sundays were the day I filled up my spiritual gas tank. This was the day the preacher was responsible for giving me fuel to last the week. Unfortunately, the message never seemed to last, and I always faded by mid-week. I finally realized that it was up to me to spend time with God every day and keep the spiritual tank full all week. Then, on Sunday, I am prepared to truly worship. I only have a little over an hour of community church to express my heartfelt thanks to the living God. I need to be focused and ready to praise him.

I decided that I would stop complaining about the parking, traffic, weather, and whatever else was bothering me because this is God's time. No matter what music is playing, I am going to let it rip. I feel sorry for the people in front of me because I know my voice is bad, but God knows I am doing the best I can. I am not going to be critical of the preacher's sermon but open my heart and let the living word of God fill my soul. I am going to concentrate and feel my Lord's pain and suffering as I take communion. Nothing is going to interfere and distract me from worshipping my God... Nothing!

Prayer: Lord, help me prepare today for this weekend's church service. It's not about what you are going to give me but what am I going to give you.

Psalm 95:6
Come, let us worship and bow down. Let us kneel before the Lord our maker...

TUESDAY
"Where Is Your Focus?"

2 Corinthians 4:18
What is seen is temporary, but what is unseen is eternal.

What is seen is temporary.

Cars, houses, clothes, fantasy football, video games, golf, NFL, etc..... Everything seen is temporary. We all become so absorbed in the world, and Satan wants to distract us from what is most important.

What is unseen is eternal.

God, Jesus, and the Holy Spirit are all unseen, and by expanding our relationship with these three spiritual entities, we can control "what is seen." How easy it is to misplace our eternal hope with the pleasures and temptations of this world.

Romans 14:10
For we will all stand before God's judgement seat.

When we stand before the living God, he will not ask us how much money we made or what kind of house we had. Our entire life will flash before us, and our mighty God will ask, "Do you know Jesus as your Lord and Savior?"

John 3:36
Whoever believes in the Son has eternal life, but whoever rejects the Son will not see life, for God's wrath remains on them.

Prayer: Almighty God, please forgive my quest for the things of this world. You are the only answer, and I want Jesus to be my Lord and Savior. Please come and take control of my life.

WEDNESDAY
Two-Minute Drill

John 15:5
"I am the vine; you are the branches.
If you remain in me and I in you, you will bear much fruit;
Apart from me you can do nothing."

I am the vine.
Jesus is the vine. Without Him, there is no life!

You are the branches.
Are you connected to the vine?

If you remain in me and I in you...
Being part of the vine means absorbing His nutrients.
Without those nutrients, there is no abundant life!

You will bear much fruit.
The life-giving nutrients from the vine will create growth.
Without those nutrients, there is no growth!

Apart from me you can do nothing.

NOTHING!

THURSDAY
"Listen!"

Proverbs 18:13

To answer before listening—that is folly and shame.

My best friend and I have breakfast twice a week. We work together, and we do discuss business, but the main objective is to talk about our personal lives. I know that when I am struggling with a problem, I can confide in him. He doesn't even have to answer, but just putting my problems into words allows me a psychological release. Many times, as he bares his soul, I am too anxious to analyze and provide my recommendations. Why am I so quick to respond instead of just listening and allowing the Holy Spirit to reveal his wisdom?

James 1:5

If any of you lacks wisdom, you should ask God…

I find myself in similar situations with my wife. I am the "fix it" guy, always looking for answers instead of just listening. Many times, she just needs to talk and clear her mind, and I can't keep from interjecting my thoughts. I need to just be quiet, let her share her heart, and pause, reflect on what she said, pray for wisdom, and decide if I need to respond or not.

James 1:19

Everyone should be quick to listen, slow to speak…

This applies to our kids too!

FRIDAY
"Guilt"

When I read about the sins people commit, I tell myself they must be talking about someone else… Who, me? No way! Wrong. Today, I realize I am a totally imperfect person and that I will continually struggle with my shortcomings.

1 John 1:8
If we claim to be without sin, we deceive ourselves and the truth is not in us.

I can ignore my inadequacies and pretend that I am not affected, but I know pride, selfishness, anger, bitterness, and many others are waiting at my doorstep. Why? Because Satan wants to separate me from the living God.

2 Corinthians 11:14
For Satan himself masquerades as an angel of light.

One of Satan's greatest deceptions is guilt. I have done some bad things in my life, and the prince of darkness wants me to think I will never be forgiven. But that is a lie from the pit of hell. Two of the more prominent "sinners" in the Bible, King David and the apostle Paul, accomplished great things for the Lord. So why can't I?

God knows we will never be perfect, and all He wants us to do is draw closer to Him each and every day so we can enjoy the abundant life He has promised us (John 10:10). I must continually come before my Lord and ask Him to make me aware of my transgressions because I want nothing to restrict my relationship to the living God. If we confess our sins and truly repent, God says he has removed our sin and purified us from all unrighteousness (1 John 1:9).

Hebrews 8:12
For I will forgive their wickedness and will remember their sins no more.

Psalm 103:12
He has removed our sins as far from us as the east is from the west.

SATURDAY REFLECTIONS
Philippians 4:12–13

I know what it is to be in need,

And I know what it is to have plenty.

I have learned the secret of being content in any and every situation,

Whether well fed or hungry,

Whether living in plenty or in want.

I can do all things through Christ who strengthens me.

Lord, as I review the past week, I remember:

....

....

....

....

....

....

....

....

....

....

....

....

....

....

....

....

SUNDAY
Proverbs 15:26–29

The Lord detests the thoughts of the wicked,
But gracious words are pure in his sight.
The greedy bring ruin to their households,
But the one who hates bribes will live.
The heart of the righteous weighs its answers,
But the mouth of the wicked gushes evil.
The Lord is far from the wicked
But he hears the prayer of the righteous.
But he hears the prayer of the righteous.

Prepare to worship and count your blessings.

....

....

....

....

....

....

....

....

....

....

....

....

....

....

....

....

Week #45
Monday: TGIM

Psalm 27:4

To gaze on the beauty of the Lord and to seek him in his temple.

While staying In Arnold, California, we were close to Yosemite National Park, and we visited there every day. After visiting the ranger station, we decided to take a short hike to one of the many waterfalls there. I worked out regularly on the elliptical and leg machines, but I was very concerned about the effect hiking would have on my surgically repaired knees. Our first hike was approximately a mile and a half up a slight incline, and my knees responded magnificently. So, the next day, we extended our hike to three miles and an increase in elevation. My legs still responded well, and we continually expanded the distance and strenuousness of our hikes.

Quite honestly, our lives took a dramatic turn after this revelation at Yosemite. Our original plan was to retire to Florida, play golf, work out, and go to the pool because I did not think my knees could withstand the wear and tear of hiking. But since Yosemite, we have been to the Grand Canyon, Glacier National Park, Zion National Park, Bryce National Park, Cedar Breaks National Monument, and many of the state parks close to Louisville. Our next destination is Big Bend National Park in Texas, and then we have Yellowstone, Acadia, Alaska, and three other parks in Utah in our sights too.

What a remarkable turn of events. Our vacations went from heading south to play golf to traveling the country to visit and see God's spectacular and miraculous creation. My wife and I love to drive and plan our trip to stop at various landmarks throughout the country. On the way to Glacier, we stopped at the Badlands and the Black Hills, and on the way back, we did some hiking in Colorado around Pagosa Springs. This country has so many absolutely outstanding places to visit, and the beauty is breathtaking. I still play golf, but I must admit that the national parks have won out, and our goal is to see them all.

Praise God!

MONDAY

"The Grand Canyon"

My wife and I love to hike and experience the beauty of God's magnificent creation. Our hiking expeditions started several years ago in Sequoia National Forest and Yosemite National Park. Seeing the largest trees in the world as well as the rock formations, lakes, and waterfalls at Yosemite was the highlight of our hiking involvement until we went to see the Grand Canyon.

We arrived at the visitor's station and discussed different options with the park ranger and then meandered to a location where we would see the Grand Canyon for the first time. As we walked through the partially wooded path to one of the viewing stations, I had no idea what I was about to see.

We went through the clearing, and there it was... I stopped in my tracks, my jaw dropped, and I gasped for air. My first thought was, "God has been here. This cannot be real!" Everyone has viewed pictures or watched documentaries or films about the Grand Canyon, but nothing compares to being there. The Grand Canyon is simply unbelievable, and all the descriptive adjectives cannot help you perceive the magnitude of this amazing wonder of the world. There is nothing comparable in all the world, so how could there be any explanation other than that a mighty and awesome God designed this-one-of-a-kind spectacle?

Genesis 1:1

In the beginning God created the heavens and the earth.

The secular world may attempt to explain this massive gorge with theories about thousands of years of erosion, but I know God carved this spectacular canyon with one swipe of his finger. Maybe he sat on the rim and doused his toes in the river, but this is his masterful work. We could feel His presence as we viewed this remarkable creation, and our hearts pounded because we knew He and His mighty Holy Spirit dwells within our very souls.

1 John 4:13

This is how we know that we live in him and he in us: He has given us of his Spirit.

TUESDAY

"Glacier National Park"

Genesis 2:1

So the creation of the heavens and the earth and everything in them was completed.

What an amazing adventure my wife and I had at Glacier National Park in Montana. We were both spellbound by its beauty and majesty. Only God could produce something that magnificent. This was no accident because I know He sculpted this for the world to see and feel His presence.

Isaiah 6:3

The whole earth is full of his glory!

Glacier National Park has many spectacular sights, but there are many right here at home. For example: My wife's joyful smile and embrace, my grandkids hug and their magic words, "I love you, Papaw," the laughter of good friends as we share memorable moments, the exhilaration of singing praise music in church, the joy of seeing a loved one baptized, going to a friend's three-year anniversary of being sober, and watching fellow Christians graduating from an intensive two-year Bible study. There are so many amazing happenings around us every day, and we *must* slow down to recognize the blessings that surround us.

Colossians 3:2

Set your mind on things above, not on earthly things.

Philippians 3:19–20

Their mind is on earthly things. But our citizenship is in heaven.

Prayer: Forgive me, Lord, for being so busy with the world. Help me focus on what is most important—your kingdom!

WEDNESDAY
Two-Minute Drill

1 John 1:9
If we confess our sins,
He is faithful and just and
Will forgive us our sins
And cleanse us from all unrighteousness.

Do you have any sin? "No," you say?
No anger, bitterness, or lack of forgiveness?
What about pride?
Do you ever think you are better than someone else?
I do! Why?
Why can't I see others through the eyes of Jesus?
Jesus loved them all the same:
Prostitutes, tax collectors, religious leaders, thieves, soldiers...
I need to get my vision checked because I see them all differently.
Many times, I think I am better than *them*!
Am I better than the cheating politician?
Am I better than the man who was unfaithful to his wife?
Am I better than the pastor who fell from grace?
Forgive me, Father, for my judgmental eyesight. Help me to remember that...

JESUS LOVED THEM ALL THE SAME!

THURSDAY
"Retreat"

John 15:19

As it is, you do not belong to the world...

My wife and I rented a cabin in the Big South Fork recreation area. Everything was perfect! It had a vaulted great room and kitchen, king size bed, and most importantly, a porch with a rocking chair. (Yes, we had an indoor bathroom too.)

On all of our previous adventures to various national parks, we had had all modern conveniences. This unit had no phone service, television, or Wi-Fi, and despite my wife's concerns, we survived. Not only did we survive, but we thrived! Mornings began with coffee, smoothies, and a Bible study on the front porch. Then we went hiking, had lunch in the forest, did more hiking, and went back to the porch to relax. We then had refreshments, prepared for dinner, and went to bed early so we could repeat the next day.

One thing we did a lot of was talking. We were not distracted by outside influences, so we just focused on each other. Why does the world (phones, video, computer, etc.) reduce our quality time with the ones we love?

We learned a valuable lesson. *We* are more important than business or entertainment, and the big question is: What are we going to do about it?

Such an easy answer... Turn it off!

1 John 2:15

Do not love the world or anything in the world.

Turn off the world, and communicate with the ones you love.

That includes our kids too.

Most importantly, that includes God!

1 John 5:4

For everyone born of God overcomes the world.

FRIDAY

"How Great Thou Art"

Genesis 1:11

Then God said, let the land produce vegetation: seed bearing plants and trees...

Several years ago, my wife and I visited the Grand Canyon and were absolutely amazed at its grandeur. No matter what pictures you see, nothing compares to actually being there and standing close to this spectacular wonder of the world. We had a similar experience recently when we visited the Black Hills in South Dakota, Glacier National Park in Montana, and Zion National Park and Bryce Canyon in Utah. The mountains and rock structures, the trees, streams, lakes, and waterfalls are unbelievable.

Job 38:4

"Where were you when I laid the earth's foundation?"

One day, we sat on an overlook and prayed and thanked God for his magnificent creation. We wondered how anyone could possibly believe that this beauty could just happen without our supreme artist and designer, the living God.

Romans 1:20

For since the creation of the world God's invisible qualities—his eternal power and divine nature—have been clearly seen...

As we sat on the mountainside, we could feel God's presence and see that His Spirit dwells in His creation. We are so very thankful and blessed to have that same Spirit dwelling within us.

Ephesians 1:13

When you believed, you were marked in him with a seal, the promised Holy Spirit...

SATURDAY REFLECTIONS
Philippians 4:12–13

I know what it is to be in need,

And I know what it is to have plenty.

I have learned the secret of being content in any and every situation,

Whether well fed or hungry,

Whether living in plenty or in want.

I can do all things through Christ who strengthens me.

Lord, as I review the past week, I remember:

....

....

....

....

....

....

....

....

....

....

....

....

....

....

....

Proverbs 15:30–33

Light in a messenger's eyes brings joy to the heart,

And good news gives health to the bones.

Whoever heeds life-giving correction

Will be at home among the wise.

Those who disregard discipline despise themselves,

But the one who heeds correction gains understanding.

Wisdom's instruction is to fear the Lord,

And humility comes before honor.

Wisdom's instruction is to fear the Lord,

And humility comes before honor.

Prepare to worship and count your blessings.

....

....

....

....

....

....

....

....

....

....

....

....

....

....

Proverbs 17:17

A friend loves at all times, and a brother is born for a time of adversity.

My wife and I attended our 13-year-old granddaughter's confirmation at St. Patrick's Catholic Church at 7:00 p.m. and got home around 9:00 p.m. I usually check my phone, but as we started getting ready for bed, I remembered that I had to review my messages. I noticed a text from Mark Magrum, who is a close friend of Al Lochner's. The message read, "Please call me. This is an emergency." As soon as I saw the message, I knew something bad had happened to my best friend Al.

Flashback of my relationship to Al Lochner:

Al was my mentor who taught me the building business almost 40 years ago. I had formed a business partnership with Omikron Construction Company to build six houses, and Al was their lead superintendent. I followed him for several months reviewing Omikron's jobs as well as mine. I learned the business from the foundation to the roof, from digging a basement to putting on shingles, and Al was there every step of the way.

After I built my six houses so I could become a registered builder, Omikron and I amicably decided to separate, and I was on my own. We had bought 12 lots in a planned community called Plainview, and we divided the lots equally. Six went to Omikron Construction Company, and six went to Amos Martin Construction Company.

I started building totally on my own and continued for the next five years. Then, I got a call from Al asking to have a meeting. We met at my office, and surprisingly, he said he had a falling out with Omikron and asked if I needed any help. Just imagine, the man who taught me the building business was now asking me for a job. What an honor! I asked him how soon he could start. That was 35 years ago, and our relationship goes much deeper than most friendships. Today's devotional will give you a glimpse into our relationship.

One week from today (Monday), I will continue with my return phone call to Mark Magrum.

362

MONDAY

"Does Absence Make the Heart Grow Fonder?"

Proverbs 12:4

A worthy wife is a crown for her husband...

Most years, I am blessed to go on a Canadian fishing trip with my best buddies. There's nothing like an early morning breakfast, all-day fishing, a relaxing dinner, and a good night's sleep. But one of the best parts of the trip is the return home. In Canada, I have no communication with my wife for seven straight days, so the first call is so very special. There's nothing like hearing her voice for the first time in a week.

Proverbs 31:11

She will greatly enrich his life.

My wife went out of town with her sister several days ago, and honestly, I am not used to being alone. Work and coaching keep my mind occupied during the day, but I definitely do not like coming home to an empty house. Something is not right. A part of me is missing. I know we will talk on the phone tonight, but we didn't have dinner together, and she is not next to me in bed. As I fall asleep, I reach over and touch her pillow and say a prayer and tell her how much she means to me. Her absence has created a cavern in my heart. A portion of my soul is missing. She will be home soon, and this void within will be filled with her love and affection, and I will be whole again.

Genesis 2:24

And they become one flesh.

TUESDAY

"Canada 2017"

Psalm 27:4
To gaze on the beauty of the Lord...
This past summer, three friends and I flew a boat plane to Lake Clear, 200 miles north of Nestor Falls, Ontario, Canada. The flight was amazing as we viewed the mass of trees and water, since there are over 250,000 lakes in this Canadian province. There was only one cabin and four people fishing a body of water over four miles long. We took in our own food, and our cook was a good ole country boy who made homemade biscuits, sausage gravy, cherry cobbler, pineapple upside down cake, French toast, grilled walleye, and steaks too (roughing it, huh?).

The fishing and camaraderie are great, the scenery is spectacular, but the most important part is just feeling God's presence in this place. After fishing for a whole day and eating heartily, I was usually in bed by 9:30 p.m. and up at 5:30 a.m. (4:30 Canadian time). Everyone else usually slept in, but my quiet time with the Lord watching the sun come up was outstanding. Looking out the window as the sky illuminated in multiple colors was so peaceful and relaxing. I praised God for His magnificent creation and would sit quietly and just listen for Him to speak. I am not very good at listening, and most of the time, I want to do the talking, so this was a really special time for me.

Proverbs 8:34
Blessed are those who listen to me, watching daily at my doors, waiting at my doorway.
When I come back to civilization, why does the world distract me from time with the most important thing in my life, my God? He has provided everything I have, and yet, many times, I forget Him and am prideful enough to think I was responsible for the outcome of the events in my life.

Psalm 106:13
But they soon forgot what He had done and did not wait for his plan to unfold.
My prayer time usually covers several themes but features very limited if any time for supplication (listening). Why am I so busy talking instead of waiting for God to speak? Lord, please make me be still, and take time to listen.

Psalm 37:7
Be still before the LORD and wait patiently for him.

WEDNESDAY
Two-Minute Drill

Bible Translations

I enjoy reviewing various Bible translations. Comparing versions sometimes give me a totally different perspective on the Scripture. On my Bible phone app, I review five different translations, including the King James Version, the New King James, the Message, the New International Version, and the New Living Translation.

Compare these verses from The Message and The New International Version

1 Timothy 4:7–8 (Message)
Exercise daily in God—no spiritual flabbiness, please!
Workouts in the gymnasium are useful,
But a disciplined life in God is far more so,
Making you fit both today and forever.
1 Timothy 4:7–8 (NIV)
Train yourself to be Godly.
For physical training is of some value,
But Godliness has value for all things,
Holding promise for both the present life and the life to come.

Here are the words that caught my attention: Exercise daily, no spiritual flabbiness, discipline, train yourself, physical training, forever, promise, present life, and life to come.

The Christian life is a marathon, not a sprint. This passage emphasizes our dependence on God's word, not just on Sundays, but every day. Otherwise, we are not prepared for the day. Just like going to the gym to train our physical bodies, we must discipline our spiritual bodies a well.

...Making you fit both today and forever.

THURSDAY
"Canada"

Genesis 1:9

And God said, "Let the water under the sky be gathered to one place, and the dry ground appear." And it was so.

As we pulled away from civilization, there was a lot of exhilaration just anticipating our time in Canada. Shortly after we crossed the border, all communication was eliminated. For the next week, there would be no phones, no television, no indoor toilets, no outside world, and no wives (just kidding, dear).

The view from the boat plane is absolutely remarkable because Canada has more lakes than any country in the world. From the air, all you see is trees and water. After arrival, unpacking, fishing all day, and then dinner, I anxiously awaited darkness and the revelation in the sky as it revealed millions of stars. It's hard to fathom that God is aware of each and every one of them.

Psalm 147:4

He determines the number of the stars and calls them each by name.

The most rewarding part of the trip was slowing down my normal hectic pace and feeling God's presence in the wilderness. I woke myself before everyone else got up so I could be alone with God and his creation. Accompanying me was my favorite devotional, my smartphone Bible app, and my journal as I entered into His presence.

This quiet time was almost surreal, and I could feel the Holy Spirit as He illuminated God's Holy Word. My wife and I agreed to exchange five cards during our time apart. Her words spoke to my very soul as I realized how she has blessed me, and I am not complete without her. God was there! This was such a special time and place, but I do recognize that I don't need Canada to find Him. If Jesus made time for a private meeting with God, shouldn't I?

Mark 1:35

Very early in the morning, while it was still dark, Jesus got up, left the house and went off to a solitary place, where he prayed.

FRIDAY
"Making Time for God"

Hosea 10:12
For it is time to seek the Lord...

Years ago, I made a covenant with God to read my Bible for five minutes a day for a year. Five minutes... just five minutes, a fairly minimal commitment to my Lord and Savior. I was not familiar with the Bible, so I started with the Gospel of John. After several months of wandering through Scripture, my mind seemed to wander, and my focus and attention span were fading. I needed a plan and a program instead of just random reading. I went to a Christian bookstore and the Holy Spirit directed me to an author named Max Lucado. He had a 365-day journaling devotional called *Grace for the Moment*. His book had a daily scripture and followed with his personal revelation of God's Holy Word. This is what I needed to confirm and honor my covenant with God.

There are so many outstanding Christian authors with daily devotionals. Charles Stanley, Tony Dungy, Billy Graham, Beth Moore, and Sarah Young are just a few. God speaks through these people. I can't tell you how many times my heart was troubled and searching for answers and the Holy Spirit revealed the answer to me through His mighty Word and the author's application.

One thing I am sure of: If you take time for God, He will take time for you.

Proverbs 8:17
I love those who love me, and those who seek me find me.

SATURDAY REFLECTIONS
Philippians 4:12–13

I know what it is to be in need,

And I know what it is to have plenty.

I have learned the secret of being content in any and every situation,

Whether well fed or hungry,

Whether living in plenty or in want.

I can do all things through Christ who strengthens me.

Lord, as I review the past week, I remember:

....

....

....

....

....

....

....

....

....

....

....

....

....

....

....

....

SUNDAY

Proverbs 16:3–9

Commit to the Lord whatever you do,

And he will establish your plans.

The Lord works out everything to its proper end—

Even the wicked for a day of disaster.

The Lord detests all the proud of heart.

Be sure of this: they will not go unpunished.

Through love and faithfulness sin is atoned for;

Though the fear of the Lord evil is avoided.

When the Lord takes pleasure in anyone's way,

He causes their enemies to make peace with them.

Better a little with righteousness

Than much gain with injustice.

In their hearts humans plan their course,

But the Lord establishes their steps.

In their hearts humans plan their course,

But the Lord establishes their steps.

Prepare to worship and count your blessings.

....

....

....

....

....

....

....

....

Week #47
Monday: TGIM

John 15:13

Greater love has no one than this: to lay one's life down for one's friends.

Mark answered the phone quickly. He told me that Al had been in an accident and that he wasn't positive, but he thought Al had been killed. Mark was on the way to the hospital, so my wife and I jumped in our car and headed that way too. Half way there, Mark called back and said Al had died, presumably from a heart attack, and ran off the road. They had already taken him to the funeral home.

This could not be happening! Al was 79 years old and had stints put in several years ago, but the doctor had given him a clean bill of health within the last two months. I told my wife right after the phone call, and she cried and hugged me. I was in shock but, unbelievably, no tears came. I immediately thought about Al and how frustrated he was with some of his family problems, his health issues, and his job situation. Al should not have been working as hard as he was, but financially, he didn't have a choice. He did not tell me the full depth of his depression, but I knew he was struggling. Our biweekly meetings always lifted him up and gave him a chance to open up about his concerns. Despite the various issues he faced, he always was upbeat because his prayer life was his strength.

The next day, I was still stunned, but during my morning devotionals, I broke down and realized how much I was going to miss him. We talked almost every day and met several times during the week, and now, he was gone. A part of my soul had just been removed and could not be replaced.

As I reflected on our relationship and his subtraction from my life, I suddenly switched gears and thought about where he was now and how he was with the Lord. Al deserved heaven, and I know he was experiencing a "peace that transcends all understanding." How blessed I was to have him for the last 40 years, and I thanked God for His timing and His wisdom to take Al and remove his suffering. I can see Jesus reaching out His hand to Al as he welcomed him into heaven. As the Lord grasped Al's hand, I can hear Him say, "Well done, good and faithful servant!"

The devotionals this week are my comments at Al's eulogy and will give you more insight into my relationship with my best friend Al.

MONDAY

"Al's Eulogy"

Most of you know how close Al and I were, and I found a scripture in 1 Kings chapter 18 verse 1 that talks about Jonathan and David. This verse seems so appropriate for my relationship with Al. The verse reads, "Jonathan became one in spirit with David, and he loved him as himself."

I've prayed and searched for what Al wants me to speak to you about today, and it can be summed up in two words:

Don't wait.

One of my favorite scriptures:

Proverbs 3:5–6

Trust in the Lord with all your heart and lean not unto your own understanding; in all your ways submit to him, and he will make your paths straight.

This morning, I woke up early and was driving to my office to put my thoughts on paper, and as I was coming down Shelbyville Road right in front of Vahalla, I could see ahead that there was a car stopped on the other side of the road right in a traffic lane with flashing lights. There was a car behind me, so I slowed down as I passed. The man was out of the car, but I couldn't tell what was going on. As I drove down the road, I questioned myself. Should I go back? I prayed about it, and I thought of Al and some of his "pick up the hitchhiker stories." Then, I pulled over and turned around, went back, and checked up on the man. He was okay, but his car was smashed because he had just hit a deer on the way to work. I knew God was telling me to stop, and He was saying…

Don't wait!

TUESDAY
"Al's Eulogy" Part 2

I saw Al last Thursday morning at our weekly Bible study. Al sat at a table close to mine, and he always propped his leg up in the empty chair next to him. I noticed the boots he was wearing. They were the same ones I put in a dumpster a couple of years earlier. I kidded him about the fact that he had on four pairs of socks to make them fit.

Our Bible study was on the end times and the rapture. I had no idea that Al would not be on this earth later that day. I had to leave at the end, and Al stayed around to talk a little longer, so I told him we would talk later, and I gave him a hug. At around 3:00 p.m., Al called and told me he was dropping off some trim at a job site. We talked briefly, and I told him that I would see him at our regular Friday morning meeting. We said goodbye, and I told him I loved him. That was our last conversation.

I know everybody in this room wishes they could see Al one more time or say, "I love you" one more time. Everybody in this room has somebody waiting to hear from you today. A phone call, a note, a text, or a visit today may be your last chance to say, "I love you..."

Don't wait!

Two-Minute Drill

Romans 12:2 (Message)
Don't become so well adjusted to your culture
That you fit into it without even thinking.
Instead, fix your attention on God.
You'll be changed from the inside out.
Readily recognize what he wants from you, and quickly respond to it.
Unlike the culture around you,
Always dragging you down to its level of immaturity,
God brings the best out of you, develops well-formed maturity in you.
Romans 12:2 (NIV)
Do not conform to the pattern of this world,
But be transformed by the renewing of your mind.
Then you will be able to test and approve what God's will is—
His good, pleasing and perfect will.

Here are the words that caught my attention: Don't become adjusted, fit in without thinking, fix your attention on God, what He wants, respond, unlike culture, dragging, immaturity, God brings the best out of you, do not conform, world, transformed, renew your mind, able to test, approve, God's will, good, pleasing, and perfect will.

Every day when we get out of bed, we have a choice: conform or be transformed. If we start our day without God, then we are telling Him we are too busy, that we don't need Him today, and that we can handle it.

Conform of be transformed.

What's your decision?

THURSDAY
"Al's Eulogy" Part 3

Al taught me the building business, and after he tutored me, I started my own company. Then, a few years later, he said he wanted to meet. He told me that he had a falling out with his employer and asked if I needed anybody. Here was the guy who taught me everything I know about building asking me for a job. I gave him a hug and asked him when he could start.

With Al on the job site, I could concentrate on sales and not worry about the end product, and we became very successful. After several years, I had some serious problems at home and was seeing a counselor. Then, some very traumatic things happened, and I rushed to my psychologist so I could get some guidance and direction. He asked me a very simple question: "Do you have a friend you can share this with?" I had lots of buddies but no one to share my heart with.

After pondering this for several days, I asked Al if he wanted to get together on Tuesdays every week to have breakfast and talk. Each week, we drew closer and closer, and eventually, we could share the demons in our lives. We started this process over 30 years ago, and then, about 15 years ago, we started meeting on Fridays too.

This has been the most rewarding experience of my life, and all it took was time. Al and I both looked forward to our meetings, and it wasn't about receiving advice from a friend. We just need to verbalize our problems and have someone listen. We could both tell when something was bothering one of us. But this isn't just for men. My wife started meeting with a friend of hers, and their bond is remarkable. So, the point of this story is this: Find someone you can confide in and talk to about your concerns, and I promise you that will anticipate meeting with them every week.

Don't wait!

FRIDAY
"Al's Eulogy" Part 4

Al and I had been meeting for a few years, and one time, he talked about his daughter and son-in-law having such an amazing experience on a weekend retreat called the Emmaus Walk. Sounded interesting, but we were both too busy. Eventually, they persuaded us to attend, and reluctantly, we went, griping all the way. This was a fantastic experience, and it was life-changing, especially for Al.

Al lived close to the church and been an altar boy for a long time, but he didn't really know Jesus. During the Emmaus Walk, he found the Lord. You see, before this retreat, Al was a good man, but after the Emmaus Walk, Al was a new man. Al used to say, "Before Emmaus, I was a spectator, and after Emmaus, I became a participator."

That reminds me of the story from the third chapter of the Gospel of John and Nicodemus. A "religious man" came to Jesus asking questions, and Jesus told him, "You must be born again." Then, Jesus said, "For God so loved the world that gave His only Son, that whosoever believes in Him shall not perish but have everlasting life."

You see, there is a difference in being good or just having an intellectual belief that Jesus walked this earth. In the book of James, it mentions that even the demons believe who Jesus is, but they don't accept Him as Lord and Savior. The most important message Al Lochner can give you today is expressed in 1 John: "And this is the testimony, God has given us eternal life and this life is in His Son. He who has the Son has life and he who does not have the Son of God does not have life."

Many of you have asked me what you could do for Al. The greatest gift you could give Al Lochner is accepting Jesus Christ as your Lord and Savior. And if you already know Him as Lord, then become more familiar with His Gospel and draw closer to Him.

Don't wait!

SATURDAY REFLECTIONS
Philippians 4:12–13

I know what it is to be in need,

And I know what it is to have plenty.

I have learned the secret of being content in any and every situation,

Whether well fed or hungry,

Whether living in plenty or in want.

I can do all things through Christ who strengthens me.

Lord, as I review the past week, I remember:

....

....

....

....

....

....

....

....

....

....

....

....

....

....

....

....

Proverbs 16:16–20

How much better to get wisdom that gold,

To get insight rather than silver!

The highway of the upright avoids evil;

Those who guard their ways preserve their lives.

Pride goes before destruction,

A haughty spirit before a fall.

Better to be lowly in spirit among the oppressed

Than to share plunder with the proud.

Whoever gives heed to instruction prospers,

And blessed is the one who trusts in the Lord.

Whoever gives heed to instruction prospers,

And blessed is the one who trusts in the Lord.

Prepare to worship and count your blessings.

....

....

....

....

....

....

....

....

....

....

....

....

Week #48
Monday: TGIM

John 3:36

Whoever believes it the Son has eternal life...

When I was 12 years old, my family and I went to sunrise service. Afterward, we went back to the church for breakfast and then prepared for our regular service. I was going to be baptized with several others, and just prior to going behind the altar to prepare, I dozed off. Our group leader received the signal, and fortunately, he nudged me. I quickly got in line and headed for the back. We had gone through a class to explain the baptismal ceremony and its significance, and I vividly remember that day. My question: Did I really believe in Jesus, or was He just another fact in my brain?

Years later, I read a story in the Bible about Jesus being met by a demon-possessed man. When he saw Jesus from a distance, he ran and fell to his knees and shouted at the top of his voice, "What do you want with me, Jesus, Son of Most High God?" This declaration created some serious conflict in my mind. If I accepted the fact of who Jesus was and so did the demon-possessed man, then how were we different? The following scripture answered my question.

Romans 10:9–10

If you declare with your mouth, "Jesus is Lord," and believe in your heart that God raised him from the dead, you will be saved. For it is with your heart that you believe and are justified, and it is with your mouth that you profess your faith and are saved.

When I was 12 years old, I had only confessed with my mouth and accepted the fact that Jesus was the Son of God. At age 25, two years into pro football and after realizing a certain amount of fame and fortune, I decided to truly give my heart to God by accepting Jesus as my Lord and Savior. At that very moment, the Holy Spirit filled my soul.

John 3:3

No one can see the kingdom of God unless they are born again.

"Prophecy"

2 Timothy 3:16

All scripture is inspired by God...

The definition of prophecy: a divinely inspired prediction.

Easter is coming, but don't forget the miraculous origin of this man named Jesus. His birth and heritage were announced 600 to 1,400 years before his birth!

Jesus would be born in Bethlehem.

Micah 5:2 (Written in 675 BC)

But you, Bethlehem Ephrathah, though you are small among the clans of Judah, out of you will come for me one who will be ruler over Israel, whose origins are from of old, from ancient times.

This prophecy was fulfilled in Luke 2:4–7.

Jesus would be born of a virgin.

Isaiah 7:14 (written 700 B.C.)

Therefore, the Lord himself will give you a sign: the virgin will be with child and will give birth to a son, and will call him Immanuel.........

This prophecy was fulfilled in Matthew 1:18–23.

Jesus would be from the line of Abraham (Genesis 22:18), a descendant of Isaac (Numbers 24:17), called out of Egypt (Hosea 11:1), born among the sorrow (Jeremiah 31:15), from the lineage of King David (Jeremiah 23:5), and as a member of the tribe of Judah (49:10).

There are no prophecies foretelling the birth of any other religious leader. There were no predictions for the birth of Mohammed (Islam), Joseph Smith (Mormonism), or Charles Taze Russell (Jehovah's Witnesses).

Jesus asked the disciples in Matthew 16:15, "Who do you say I am?" Simon Peter answered, "You are the Christ, the Son of the living God."

As we prepare for Easter, Jesus is asking each of us, "Who do you say I am?"

TUESDAY
"The Gifts of Easter"

The Easter season is so special with family celebrations, church, Lenten commitments, and quiet moments to contemplate and reflect on Jesus' sacrifice and God's restoration of life to our Savior. One of the many blessings we become aware of during the Easter season is God's all-encompassing love and his gift of grace.

Ephesians 2:4–5

But because of his great love for us, God, who is rich in mercy, made us alive with Christ even when we were dead in transgressions—it is by grace you have been saved.

Jesus did not come because I was deserving. I am totally and absolutely unworthy of his sacrifice. All my attempts to be a good person have not made me righteous enough to receive God's mercy and grace.

Romans 3:23

All have sinned and fall short of the glory of God...

Grace is a gift, and I didn't earn it. It's not about what I do for God but why I do it for God. The Pharisees and Sadducees, with all their pompous righteousness, are proof that obedience to the law doesn't necessarily mean your heart is right. We choose to accept God's grace and be faithful because we love the Lord and want to honor Him with our behavior. The only way for me to remain obedient is to grow closer to the source of my faith, God.

So, how do we improve our relationship to the Lord? By spending more quality time with Him! Church on Sunday only fills us temporarily and is not enough because the world bombards us and weakens our spiritual strength. How many times have you had a very inspirational weekend service, but as the week evolves, your Christ-like attitude fades and disappears? Our daily routines must include time with the Lord so we can continually fill our spiritual gas tank. If we neglect our time with God, we are basically telling the Lord, "Thanks for Sunday, but I'll take it from here."

Hebrews 11:6

He rewards those who earnestly seek him.

WEDNESDAY

Two-Minute Drill

Mark 15:24
And they crucified Him.

Jesus was also scourged before He was nailed to the cross.
His back was a bloody mess, and the nails in His wrists and ankles were tremendously painful.
Death could have been from loss of blood or suffocation because the lungs usually collapsed.
Our Savior lived close to six hours on the cross before He died.
While He was dying:

Mark 15:24
Dividing up his clothes,
They cast lots to see what each would get.

Our Savior looked down, and the Roman soldiers were gambling for His clothing.

Mark 15:31
The chief priests and the teachers of the law
Mocked Him among themselves.

Jesus withstood all the ridicule so that we might live!

PRAISE GOD!

THURSDAY
"Easter 2016"

As I reflect back on the last days before our Lord was crucified, I wonder how I would have reacted to the various events leading up to his death. I would like to think positive thoughts about myself as he endured such great suffering, but I know at one time in my life, that would not have been the case. If I had been there, would I have welcomed Jesus into Jerusalem?

Mark 11:8–9

Many people spread their cloaks on the road... "Hosanna!"

Would I have fallen asleep in the garden?

Mark 14:37

"Could you not keep watch for one hour?"

Would I have betrayed him like Peter?

Mark 14:72

"Before the rooster crows twice you will disown me..."

Would I have been part of the crowd yelling for justice?

Mark 15:14

But they shouted all the louder, "Crucify him!"

Would I have stood at the foot of the cross and questioned him?

Mark 15:31

"He saved others," they said, "but He can't save himself!"

Would I have been a skeptic and walked away from the cross and said he was just another man?

John 20:25

Unless I see the nail marks in his hands and put my finger where the nails were, and put my hand into his side, I will not believe.

At one time in my life I cursed, shamed, and deserted Jesus, and despite all my faults, He still died for me. I was so unworthy, and yet, He endured all the torture and suffering just for me.

Romans 5:8

But God demonstrates his own love for us in this: While we were still sinners, Christ died for us.

FRIDAY

"I Was There"

John 11:43

Jesus called in a loud voice, "Lazarus, come out!"

I was there when this man called Jesus raised a man from the dead. This man had been dead for four days, and I saw him walk out of the tomb with his grave clothes.

John 12:13

They took palm branches and went out to meet him shouting, "Hosanna... Blessed is the King of Israel!"

I was there yelling "Hosanna in the highest!" This man had to be the Messiah.

Luke 22:40

On reaching the place, [Jesus] said to them, "Pray that you will not fall into temptation."

I was there in the garden, and I could not keep my eyes open.

Luke 22:59

"Certainly this fellow was with him, for he is a Galilean."

I was there in the garden when they arrested Jesus and took Him away. I followed from a distance, and someone accused me of being one of his followers. I denied I had ever seen him.

Matthew 27:17

Pilate asked them, "Which one do you want me to release to you: Barabbas, or Jesus who is called Messiah?"

I was there when he stood before the governor, and I heard him ask the question, but I was too afraid to say anything.

Luke 23:34

"Father forgive them, for they do not know what they are doing."

I was there as Jesus was dying on the cross, and even though I had fallen asleep, denied him, and remained silent in front of his accusers, He looked at me and asked his Father to forgive me.

Mark 15:39

"Surely this man was the Son of God!"

SATURDAY REFLECTIONS
Philippians 4:12–13

I know what it is to be in need,

And I know what it is to have plenty.

I have learned the secret of being content in any and every situation,

Whether well fed or hungry,

Whether living in plenty or in want.

I can do all things through Christ who strengthens me.

Lord, as I review the past week, I remember:

....

....

....

....

....

....

....

....

....

....

....

....

....

....

....

Proverbs 30:5–9

"Every word of God is flawless; He is a shield to those who take refuge in Him.
Do not add to His words, or He will rebuke you and prove you a liar.
Two things I ask of you, Lord;

Do not refuse me before I die: Keep falsehood and lies far from me;

Give me neither poverty nor riches, but give me only my daily bread.

Otherwise, I may have too much and disown you and say,

"Who is the Lord?"

Prepare to worship and count your blessings.

....

....

....

....

....

....

....

....

....

....

....

....

Psalm 37:7

Be still before the Lord and wait patiently for him...

Darryll Davis, the executive director of Proclamation of the Word prison ministry, sent me a text challenging me to 45 minutes this week in solitude with God. Most every morning, I spend time with the Lord, reading several devotionals and praying. The majority of that time is absorbing God's word or talking to Him, However, I usually don't spend any extended length of time just listening. I asked myself when the last time was that I was really totally alone with God and had no phone or agenda. No reading, talking, or writing but just being still and quiet and listening to the God of the universe. Rarely have I searched for someplace quiet or even sat on my back porch and spent an extended time in silence and contemplation.

Psalm 46:10

Be still and know that I am God.

Easter is so close, and I am going to commit to a 45-minute silent time once a week with the Lord. There are approximately 16 waking hours in a day, which is 112 hours a week, so 45 minutes is less than .oo6% of my time commitment. Jesus sacrificed so much more, and yet, I still hesitate because I am too busy. Well, I am going to make a covenant with God, a sacred promise with my Lord for the next few weeks to find a place to be alone and silent for 45 minutes once a week with my God.

Prayer: Jesus, my precious Lord and Savior who sacrificed everything and died for me, I'm not too busy for you. I'm in!

How about you?

Too busy?

Will you join me?

MONDAY
"Calvary (Golgotha)"

Luke 23:26

As they led him away...

Three crosses, two criminals, and the innocent Son of God, who sacrificed His life for mankind.

The two lawbreakers are no different than you and I. Maybe we haven't committed malicious crimes, but we are sinners just like them. One of the evildoers hurled insults at the Savior of the world, expressed no remorse, and sneeringly commented, "Aren't you the Christ? Save yourself and us!"

The other felon accepted his offenses and defended our Lord and then said, "Jesus, remember me when you come into your kingdom." Jesus responded, "I tell you the truth, today you will be with me in paradise."

Today is just like that day 2,000 years ago. We are all in a survival mode on the hill of Calvary we call life. We struggle with our sinful lives and must ultimately make a decision. We can reject or accept Jesus. With your *mind,* you can just intellectually believe that Jesus was the Son of God and that He was resurrected from the dead, or you can sincerely ask Jesus to come into your *heart* and truly accept Him as your Lord and Savior. The decision is so critically important, and yet, so radically simple. There are no credentials necessary, no requirements for purification, and no official statements to sign.

All the God of creation wants is your heart (Romans 10:9–10).

One of the criminals chose Jesus. What's your choice?

Prayer: Lord God, today, this day, I am asking you to come into my life and take control. I cannot continue to live my life without you. I know I have sinned against you. Please forgive my trespasses. My heart is yours. Show me how to live for you and not the world.

TUESDAY
"Easter"

1 Peter 1:3

Praise be to God and Father of our Lord Jesus Christ! In his great mercy he has given us new birth into a living hope through the resurrection of Jesus Christ from the dead.

The disciples had followed Jesus for several years, but they certainly didn't expect him to be crucified. Jesus informed them at the last supper that he would suffer, but they did not understand. He announced, "You will all fall away" (Mark 14:27). He also disclosed this: "But after I have risen, I will go ahead to Galilee" (Matthew 26:32).

Did they believe him? Thomas refused to accept that Jesus rose from the dead: "Unless I see the nail marks in His hands and put my finger where the nails were and put my hand into His side, I will not believe it" (John 20:25).

When you pause and contemplate Good Friday and Easter, what comes to mind?

The ludicrous trial and condemnation? The flogging, beating, and crown of thorns? The crucifixion? The resurrection? His appearances after death?

We celebrate Easter because our Savior rose from the grave so we would have hope.

Jesus was a great prophet and teacher, but without the resurrection, there would be no hope (1 Corinthians 15:12–19).

There would be no hope for eternal life.

There would be no Holy Spirit (John 7:39).

Without Jesus in our lives, there is no hope.

1 John 5:11–12

God has given us eternal life, and this life is in His Son. Whoever has the Son has life; whoever does not have the Son of God does not have life.

WEDNESDAY
Two-Minute Drill

Mark 15:26

The written notice of the charge against Him read:

The King of the Jews.

The Savior of the world was ridiculed and mocked.
He could call a legion of angels, and they would rescue Him,
But instead, He endured all the pain and suffering so you and I would have a
chance to live!

Mark 15:29–30

*Those who passed by hurled insults at him, shaking their heads and saying,
"So! You who are going to destroy the temple and build it in three days,
come down from the cross and save yourself!"*

Surrounded by all these disrespectful people.
He suffered their insults for me!

Mark 15:39

*And when the centurion who stood there in front of Jesus,
saw how he died, he said,
"Surely this man was the Son of God!"*

As you review God's Holy Word,

And all the prophecies about Jesus,

You must agree

"Surely this man was the Son of God!"

THURSDAY
"Easter Reflections"

Why did Roman soldiers guard Jesus' tomb?

Matthew 27:62–65

The Pharisees went to Pilate. "Sir," they said, "we remember that while he was still alive that deceiver said, "After three days I will rise again." So give the order for the tomb to be made secure until the third day.

Luke 9:22

And he said, "The Son of Man must suffer many things and be rejected by the elders, the chief priests and the teachers of the law, and he must be killed and on the third day be raised to life."

Did Jesus really come back from the grave?

Mark 16:14

Later Jesus appeared to the Eleven as they were eating...

Luke 24:36

Jesus himself stood among them and said to them, "Peace be with you."

John 20:27

Then he said to Thomas, "Put your finger here; see my hands. Reach out your hand and put it into my side. Stop doubting and believe."

1 Corinthians 15:6

...he appeared to more than five hundred of the brothers and sisters at the same time...

Of all the spiritual leaders in the world, there is only one prophet that returned from the dead—not Mohammed, Confucius, Hindu or Buddhist monks, Brigham Young, or John Smith......only JESUS!!

"The Gift of Easter: The Holy Spirit"

John 16:7

Unless I go away, the Advocate will not come to you; but if I go, I will send him to you.

Jesus' death, burial, and resurrection proved that He was the Messiah. But many did not believe and refused to accept the fact that He was alive. If you recall, the disciples were in hiding from the Jews when the Lord appeared to them (John 20:19). Jesus was aware of His follower's weaknesses, and He knew it was absolutely imperative for them to receive His supernatural strength to endure the onslaught of the world.

John 20:21–22

Again Jesus said, "Peace be with you! As the Father has sent me, I am sending you." And with that He breathed on them and said, "Receive the Holy Spirit."

When I accepted Jesus as my Lord and Savior, I expected some explosive occurrence to signify my commitment to him. There were no lightning bolts or flashing visions, but I knew I had trusted God with my heart. Even though there was not a miraculous supernatural moment, I know that day that God breathed new life into my very soul.

Why do we need the Holy Spirit?

John 14:26

But the Advocate, the Holy Spirit, whom the Father will send in my name, will teach you all things and will remind you of everything I have said to you.

Throughout the Old Testament, from Genesis to Malachi, we see the disobedience of God's people and their inability to consistently follow the Lord. They were not capable of following God's plan for their lives without divine assistance. Multiple times in the Old Testament, the people are portrayed by the following scripture, "Once again, they did evil in the eyes of the Lord."

Without the Holy Spirit, we are those people!

1 Corinthians 2:14

The person without the Spirit does not accept the things that come from the Spirit of God...

SATURDAY REFLECTIONS
Philippians 4:12–13

I know what it is to be in need,

And I know what it is to have plenty.

I have learned the secret of being content in any and every situation,

Whether well fed or hungry,

Whether living in plenty or in want.

I can do all things through Christ who strengthens me.

Lord, as I review the past week, I remember:

....

....

....

....

....

....

....

....

....

....

....

....

....

....

....

....

SUNDAY
Isaiah 40:28

Do you not know?

Have you not heard?

The Lord is the everlasting God,

The Creator of the ends of the earth.

He will not grow tired or weary,

And his understanding no one can fathom.

And his understanding no one can fathom.

Prepare to worship and count your blessings.

....
....
....
....
....
....
....
....
....
....
....
....
....

Week #50

Monday: TGIM

Christmas Reflections

Matthew 1:23

"The virgin will conceive and give birth to a son, and they will call him Immanuel" (which means "God with us").

Christmas is such a special time of the year and has always been my favorite. There were no spectacular gifts as a child. Just things I needed more than things I wanted. I did get a microscope once, and I remember when my Mom left the house, I searched high and low to find it and never did, but Santa brought it anyway. My cousin got a car set and I got clothes, but there were no complaints.

I remember my son's eighteenth Christmas. He had worked hard at school as a senior, and we surprised him with a shiny new red Camaro. We planned it so his grandfather would drive it up and put it in the driveway after we had finished opening the majority of the presents. I never will forget his face. The joy of Christmas is seeing everyone's happiness and joy. There is nothing comparable.

My most memorable Christmas was in 1994. Five years previous, I had gone through a very traumatic divorce. My kids were hurt, and so was I. The scars were deep, and I assumed I would never marry again. I dated for a while and then met a younger woman through some business dealings, and she had never married.

We started spending a lot of time together, and I told her from the beginning that my kids were my number one priority. We dated for five years and only had one major disagreement during that time. Money was tight due to the divorce, and I could not afford an expensive ring. I had a friend in the jewelry business, and I went to see him and explain the circumstances. He had a great idea and suggested buying a beautiful zirconia diamond, and when the money rebounded, he told me to come back and see him. I bought the ring, and I still wasn't sure if I wanted to ask her, but on that Christmas Eve, I gave it to her. I remember the tears flowing down my face as I asked her to be my bride. She accepted even when I told her it was a fake diamond. She had put up with me for five years, and I am so glad she waited.

I Praise God every day for my soul mate.

We are one!

MONDAY

"Christmas Preparation"

1 Peter 1:13

Therefore, prepare your minds for action.

I love the holidays, but Christmas can sure get hectic. I get so absorbed in all the events as well as the strategic planning and shopping for presents. Every year, I always catch myself forgetting the reason for the season. Why do I let the holidays overwhelm me? You know why? Because I let it happen. This year is going to be different. Scripture tells me exactly what to do:

Psalm 46:10

Be still, and know that I am God.

If I don't slow down and pause for time alone with God, I am just asking for more distraction. I am going to spend more time with God and remind myself of the real meaning of Christmas. Our Lord was busy preaching and performing miracles, but how did Jesus slow down and focus on what was important?

Mark 1:35

Before daybreak the next morning, Jesus got up and went out to an isolated place to pray.

When I get hung up in traffic or have to wait at the checkout, I am going to pause and praise God and thank him. Even Jesus, after the chaos of feeding the five thousand, dismissed his disciples and...

Matthew 14:23

He went up to the mountainside... to pray.

How do I stay focused just like our Lord did the night before he selected the 12 disciples?

Luke 6:12

One of those days Jesus went out to a mountainside to pray, and spent the night praying to God.

TUESDAY

"Believe It or Not!"

2 Peter 1:21

For prophecy never had its origin in the human will, but prophets, through human, spoke from God as they were carried along by the Holy Spirit.

As we look back 2,000 years ago, our only proof of the birth of Jesus is the authentic documents passed down over the centuries. The Bible has more manuscripts and scrolls to support its validity than any other book in all antiquity. The Bible is full of prophecies made hundreds of years before they happened, including many predictions related to the birth of Jesus.

Isaiah 7:14

Therefore the Lord Himself will give you a sign: The virgin will conceive and give birth to a son, and will call him Immanuel.

This statement was made 700 years before the birth of Christ. The people of Isaiah's generation must have thought he was absolutely crazy… A virgin with a child! Another 700-year-old prophesy predicted the birthplace of Jesus.

Micah 5:2

"But you, Bethlehem Ephrathah, though you are small among the clans of Judah, out of you will come for me one who will be ruler over Israel…"

The genealogy of Jesus is reviewed in Matthew 1:1–17 and, this supports the 1,000+-year-old prophecy regarding the Messiah being a descendant of Abraham:

Genesis 22:18

"…and through your offspring all nations on earth will be blessed…"

These are just a few of the 100+ prophecies related to the birth, life, and death of our Lord and Savior. God revealed His plan in a miraculous book we call the Bible.

John 20:27

"Stop doubting and believe."

2 Timothy 3:16

All scripture is God-breathed…

Merry CHRISTmas!

WEDNESDAY

Two-Minute Drill

"What Are the Odds?"

In my previous devotional, I discussed the uncanny accuracy of the prophecies concerning the birth of Jesus. Many of these prophecies were written at least 1,000 years before the birth of Our Savior. Here are just a few, so take some time to look these up and realize how there was only one person, Jesus Christ, who could fulfill these amazing predictions:

1. Promised through the seed of Abraham:
   Old Testament Prophecy: Genesis 22:18
   New Testament Fulfillment: Matthew 1:1

2. Born of a virgin:
   Old Testament Prophecy: Isaiah 7:14
   New Testament Fulfillment: Matthew 2:11

3. Worshipped by shepherds:
   Old Testament Prophecy: Psalm 72:9
   New Testament Fulfillment: Luke 2:9

4. Flight to Egypt:
   Old Testament Prophecy: Hosea 11:1
   New Testament Fulfillment: Matthew 2:13-14

5. He will be called Lord:
   Old Testament Prophecy: Psalm 110:1
   New Testament Fulfillment: Luke 2:11

6. He is the Son of God:
   Old Testament Prophecy: Psalm 2:7
   New Testament Fulfillment: Luke 3:23

Our God is an awesome God.

THURSDAY
"Gifts"

Matthew 2:11

Then they opened their treasures and presented him with gifts of gold, frankincense and myrrh.

My wife starts preparing and planning the gifts for the kids and grandkids months before Christmas. She starts squeezing information out of everyone around Halloween and puts a lot of thought into it so the gifts will be meaningful. Everyone wants the person opening the present to be surprised and super excited. Very rarely do they ever talk about last year's presents, but that's okay because I still get so much pleasure in watching their reaction to each and every gift. Do you remember anyone who turned down a present or refused to open one?

How does God feel when He offers the gift of His Son and we say, "No, I don't need you"? At one time in our life, we all said, "No thanks, quit bugging me, I am too busy." Then, one day, we realized our hopelessness and decided to accept the greatest gift we would ever receive... Jesus. All the remarkable presents we have received in our lifetime mean nothing in comparison to God's gift of eternal life.

Romans 6:23

The gift of God is eternal life in Christ Jesus our Lord.

The best present we can give each other is sharing the gospel of our Lord and Savior Jesus Christ. Christmas gifts will not be discussed when we stand before the Lord on Judgement Day (2 Corinthians 5:10). The only question will be:

Do you know Jesus?

FRIDAY
"The Masters"

Isaiah 2:3

He will teach us his ways, so that we may walk in his paths.

What an overwhelming surprise it was this past Christmas when my wife gave me two tickets to a practice round at the Masters Golf Tournament in Augusta, Georgia. She said I could take anybody, and I quickly responded, "You are going with me because you will not want to come home." After being there last week, she said that we are going back every year until we can't walk, and even then, we are getting motorized wheelchairs.

There really is no place in the world quite like the Masters. As I walked the immaculately maintained course, I thought about two characters in the Old Testament that actually walked with God.

Genesis 5:24

Enoch walked with God...

Genesis 6:9

Noah was a righteous man... he walked faithfully with God.

Can you imagine walking the hallowed grounds of Augusta with the creator of the universe? If only I had a special place like this to be with God every day. Then I realize that the Masters is a phenomenal place, but I actually have access to God every morning. I have his instruction book, the Bible, and prayer, and I can walk with my Lord and Savior every day if I just take the time. Some days, I wake up late and get too busy to walk with God, and I am a different person on those days. Not only do I miss my time with the Lord, but I think he misses me too. If I am too busy for God, then I am too busy!

Micah 6:8

And what does the Lord require of you? To act justly and to love mercy and to walk humbly with your God.

SATURDAY REFLECTIONS
Philippians 4:12–13

I know what it is to be in need,

And I know what it is to have plenty.

I have learned the secret of being content in any and every situation,

Whether well fed or hungry,

Whether living in plenty or in want.

I can do all things through Christ who strengthens me.

Lord, as I review the past week, I remember:

....

....

....

....

....

....

....

....

....

....

....

....

....

....

....

SUNDAY
Isaiah 40:29–31

He gives strength to the weary

And increases the power of the weak.

Even youths grow tired and weary,

And young men stumble and fall;

But those who hope in the Lord

Will renew their strength.

But those who hope in the Lord

Will renew their strength.

Prepare to worship and count your blessings.

....
....
....
....
....
....
....
....
....
....
....
....

Week #51

TGIM: MONDAY

"Were You Ready?"

2 Timothy 4:2

Preach the word; be prepared in season and out of season; correct, rebuke and encourage—with great patience and careful instruction.

Wow! What a Christmas! All my family members were at church service on Christmas Eve, and we had a party afterward. Then, Christmas day with my wife's family was absolutely awesome. There was a special spirit at both gatherings, and you could feel the joy and everyone's love for each other. Why was this Christmas so different? Why? Because we worked at it! My wife and I promised each other several weeks before Christmas that we would focus each day on the reason for the season, and we were so much more prepared, especially spiritually. There was no rush. Sure, there were some last-minute gifts, but most of the packages were wrapped ahead of time. I had five gifts for my wife, which I normally wrap on Christmas Eve, but this year, I decided to finish one a day a week before the big day.

I realize now why this Christmas was so special: time. Our devotionals every day included an emphasis on the birth of our Savior, and we were more available to hear his indwelling Holy Spirit. When you think about it, the best gift we can give God is time. Time... It's such a precious commodity, but we get so busy with the world, and the first one we squeeze out is God. It's up to me to give Jesus focused attention every day—not just before Christmas.

Prayer: Lord, for the past several weeks, my attention was focused on the real meaning of Christmas. Your Spirit was apparent this year because I requested your presence every day. Keep me committed to time with you each and every day because I know if I start my day with You, I will magnify the Spirit of Christmas all year round.

Hosea 10:12

For it is time to seek the Lord...

Monday
"Christmas Gifts 2016"

Psalm 16:11

You have made known to me the path of life.

My wife has blessed me with some amazing Christmas gifts over the years, including taking me to Richard Petty driving school and buying me Masters Golf tickets. This year, she got me tickets to the U.S. Open golf tournament.

These are all unbelievable presents, but the most important gifts I have received were not at Christmas. I accepted my two greatest gifts at a chapel service in Oakland, California. As our speaker finished, he prayed and said that if anyone wanted Jesus Christ as their Lord and Savior, all they had to do was ask Him to come into their life and take control. I humbly came before God, and told Him I did not like the life I was living and that I wanted Him in charge. On that day, I received the gift of *eternal life* and the *Holy Spirit.*

John 3:16

For God so loved the world that he gave his one and only Son, that whosoever believes in him shall not perish but have eternal life.

Ephesians 1:13

Having believed, you were marked in him with a seal, the promised Holy Spirit

When I left that meeting room, I had no idea I had received these two supernatural gifts, but I know that that day in Oakland, California, my life had been changed forever. Yes, there have been many blessings and many trials since that day, but I know that God's Spirit dwells within me and that I will live with Him for all eternity.

Some of you reading this have not yet asked Jesus to be your Lord and Savior, and you can take this change to make this your most memorable new year ever. I realized that day in Oakland that I was a hopeless sinner and that God loved me anyway. All he wanted was my heart.

Revelation 3:20

Here I am! I stand at the door and knock. If anyone hears my voice and opens the door, I will come in and eat with that person, and they with me.

He is at the door, just waiting for you to ask him in.

TUESDAY

"Happy *Christmas* Eve"

Proverbs 15:13

A happy heart makes the face cheerful...

This is going to be a tough Christmas for a lot of people who are going through some hard times. I have a friend who lost his wife recently, and I will miss my best friend Al this Christmas. The good news is I know they are both having a Christmas celebration dinner with Jesus.

There are other problems during the holidays too. People with broken families, marital difficulties, trouble in the workplace, disputes with close friends, parents with aging complications, and more. We need to empathize and be compassionate, but we can't lose our joy during the Christmas season.

1 Thessalonians 5:18

Give thanks in all circumstances; for this is God's will for you in Christ Jesus.

I remember going through some tough times in my life and consulting a psychologist for advice. My background as a dependent child of an alcoholic had shaped my personality, and all I wanted was peace and tranquility. The counselor listened to my situation and he gave me this important advice: "You can't control other people's happiness." This was startling news for me, since my goal was to make everyone happy. If someone close to me is unhappy, does this mean I just ignore them and continue in my own joy? No. I try doing everything possible to help them with their concerns, but they have a responsibility too. I will continue my empathetic counseling, but they are not going to control my happiness!

John 16:22

And no one will take away your joy.

My wife and I are currently going through a tough family crisis, and we will do everything in our power to help our family members survive and thrive, but they are not going to control my happiness in this holiday season. I want people to see Jesus in me and feel my concern, but they also need to be part of my joy. Despite my unworthiness, Jesus came to earth for me, and I am going to *celebrate* His birth, and nobody is going to slow me down.

Come, Lord Jesus, come!

WEDNESDAY
Two-Minute Drill

Revelation 3:20
Here I am! I stand at the door and knock.
If anyone hears my voice and opens the door,
I will come in and eat with that person, and they with me.

I remember standing at the door for many years, but I thought I was not good enough to open the door.

Then, someone told me Jesus wanted me just as I was... sins and all.

And, praise God, I finally opened the door, and Jesus came into my life.

Why did I wait so long?

The day I received Him, I was blessed with two unbelievable gifts:

John 3:16
For God so loved the world that he gave his one and only Son,
That whosoever believes in him shall not perish but have eternal life.

Ephesians 1:13
Having believed, you were marked in him with a seal,
The promised Holy Spirit

ETERNAL LIFE AND THE HOLY SPIRIT.

THURSDAY

"Preparing for Christmas"

Matthew 3:3
Prepare the way for the Lord...

I asked my wife what we needed to do to prepare for Christmas: She responded with a list: presents, menu, tree, grocery, church, house, and parties. So much to do, and so little time. How do you accomplish everything and still honor our Lord and Savior?

Here are some specific things my wife and I have decided to do:

1. **Pray.** I know I am not capable by own power to concentrate and focus on the birth of my Savior without God's help, so I set my alarm clock one minute early, and as I roll out of bed and set my feet on the ground, I pause and ask the Lord to assist me in being more aware of *his* birthday.

2. **Plan better!** I know the things I need to get done, and I need to have a quiet time during the day to refocus and *slow down*. At lunch, I pause and reflect on Bethlehem, Mary, the stars, and the cry of the newborn baby Jesus!

3. **Make the car a place of worship!** Everyone will be in the car alone or with family or friends, so turn on the Christmas music or have a quiet time and praise God for all your blessings and thank Him for sending His Son.

4. **Remember that the devil is trying to keep you from focusing on the reason for the season.** When you panic and start pulling out your hair over the fact that you have so much to do, just picture Satan laughing with all his little demons about how he has accomplished his goal of distraction.

5. **Watch Christmas movies with the family even if you have seen them before.** Watch *White Christmas, A Christmas Story, It's a Wonderful Life, Miracle on 34th Street*, and so many more.

6. **Go to Christmas plays, choir recitals, and Christmas musicals.** Even if it is not at your church, they will I let you in. Plan your Christmas Eve service.

7. **Call or visit someone and wish them a Merry Christmas.** Let them know that they are important to you. Make someone feel special!

Isaiah 9:6
For to us a child is born, to us a son is given...

Merry CHRISTmas!

Imagine You Were a Shepherd in the Field

Luke 2:8–9
And there were shepherds living out in the fields nearby, keeping watch over their flocks at night. An angel of the Lord appeared to them, and the glory of the Lord shone around them, and they were terrified.
It was the dark of the night in a huge open field, and I was minding my own business, watching my sheep, and suddenly, the sky lit up and blinded me and my fellow shepherds. Where should I run? There were no caves or rocks to hide behind, and as I prepared to escape…

Luke 2:10
But the angel said to them, "Do not be afraid. I bring you good news that will cause great joy for all the people. Today in the town of David a Savior has been born to you; he is the Messiah, the Lord. This will be a sign to you: You will find a baby wrapped in cloths and lying in a manger."
So, we finally calmed down and stopped running and felt the radiance and calmness of the angel, and then…

Luke 2:13–14
Suddenly a great company of the heavenly host appeared with the angel, praising God and saying, "Glory to God in the highest, and on earth peace to men on whom his favor rests."
We were ready to head for the hills again, but the sound of heavenly host is so uplifting, peaceful, and joyful that you can feel your skin vibrate with anxious anticipation. We didn't know what to do after that.

Luke 2:15–16
When the angels had left them and gone into heaven, the shepherds said to one another, "Let's go to Bethlehem and see this thing that has happened, which the Lord has told us about." So they hurried off and found Mary and Joseph, and the baby, who was lying in the manger.
We arrived and realized that we were the only ones who were witnessing the amazing birth of our Savior. How could this be? He's a king, and nobody was there. He was lying in a stable, but there was something supernatural there. You could feel a special presence, and I have never seen the animals so calm yet excited. I don't want to ever forget that feeling. It was so peaceful, and I was overwhelmed with joy and love. Surely, this is the Son of God!

SATURDAY REFLECTIONS
Philippians 4:12–13

I know what it is to be in need,

And I know what it is to have plenty.

I have learned the secret of being content in any and every situation,

Whether well fed or hungry,

Whether living in plenty or in want.

I can do all things through Christ who strengthens me.

Lord, as I review the past week, I remember:

....

....

....

....

....

....

....

....

....

....

....

....

....

....

....

....

SUNDAY
Isaiah 40:31

But those who hope in the Lord will renew their strength.

They will soar on wings like eagles; they will run and not grow weary,

They will walk and not be faint.

They will soar on wings like eagles;

They will run and not grow weary,

They will walk and not be faint.

Prepare to worship and count your blessings.

....

....

....

....

....

....

....

....

....

....

....

....

....

....

Week #52
MONDAY: TGIM
"It's Never Too Late"

John 3:16

For God so loved the world...

On New Year's Day, I try to review the previous year and make resolutions to change some things and be a better person. In years past, I know I have prayed to be more forgiving, more generous, more empathetic, more aware, etc.

Why do we want to improve?

Will God love us more?

It wasn't that long ago that I was not a very good person, and even now, I have my moments. But despite my wickedness, I finally understand that...

God still loves me.

He loved me enough to send His Son to die for me.

Why did he die for me? I wasn't worthy. You see...

I was the one in the crowd yelling, *"Crucify Him."*

I was the one who nailed Him to that cross.

And yet, despite the evil within me, He died that I might live.

John 3:16

...that he gave his one and only Son, that whoever believes in him shall not perish but have eternal life.

Prayer: Lord, I know there are many areas of my life I need to work on. I can't do it on my own. I need you to help me be the person you want me to be. I know that if I spend more time with you and in your word, you will show me how to live.

Psalm 40:3

He put a new song in my mouth, a hymn of praise to our God.

As you evaluate the New Year and a potential resolution, I want you to think about something specific you can sacrifice for God's glory. The item I am thinking about is something you can't buy at the store and does not cost anything. You don't have to give away something you own or paint a picture or sculpt a statue. However, there just never seems to be enough of this particular possession. But we seem to find it when we need it. This item never runs out and exists for all eternity. What is it?

Ecclesiastes 3:1

There is a time for everything...

Time is the cheapest commodity on earth, and yet, it is the costliest. Whose life will be sacrificed because someone did not take enough time with them? Who will we miss saying goodbye to because we didn't have enough time? Which ball game, church service, birthday party, piano recital etc. will you miss because there was not enough time? We think we have plenty of time, but we never utilize what we have.

1 Corinthians 7:29–31

Time is short.... For this world in its present form is passing away.

We say we can't do it, but we must remember...

2 Corinthians 5:17

Therefore, if anyone is in Christ, the new creation has come: The old has gone, the new is here!

We are made new in Jesus Christ, and we can do anything because we received...

Ezekiel 18:31

A new heart and a new spirit...

This year, sacrifice more time for the God of all creation. He will direct your paths if you make time to listen to him

TUESDAY

"New Year Challenge!"

2 Peter 3:18

But grow in grace and knowledge of our Lord and Savior Jesus Christ.

I challenge you to try this for one week and then make your New Year's resolution:

Spend five or more minutes with God every morning for a week! Not a year, but just for a week. If you commit to this regime for just a week, you will realize how desperately God wants to speak to you. When you wake up and you roll out of bed, before you turn on the light, pause and say a short prayer:

"It's dark, and the world I face today is even darker. Help me, Lord, to absorb your light by illuminating your word into my very soul. I can't fight this world without you, so please lead me and guide me on your path and not mine."

Then, you start the coffee, take a shower, get dressed, fix your coffee, sit down, and spend five or more minutes with the God of the universe. For the next few minutes, your only priority is learning from the Master Educator, the one who created you. Here are some options: read the Bible (Gospel of John), open the Bible app on your phone and review various devotionals, let your mind be totally quiet and listen, give thanks for all your blessings, start a Bible study, or write down your prayer.

God speaks, but we must listen and seek Him daily. If we do not ask for His guidance every day, then we are telling Him that we can do it on our own and that we don't need His advice.

A quote from Marshall Segal: "The clarity we need to make difficult decisions today, especially as we enter another year, comes not mainly from meticulous planning or budgeting or scheduling, but from lifting our eyes up to God—knowing Him more through what He says (in His word), waiting on Him in prayer, deepening our joy in Him."

John 10:27

My sheep listen to my voice.

WEDNESDAY

Two-Minute Drill

Genesis 1:1

In the beginning God created the heavens and the earth.

God was in the beginning of everything.

He was my beginning too—

Not just my physical birth,

But He is responsible for my spiritual birth.

Without Him, I have no hope.

Eternal life awaits me when I leave this earth.

Had I not accepted Jesus Christ as my Lord and Savior, then eternal death was my destiny.

If He has given me life, then why do I neglect Him?

Every day is a new beginning.

I have a choice every day.

Begin with the One who gave me eternal life or start without Him.

We all must decide.

With Him or without Him?

What is your choice?

Joshua 24:15

Choose for yourselves this day whom you will serve…

THURSDAY

"The New Year"

Proverbs 28:13

Whoever conceals their sins does not prosper, but the one who confesses and renounces them finds mercy.

You read the first part of this scripture and you say to yourself, "I know plenty of people who are not right with God, and they are very prosperous."

Webster's has three definitions for prosperous:

1. Auspicious, favorable
2. Marked by success or economic well-being
3. Enjoying vigorous and healthy growth; flourishing (I like this one.)

Isaiah 59:2

But your iniquities have separated you from your God.

Concealed sin creates a separation from God. I have felt it before... We all have. I knew I was immersed in sin and felt so distant from my God. My soul was calling me back to restore my relationship with my Lord. The Spirit hadn't left, but I knew it wasn't the same. I knew what I had to do, but I kept avoiding the reality of abstaining from sin. I wasn't spending time with the Lord like I did before. God was like a friend who moved across the country, and we had lost touch.

James 4:7

Resist the devil, and he will flee from you.

I remember the day I confessed my sin and finally decided to say no more. I could feel God's Holy Spirit rescue me and restore my faith. What a glorious feeling to know I had truly repented and that my great God had forgiven me and "renewed a steadfast spirit within me" (Psalm 51:10).

Now that's what I call prosperous!

Proverbs 28:25

Those who trust in the Lord will prosper.

Am I enjoying vigorous and healthy growth? Am I flourishing?

FRIDAY
"New Year's Resolution"

Exercise... Lose weight...

The YMCA is always crowded from January 1 until the middle of February. Everybody commits to more walking, running, workout videos, new equipment, protein shakes, cod liver oil, or anything else to help them lose weight and get in shape. This kind of resolution takes time and a serious commitment. Our physical bodies need training and discipline, and so does our Spirit.

1 Timothy 4:7
Train yourself to be Godly.

Why do I let the world absorb me and neglect the living God? The answer is so simple: Time. Just like working out at the YMCA, I have to commit time to the Lord. If I don't start my day with the Lord, then I can't be the man He wants me to be. If I forget Him in the morning, then basically, I am saying, "I don't need you. I can handle the world on my own today." That's why I have to train my spiritual nature just like I do my physical body.

1 Corinthians 9:25
Everyone who competes in the games goes into strict training.

Several years ago, I was challenged to spend five minutes a day with God for a year. Occasionally, I would forget, but as I got in bed, I would remember my covenant promise and get up and have some late-night quiet time. Now, I meet with the Lord before the day begins. I am anxious to be there because I know He will speak to me and reveal to me how to be more like Jesus.

Psalm 143:8
Let the morning bring me word of your unfailing love...

This is a great quote: "When I wake up in the morning, I picture myself as an empty cup, and I am going to fill the cup with Jesus."

Colossians 3:16
Let the word of Christ dwell in you richly...

SATURDAY REFLECTIONS
Philippians 4:12–13

I know what it is to be in need,
And I know what it is to have plenty.
I have learned the secret of being content in any and every situation,
Whether well fed or hungry,
Whether living in plenty or in want.
I can do all things through Christ who strengthens me.

Lord, as I review the past week, I remember:

....
....
....
....
....
....
....
....
....
....
....
....
....
....
....
....

SUNDAY
Isaiah 44:24

"This is what the Lord says—

Your Redeemer,

Who formed you in the womb:

I am the Lord,

The Maker of all things,

Who stretches out the heavens,

Who spreads out the earth by myself,

Prepare to worship and count your blessings.

....

....

....

....

....

....

....

....

....

....

....

....